THE HIGH-INCOME MORTGAGE ORIGINATOR

Sales Strategies and Practices to Build Your Client Base and Become a Top Producer

RICHARD GIANNAMORE
with
BARBARA BORDOW OSACH

BICENTENNIAL
1807
WILEY
2007
BICENTENNIAL

John Wiley & Sons, Inc.

Published by John Wiley & Sons, Inc., Hoboken, New Jersey.
Published simultaneously in Canada.

Bicentennial logo: Richard J. Pacifico

For general information on our other products and services please contact our Customer Care Department within the U.S. at (800) 762-2974, outside the United States at (317) 572-3993 or fax (317) 572-4002.

Wiley also publishes its books in a variety of electronic formats. Some content that appears in print may not be available in electronic books.

Library of Congress Cataloging-in-Publication Data:

Giannamore, Richard, 1941–
    The high-income mortgage originator : sales strategies and practices to build your client base and become a top producer / Richard Giannamore, with Barbara Bordow Osach.
        p. cm.
    Includes index.
    Published simultaneously in Canada.
    ISBN 978-0-470-13731-4 (cloth)
        1. Mortgage brokers—United States.   I. Osach, Barbara Bordow, 1951–   II. Title.
    HG2040.5.U5G54 2008
    332.7'20688—dc22   2007016883

Printed in the United States of America.

10 9 8 7 6 5 4 3 2 1

To Paula, my soul mate, inspiration and motivation for life!

R.G.

To my parents, Norma and Burt.

B.B.O.

LIST OF DOWNLOADABLE FORMS

The following are tables and figures within the book that can be downloaded from www.download.tomortgageservices.com and customized for your personal use.

CONTENTS

PART THREE
Wrap Up

PREFACE

Why now? When the idea for this book was presented to me, I thought the timing was rather odd. After a long period of seemingly endless low interest rates and inventive (though not necessarily constructive) ways to reduce monthly mortgage payments, it was apparent that the boom that had brought success to so many had to end. While the crash that eventually resulted in tens of thousands of originators, brokers, and lenders going out of business had not yet peaked, the signs pointed to the coming of a severe downturn in the residential mortgage market. So why write a book guiding people into the industry now?

The more I thought about it, though, I realized that this was exactly the right time for a book that addresses the practices and strategies for survival and growth through the rough spots and the smooth.

I started thinking about what has allowed my mortgage firm, Mortgage Services, Inc., to enjoy over 20 years of growth in spite of industry ups and downs. Larger firms, some nationally known, hadn't weathered the storms. What allowed us to? It wasn't that we had more or better information or knowledge about the industry and markets. It wasn't that we had better products to sell (you'll learn that we all get our money from the same sources). So what was it? And, how could I share this strength with those already in the business, and with those considering mortgage origination as a new career?

I set out to provide down-to-earth, real live conversations and training to give the novice not only a good foundation of information about the business of originating loans, but also provide both the novice and the established originator with the tools to allow them to sell effectively and generate business, no matter what the market conditions are.

I'm a firm believer in measuring and tracking actions and results to make informed strategic and tactical decisions, and I started looking at the sources of our business. In an industry not known for its customer loyalty, we enjoy an extraordinarily large percentage of our business originating from past customers and referrals. I also know that our marketing efforts result in a steady stream of in-bound calls—prequalified leads—regardless of market conditions. How are we able to do that? What makes us different?

What enables us to attract new customers and keep existing ones? It is a combination of what we know, what we do, and who we are in our interactions with prospects and customers.

Many books can tell you what you need to know about mortgage origination. Rather than focusing the extensive technical information in this book around the completion of forms, as many books do, I thought it most useful, particularly for the novice, to introduce the technical material in the context of numerous interactions with prospects and clients. Not satisfied with telling you what you need to know, I include overviews of the industry and loan process to explain why you need to know it, and how and why the information you collect is used in the loan process.

In addition to what a mortgage originator has to know, people considering entering the business want to know what a mortgage originator *does*. You walk into your office and sit down at your desk—then what? In addition to taking you step-by-step through the loan process with a prospect, the book offers simple-to-use tools and clear procedures to track specific actions, measure and interpret your results, and take corrective actions to improve your effectiveness at every step. A "Day in the Life" lays out a schedule of daily activities that covers all the bases for building a solid base of loyal clients.

High-income mortgage originators are sales people. Even if you have never sold anything in your life, you can learn to sell. My first sales job was a disaster. The cold sweats, the upset stomachs, dry mouth, and damp palms made things harder than they had to be. Over the course of 40 years I learned to sell, and sell very, very effectively, and so can you. This book gives you the benefit of all my experience—my mistakes as well as my successes—so that it won't take you 40 years to have the skill and confidence to close most of the prospects with whom you talk. Beginning with lead-generation to bring business to you, the book provides cases and examples that result in effective marketing campaigns. Again, using the loan process as the structure, the book provides scripts and insights into a way of thinking that get to the heart of what is important to prospects, so that without pressure or gimmicks they willingly move forward at every step in the process.

Finally, I know that it is our customer-focus and integrity—doing what we say, when we say, the way it should be done—that really make the difference. We recognize that every interaction is an opportunity to demonstrate professionalism and a genuine interest in our prospects and customers, and doing so builds the trust and respect for which our customers acknowledge us with their loyalty and referrals. Each chapter addresses the mind-set—for both the prospect and the originator—that builds relationships and closes deals.

By addressing the three ingredients that make us successful regardless of industry ups and downs—knowledge, process, and attitude—this book not only gives beginners a quick start on the path to financial freedom and success, earning money as they learn, but provides an enduring source of references, examples, and business practices to bring any mortgage originator to new levels of achievement and success. Tips, advice, and best business practices in each chapter create a solid foundation to establish and grow a customer base and a thriving, money-making business. Combined with solid and complete information about mortgage instruments, the book's practical, step-by-step business orientation prepares readers for the marketing, selling, and customer relations activities needed to attain success quickly.

ABOUT THE AUTHORS

Richard Giannamore is president and CEO of Mortgage Services, Inc. (www.tomortgageservices.com), which he formed in 1986 with little more than determination. Mortgage Services, Inc. is a full-service mortgage brokerage firm that prides itself on outstanding service to customers purchasing or refinancing homes.

Mr. Giannamore has over 45 years of experience as an entrepreneur, salesman, and transformational seminar leader. He is also CEO of Financial Program Strategies, Inc., and creator of the $-Road to Riches-$® programs, (www.roadtoriches.com), which began as information-based financial education seminars for his mortgage customers.

Mr. Giannamore lives in Connecticut with his wife, Paula.

Barbara Bordow Osach is Mr. Giannamore's assistant, a consultant to Mortgage Services, Inc., and a Facilitator of $-Road to Riches-$® programs (www.roadtoriches.com). She is a Boston University graduate with a BA in English Language and Literature, and has an MBA from New York University. In a 32-year Information Technology career as a Business Systems Analyst, consultant, and Director of Applications Development, she earned a reputation as a fluent translator of technical information into business-language documentation and training material (and vice versa). Ms. Osach has worked extensively in many industries, including 14 years in broadcast television. She lives in Connecticut, and has two sons, Dan and Drew.

INTRODUCTION

The book is divided into three parts. "Part One—What You Should Know" provides an overview of the industry, the mortgage loan process, and the interests and motivations of all the major players in the business. This information creates the foundation for understanding the technical details of mortgage origination and motivating factors for both borrowers and lenders.

"Part Two—The Mortgage Selling Cycle" takes you step by step, one chapter at a time, through the mortgage sale process, beginning with lead generation, through selling a proposal and leveraging your customer relations.

The final section of the book, "Part Three—Wrap Up," focuses on postsale activities through closing.

Part One—What You Should Know

Chapter 1, "Mortgage Originator—The Best Job in the World," sets expectations for the book and for your career as a mortgage originator. "A Day in the Life" answers the question "But what do mortgage originators *do?*"

Chapter 2, "Big Picture: Understanding the Mortgage Loan Process," is a high-level view that begins with the reasons borrowers seek mortgages, their concerns and their goals. Case studies illustrate the different roles an originator plays with customers in different financial circumstances. The chapter describes each step in the loan process, beginning with your initial contact with a prospect and moving on to collecting and analyzing information and goals, selling a proposal, and submitting a loan for processing. The chapter then follows the loan once it gets to a lender, from underwriting through approval and closing. The chapter closes with maintaining relationships with clients, and recaps key points to remember as you read the rest of the book.

Chapter 3, "Players: Defining Your Interests and Those of Borrowers, Lenders, and Brokers," concludes the general information part of the book and explains what motivates the key players in the process—borrowers, investors who impact pricing, lenders, brokers, originators, processors, and underwriters. When you understand their specific interests, you can address their concerns, respond to their needs and provide extraordinary service.

Part Two—The Mortgage Selling Cycle

"Step 1: Generating Leads, Prospecting, and Keeping Score" (Chapter 4), focuses on how to bring in the business. It compares marketing media such as mail, phone, advertising, and networking, and provides tracking tools. Scripts and sample letters target markets based on the borrower motivations described in Part One. Tracking forms measure your effectiveness and interpret your results to improve your lead generation.

"Step 2: Moving a Lead to a Prospect" (Chapter 5), shows you how to make a great first impression when you begin the sales conversation. If you've never sold anything before, this chapter illustrates how to avoid eight mistakes rookie salespeople make. Even if you consider yourself a seasoned sales pro, these cautionary examples will remind you of good practices to maintain. Sample scripts, aimed at getting the go-ahead to fill out a mortgage application, are annotated with explanations of sales strategy. A unique commitment rating system allows you to tailor your actions in response to the lead's readiness to move ahead. The chapter closes with operating practices for success, including tracking actions and results.

"Step 3: Facts and Forms—Taking the Mortgage Application" (Chapter 6), approaches the Uniform Residential Loan Application (Form 1003) as a sales tool, not merely a data collection form. Building on the industry overview and player motivation in Part One the chapter takes two passes through the form. The first looks at the information in each section of the form and tells you the information you need at this stage and why you need it. The second pass interweaves the application sections with a conversational script that builds your relationship with the prospect and sets the stage for developing a proposal that effectively addresses the prospect's needs and goals. Again, the chapter ends with tools to track your results and highlight areas for improvement.

"Step 4: Interpreting Ratios and Credit Scores, Building Trust" (Chapter 7), teaches you to interpret the information you collect and assess the borrower's qualification for a loan. A unique qualification rating system, when combined with the commitment rating, directs you to the appropriate next conversation with the prospect. Annotated scripts for each scenario set up the next conversation and interaction. The chapter concludes with key operating practices for success.

"Step 5: Determining the Right Product for Your Prospect" (Chapter 8), delves into the details of loan products, rate sheets, and pricing. You match borrowers' needs and goals with the products that are right for them. You learn how to help transform the borrower who does not qualify for a loan into a future customer.

"Step 6: Selling a Proposal that Makes Sense" (Chapter 9), instructs you in ways to present your proposal. Based on the commitment and qualification rating systems, annotated sample scripts prepare you for a variety of circumstances you are likely to encounter, including common objections, and how to overcome them. You learn to assess your performance to improve your effectiveness.

"Step 7: Creating a Customer Relations System" (Chapter 10), establishes a schedule of communications with your customers that begins while the loan is being processed and continues for a year after their closing. Sample letters (which can be downloaded and customized) are provided for each of the major milestones. The chapter explains how to manage your customer relationships without spending a fortune.

Part Three—Wrap Up

Chapter 11, "The Loan Package: Preparing the Loan for Processing," covers additional information needed to complete the Uniform Residential Loan Application, Good Faith Estimate, and other loan package documents submitted to a lender. A self-assessment form highlights your effectiveness in preparing the client to move forward.

Chapter 12, "Brokers and Lenders: Identifying and Serving Their Needs," follows your loan package through the hands of a File Processor, Closing Specialist, and underwriter. It warns you of things that can go wrong, and instructs you on how to avoid or correct them. Tracking tools keep you informed through the closing and receipt of your compensation.

Chapter 13, "The Wrap Up: Closing the Loan," describes the closing documents and process so you can fully inform and prepare your client.

Chapter 14, "Next Steps Toward Your Future," explores two options—starting a mortgage business, or finding the right firm with which to work. Six critical interview questions give you insights into characteristics of a mortgage company that will support your long-term success.

No matter what stage you are at in your career as a mortgage originator, periodically reference the book after you read it, to hone your selling skills and raise the bar on service excellence. Use the proven combination of knowledge, process, and attitude for staying power through downturns in the market, and to develop your competitive advantage in better times. Good luck!

ACKNOWLEDGMENTS

My wife Paula has made my success possible. Her unselfish giving inspires me to generosity. She takes care of me, totally and completely, in every aspect of my life, all the time. And she does it all gladly, and without being asked. Without her, I would be lost.

I want to acknowledge Ron Giannamore, my "middle" son, who has been with me in the mortgage business from the beginning and through all its ups and downs, for his willingness to listen to his old man. He and Don Polletta have been the guinea pigs since 1984 in the mortgage business. They have given me a true appreciation of what it means to be an entrepreneur, and they are consistent sources of ideas. I know I can count on them to be one hundred percent for the company and for our customers, even when we disagree (sometimes rather heatedly) on the appropriate course of action. Thank you for your contributions to the book, particularly the sales and marketing topics. Special thanks to Donnie for asking, "How's the book going?" throughout the process.

All of the people at Mortgage Services, Inc. contributed to this book through their work, envisioning and articulating the attributes of the best company in the world. Special thanks to originators Cindy Lang and Dorothy Suter for their stories, input, and feedback as the book was being written. Thank you also to Seya Jorawar and Robert Likorama for their input on the role of the originator in the back end processes. And thank you to Deb Apostolik and Phyllis Savoir for taking good care of our customers.

Thank you to Michael Snell, my agent, for bringing this project to me while working together on something completely different, and for pitching to our editor at Wiley, Richard Narramore, who provided valuable input and guidance.

Finally, thank you to Barbara Osach, who brings clarity to my words, making my ideas accessible. Thank you for your service and contribution, your integrity and your partnership in bringing these principles to the printed page.

PART ONE

What You
Should Know

CHAPTER ONE

Mortgage Originator—The Best Job in the World: How to Make Lots of Money Selling Money and Fulfilling Dreams

Congratulations! You are going to learn about the best profession in the world. One in which your earning power is unlimited, *you* determine what your income will be, and you help people to fulfill their dreams. This book is about mortgages, about success, about having freedom, and about making a difference for people. What could be more satisfying than providing the means for a young couple to buy their first home, or for a parent to fund a child's college education? How does it feel to see a hard-working family get a fresh start by helping them lift the crushing weight of credit card debt? Or to know that you are instrumental in helping someone turn a great idea into a budding new business? Wouldn't it be gratifying to help an elderly couple supplement their income so they can continue to live comfortably without worries about losing the home in which they raised their family? This is what mortgage originators do—and they make a great living along the way.

There is not one thing in this book that you can't do. Not one. How do I know? Because with no money, only a high school education, and the determination to succeed, I was able to create a lucrative mortgage business that supports me and employs others, has continually grown over 20 years, and now does business in 36 states. If I could build a business from nothing, then you, building on the decades of experience and insights that have gone into the creation of this book, can be a high-income mortgage originator.

Expectations: Getting What You Want

What do you want? Do you want to be your own boss? Do you want to make a lot of money? Do you want to be the one to say how much you earn? Do you want to meet new people and help them solve problems? Do you want to work in an industry that will challenge your ingenuity, creativity, and resourcefulness? Do you want the security of knowing that no matter what economic ups and downs occur, you have the skills, knowledge, and confidence to create your own opportunities and continue to grow your income? If so, then this book will launch you into a career that has all that and more. And it will give you all the information, tips, tools, and practices you need to become a high-income mortgage originator.

Dolores was 45 years old, single, living in Boston. A graduate of an Ivy League business school, she was a manager with the company she had been with for 17 years. She made a very good income, had a savings plan, health benefits, paid vacation and holidays, and was only three years from being fully vested in the company pension plan. She was usually upbeat and light-spirited, except when she talked about her job. Then out came a stream of complaints about boredom, political shenanigans, and lack of advancement opportunities. One year her annual review coincided with the expiration of her apartment lease, and I asked her if she wanted to leave Boston and come to work as a mortgage originator in my company. She hesitated a bit, and said she didn't know anything about mortgages and had never sold anything before. We talked at length over several weeks. I knew she could learn to sell and learn about mortgages. After all, I had done it, and she was a lot smarter than I was, and she had a better personality to boot!

She took the plunge. People thought she was nuts to quit her "good" job. But she wanted the freedom to determine her own future and the earning power that being a mortgage originator would afford her. She packed up her belongings, bought her first home (on a no-down-payment, low-interest fixed-rate mortgage), and started training as an Application Specialist, calling customers and prospects and completing mortgage applications for them. In the process, she learned how to sell. She learned what makes a script effective (it isn't just the words), how to remain confident in spite of rejections, and how to deal with difficult prospects and turn them into appreciative customers. And she did it using the tools and advice and information that are now available to you in this book. She is creating new marketing opportunities for herself, and soon will be training others coming into the business. The friends she stays in touch with, those who thought she was crazy to make the move, don't see a nut—they see a confident, prosperous woman in control of her financial future and her career, and proud of it.

Being a high-income mortgage originator is not for everyone. You'll have to make your own decisions and adjust to being compensated for the results you produce rather than for the time you put in. And you will have to think creatively as the day passes quickly with a variety of activities. Does all this sound good? If so, I know that anyone who is committed to succeed can succeed.

It's About Selling

Yes, this business is about mortgages, interest rates, and credit scores. But when you sell a mortgage, you sell money, and the great thing about selling money is that everybody needs some. There is always a demand for mortgages. Every year millions of people buy homes, many for the first time, and almost without exception, every one of them will buy a mortgage from someone. Why not from you?

You don't need years and years of schooling or training to get started, but as with anything else that is new, you need a willingness to learn. It is not just about mortgages and application forms, which this book explains to you, clearly, and simply. After all, what good is all that information if you don't know how to bring in the business—if you don't have any mortgages to originate? In addition to all the nuts-and-bolts information you need, the book shows you how to sell mortgages and how to create new business, build a client base, and generate a career that can last you a lifetime—if you choose.

Even if you've never sold anything, you can learn to sell mortgages. When I started selling over 40 years ago, I was shy, self-conscious, terrified, and terrible at selling. It took me a long time to find a very simple, very effective way to talk to people so that now they say "yes" 95% of the time, no matter what I am selling. You don't have to go through years of struggle as I did. I've sold everything from freezer plans to alarm systems, correspondence courses to flowers, vacuum cleaners to swimming pools, and selling mortgages is the easiest of all. All the lessons of my experience have gone into producing the materials you need to learn to present yourself and your products effectively, and they are all here in this book. You can download and customize presentation scripts, marketing letters, and client and activity tracking forms, which are explained in detail in the book. And if you take the recommended actions, you will develop the mindset and confidence to present yourself professionally and effectively, even with tough customers.

You don't even have to be great at math! It isn't hard or complicated. The book explains in language that is easy to understand what calculations you do have to understand, what they are used for, and why they are important to you and your client. The abundance of automated calculators on the Internet, special function calculators, and software programs means that math mechanics are much less important than they were when I started in the business. The book provides examples you can use as models for calculating your deals. Most important, you will learn what the numbers tell you, so that you can create appropriate solutions for your customers.

Being a mortgage originator is not about making a quick buck in an easy market. It is about having the staying power to weather the changes in any market—not only to survive economic downturns, but also to move into new opportunities. You will learn what to do as a mortgage originator, but also how to build a base of clients, retain them, and develop them into a gold mine of referrals and new business. The book explains how to get more business at each step in the mortgage process. You learn to provide excellent service by addressing the concerns and motivations of borrowers and lenders. You learn how to attract customers and earn their trust and confidence, helping them to move forward. And of course you learn in detail the information you need to take applications and bring loans to closing.

Using the strategies and practices of this book, you will do more than earn a living. You will build and create the life you want—the life you deserve to expect! How long it takes is completely up to you. How much do you want, and how fast are you willing to implement the book's recommendations to generate leads and convert them to commissions? That's one of the best things about being a mortgage originator: You call the shots.

Learning the Ropes

When I started my company, Mortgage Services, Inc. in 1986, I didn't know much about mortgages. I had started with a job as a trainee with a bank, and I learned as I went. Within a few months I ventured out on my own, knowing that I needed to understand much more than just mortgages. I had to generate business, know where to find customers and how to qualify them, and keep the records I needed to build and run an efficient and effective business. I couldn't just sit back and wait for people to come to me. Being a mortgage originator is being a salesperson, and I had to do what every salesperson had to do—get out there and sell the business and sell myself.

When you learn from your personal experiences, you develop a solid foundation that other forms of learning often cannot provide, which allows you to adapt to changing conditions. The mortgage industry changes constantly, which is one of the reasons it remains interesting and challenging for me, even after 20 years. It is subject to federal, state, and local legislation and regulation. It is buffeted by economic factors such as the strength of the housing markets and changing interest rates. It is creatively expanding with new products and new markets as the fiercely competitive lending institutions find a competitive edge. Despite this, you don't have to know everything before you get into action. This book follows the same "learn it as you need to apply it" approach that allowed me to start a company, build it and keep it going for over 20 years, in an industry where people come and go with changes in the wind. With few barriers to entry and lots of money to be made, the mortgage industry is appealing, but many people who enter it are not prepared to sell, and some get stopped by the technical knowledge needed to succeed. The book's tools and explanations are designed to get you into action quickly, learning sales techniques and technical information as you go, without being overwhelmed by every possible variation and kink or twist the process could take. The index and glossary provide easy access for referencing all the material, any time you need it.

An Overview

Part One of the book describes with broad brushstrokes the mortgage process from origination to closing, and the larger factors that determine the market, pricing strategies, and ultimately your compensation and earning potential. You don't need to study this information to learn it. Its purpose is to give you a perspective that will support you in knowing that the decisions made about your loans are not personal—you are part of something much larger. Armed with this background material, you will be able to apply your understanding to any set of circumstances and conditions that you encounter when doing business as a mortgage originator.

Part Two focuses on the details of marketing, mortgage applications and loan products in the context of selling, building client relationships, and becoming an effective closer. Each chapter focuses on one step, in sequence, in the selling process from prospecting to closing. Each chapter explains not only the information you need and the actions to take, but why everything you do is important to closing deals. You learn to evaluate your customers' motivation, qualification, and readiness to move forward at each critical decision point, so that you will be able to identify and address any concerns or obstacles. Examples and case stories illustrate the material and demonstrate both winning strategies to adopt and common pitfalls to avoid. And each chapter provides tools and procedures to track your actions, evaluate effectiveness and take corrective action when necessary. Technical information, customer-focused salesmanship, and objective results evaluation—these are the winning combination that will make you a high-income mortgage originator.

Part Three wraps up with post-sale activities and a discussion of your career options as a mortgage originator. Whether you continue to work for a broker or lender or decide to strike out on your own, you will learn the pros and cons, opportunities and costs of each option.

Making a Difference, One Loan at a Time

One thing I've learned in my 20 years in the business is that no two mortgages are the same. You might think a 30-year fixed is a 30-year fixed—and it is. But to each of your customers their mortgage is a unique, powerful, and important financial tool—and you hold the key. For one young family, it meant being able to add on to their home so that they could have the wife's mother closer to them. For a young man it represented the end of nine months of earnest credit repair and the end of high-interest loans, creditors calling, and being afraid a repo agent would claim his car. For a middle-aged couple it meant the pride of owning a home and being able to stay where they were and keep their kids in the same schools when their rental converted to a condo. For a 50-something manager it meant escaping 30 years of corporate drudgery with seed money to start a business of her own. For a retired widow it meant a new boiler and much-needed repairs for a porch, without dipping into her retirement nest egg.

The relationships you make during a loan transaction are the future of your business. Anyone can "do a loan" but when you make a difference for people, they tell others, and when they need another mortgage, they remember, and they call you first. The stories are endless. Over and over, you meet people with different circumstances and different dreams, and all of them are looking for help. Getting to know them, their stories, and their aspirations has been a rich part of my career, and a rewarding one. If you can read, if you can speak, if you can think, you can originate mortgages. If you have integrity, a genuine interest in helping people, the desire and motivation to succeed, and the information, tools and structures this book provides to support you, you can be a high-income mortgage originator.

Choosing a Company, Getting Training, Deciding How Much You Want to Earn

One of the things I love best about being a mortgage originator is being master of my own future. You can be master of your future. It starts with a decision about how successful you are willing to become. Yes, willing. The mortgage industry is a multi-trillion-dollar industry—trillion! That's a lot of money going into mortgages, and a lot of money paid to those who keep the pump primed—the mortgage originators. You will be able to achieve whatever income level you are willing to work for.

You don't have to do it alone. There are tens of thousands of mortgage brokerage firms and lending institutions looking for motivated people to originate loans. Most institutions do not require a college degree, and many require no related experience. On-the-job training is standard. You can work full-time or part-time, salaried or commissioned, or a combination. Some institutions offer health and retirement benefits. As a beginner in the industry, you should find an established company with a good reputation. They already have contacts with lenders and others, and have the administrative systems and personnel in place to support you, so that you can concentrate on learning the trade and building your client base. Regardless of the situation that attracts you, this book will give you a competitive edge, so you can ask the right questions when you interview and hit the ground running, to begin earning commissions and bonuses very quickly.

Most firms pay a commission based on the number of closed loans you originate. Some (usually direct lenders like banks) pay a salary. Some, like my firm, pay a combination of salary and commissions and bonuses. Some firms offer "split" commissions, where they split the profit on each closing with you. In exchange, they may expect you to generate all the prospects, leads, and applications on your own, at your own expense.

Other firms, like mine, do extensive marketing that results in prospects and leads who call you. We also encourage, through additional bonuses, new marketing ideas and actions that have our loan originators generating their own business. Wherever you decide to work, this book will prepare you to ask the questions that will give you a clear understanding of the opportunity, the responsibilities, and the compensation structure you can expect, so there are no unpleasant surprises after you start working. Ultimately, as a mortgage originator your income depends on one thing and one thing only—how much you produce.

Also included in this book are tools and instructions to track your progress and measure your effectiveness at all process milestones. You will identify your strengths and weaknesses and make necessary adjustments before you get into trouble. While the strategies and operating practices in the book are tailored to mortgage origination, the skills you develop as you apply the information are valuable in any position where salesmanship, integrity, and customer service are important—virtually anywhere.

Opportunities for advancement abound within the industry, and the foundation and successful practices you master as a high-income mortgage originator will serve you well in all of them. Whether you stay in origination and grow your customer base, take on more independence and more responsibility with the firm you work with, or decide to strike out on your own as I did, you have the power to call the shots. Your future can be anything you are willing to commit yourself to.

Being a mortgage originator is about generating sales, caring for customers and following up on details. It's also about your freedom and independence, and that's exciting. It is about having control of your financial well-being. No need to kiss up to a boss you don't like or who can't do the job he is evaluating you on doing. No more office politics or frustrating salary range caps. Every paycheck reminds you that your initiative, creativity, and performance are valued and appreciated.

A Day in the Life of a Mortgage Originator

Yes, but what does a mortgage originator *do*? You do many different things. A mortgage originator has relationships with many people who are at different points in the selling cycle (described at length in Part Two). The activities and daily actions for each stage of a loan are different, and the successful mortgage originator tends to all of them. A typical day is never typical, because every loan is different. Every customer has particular needs and concerns, and markets and products change all the time. The variety of activities and situations you deal with keeps you on your toes, and time passes quickly. At the end of the day you can look back at your stats and take satisfaction in knowing exactly what you have accomplished.

The morning begins with calls related to loans "in process." You call an employer for a verification form for one of your clients. Or you follow up with an appraiser prior to receiving the written report. You lock rates and gather loan documentation to keep the process going. And you call clients to let them know what's going on, to stay in touch and answer any questions or concerns they have.

Once the in-process files are moving, you turn your attention to generating new applications, beginning with calls to past customers. You may have sent out a mailing, which you are now following up. Or you are just calling to see how your clients are doing, offer your services, and ask for referrals. Or, you call past customers who are in mortgages that had a short fixed rate that is about to convert to adjustable, to let them know their options and what you can do for them. You call clients who recently closed a loan, to ask how it went and to ask for referrals. Staying in touch is very important—a satisfied customer is the best marketing and advertising there is.

Next, you move on to generate new business. Cold calls keep you sharp, so that when someone calls you in response to your marketing efforts, you are on your game and can convert the incoming call to an application. You keep statistics of your calls—how many people you spoke to and how many applications you took. You track your improvement over time. You record your presentations and listen to your interactions to train yourself in the sales techniques you learn in this book. You quickly develop a keen ear for the things that work and the things that don't, and you become masterful on the phones. (I know this may seem hard to believe, but I promise you, if you do this, you will overcome your anxiety and develop mastery.)

Next you move on to processing applications, pulling credit reports from today's applicants, reviewing yesterday's credit reports, and discussing the reports with clients to set them up for the next steps in the process. In these credit call conversations you develop relationships with clients based on trust and integrity. You also learn to recognize whether clients are ready to move to the next step, and if not, what you need to do to get them ready.

Then, you turn your attention to preparing proposals for clients. You review rate sheets, evaluate the clients' motivation and qualifications, call lenders for quotes on different loan products, and prepare alternatives and recommendations. You call clients to review the proposals with them, and to ask for the go-ahead, thus closing the sale. You track your conversion ratios and take corrective actions as needed.

Later you prepare loan packages for the proposals you sold, schedule appointments to review the package with the client, obtain signatures, collect application fees, and ask for referrals. You may visit clients' homes to obtain signatures and review the loan package documents, and then return to the office to submit the package to a processor.

You'll prepare for upcoming closings you have scheduled, reconcile the closing settlement statement with the Good Faith Estimate. You call your clients to prepare them for the closing, and ask for referrals. You update your records for future correspondence with your client to set up a schedule of automatic, regular communication with them.

On occasion, in the evening you attend a networking event, put on a seminar for first-time homebuyers or a credit repair program, or take a course to improve your knowledge and skills.

Before bed, if you sit back and think about it, you have the satisfaction of knowing that as a result of your efforts today, someone else's life is better. Imagine the confidence and power of knowing you are in control of your future. Imagine the freedom and power that come with being responsible for the results you produce and the unlimited income you can generate. All this is yours for the taking. Let's begin.

CHAPTER TWO

Big Picture: Understanding the Mortgage Loan Process

O btaining a *residential mortgage* is one of the most important financial decisions people make in their lifetime. This chapter begins with a look at why people buy mortgages, and you will see that borrowers' goals can be quite different. The chapter moves next to a high-altitude look at the loan process for two main types of residential mortgage transactions: *purchase* and *refinance*. While both follow the same basic process flow from *application* to *closing*, each has unique and specific requirements. This chapter focuses on the similarities, leaving the differences for later chapters.

When you understand what motivates a borrower, how the process works, and the role of each of the major players, you can efficiently provide loan products that make sense and lead to closings. And that is how you become a high-income mortgage originator.

Borrowers: Understanding Events That Motivate Them

People need or want money for all sorts of things: paying monthly bills, buying a home or a car, paying for an education, medical expenses, home improvements, and vacations to name a few. Regardless of the specific use for the money, a mortgage is a powerful financial tool that allows people to own homes and turn the *equity* value of a home into cash. We are going to look at four primary motivation categories and the events that trigger them: purchase, cash out, cash flow, and risk mitigation. When you understand the motivation that is most important to your borrowers, you can find the right loans for them, and effectively move them through the mortgage process to closing.

Purchasing a Home

Buying a home is one of the most exciting events in life. Whether you are looking for the perfect starter home, upgrading as your family or income grows, or down-sizing as your needs and income shrink, the experience of buying a home is filled with excitement, hope, and expectation. Financing the purchase can present challenges and concerns, but the knowledgeable *mortgage originator* prepares borrowers and guides them smoothly through the process from beginning to end. In this section we look at mortgages for home purchases, both for first-time homebuyers, and for people selling their present home and buying another.

First-Time Homebuyers

For most people, the purchase of their first home is a major milestone in their lives. Especially in the United States, owning your own piece of property is a fundamental element of the American dream. Annually, some 1.1 million people buy their first homes.

By the time they come to you, the mortgage originator, first-time homebuyers have most likely been working with a *real estate broker* or *agent* to find the home of their dreams. In order to know that they are shopping in the right price range, an agent or broker may advise prospective homebuyers to *prequalify* for a mortgage. Prequalification is a preliminary assessment of the amount of money a bank or other lender is willing to loan the homebuyer. *Preapproval* goes a step better; it is a commitment from a lender to provide funding, assuming the property meets certain requirements.

Preapproval serves all parties well. Knowing the amount of money a lender will provide, plus any money the buyer already has for a *down-payment* gives the buyer a ballpark price for a home he can afford. The broker or agent can focus on properties for which she knows the buyers will be able to get financing, and knows that when the time comes, obtaining a mortgage will not be an obstacle in closing the deal (there may be other obstacles, but financing won't be one of them). And a potential seller, interested in getting out of his property, is looking for a deal that will close quickly. Preapproval may help the buyer in negotiations over the purchase price. For the seller, knowing that a buyer has been preapproved provides assurance, again, that financing will not be an obstacle in the closing.

Patty and Craig Norman were finally about to reap the rewards of years of hard work during which they scraped by as Craig completed law school and Patty did office work for a small textile company in New York City's garment district. Craig had landed a good job with a law firm in one of Connecticut's largest cities, and he and Patty couldn't wait to get out of the dark, dreary, cramped studio apartment on West 13th Street that had been their home for the last six years.

They connected with Sheila, a veteran real estate agent, and began looking for homes in an upscale suburb of the city where Craig would be working. When they saw the bright three-bedroom sprawling contemporary on Forest View Drive, they knew it was where they wanted to live. Patty could already see herself happily planting a garden in the private, sunny backyard. The seller, a recently promoted division manager for a housewares manufacturer, was relocating his family to Chicago. The seller had already found a new home, and he and his wife were consumed with the logistics of moving, transitioning job responsibilities, preparing their two small children for the change, and finding contractors and suppliers 1000 miles away to prepare their new home for their arrival. Thrilled and excited, Patty and Craig stretched, and made an immediate offer for what they thought they could afford, nervous about whether they would be able to.

Sheila came back with some disappointing news. The seller had accepted another offer. She also gave Craig and Patty good advice: apply for preapproval for a mortgage. Patty was hesitant—she was afraid they wouldn't qualify, and she'd never have that garden. Sheila assured her that it was better to know sooner rather than later, and sent the Normans to me.

Craig and Patty had been smart and responsible during those lean years. They had managed to pay their bills on time, save a little money, and avoid debt while Craig was in school. Their credit was very good. They had avoided tapping into a small sum of money Craig's grandfather had left him that they would use for a down-payment. I was able to get them preapproval for a 30-year fixed at a good rate, giving them the assurance they could afford a home where they wanted to live, and Patty would have her garden. With this confidence and Sheila's help they began looking in earnest for another home they loved.

About two weeks later, Sheila called Craig with a surprise. The house on Forest View Drive was on the market again. The deal had fallen through because the buyer couldn't get financing. Patty and Craig couldn't believe their good luck and made their offer for the second time. The seller, with one foot in Connecticut and one in Chicago, was now only weeks from beginning his new job, and above all else, did not want to be in this position a second time. Sheila let him know that the Normans' financing had already been preapproved, and despite another slightly higher offer, he accepted theirs. Within six weeks the Normans were in their new home, and Patty was planting daffodils and tulips for the following spring.

Homebuyers, particularly first-time homebuyers, are excited and nervous. They want to know that they are doing the right thing, making the right choices. Once they find the home they love, they don't want to be in a position where there is a question about obtaining approval for a mortgage or where they are at risk of losing the home. Chances are they know little about the process for acquiring a mortgage, and they hope they made the right decision. It is in the agent's best interest to help the buyer secure funding. If the deal falls through, the agent will not get a commission. Sometimes a real estate agent will recommend a lender or loan originator to the buyer. An agent is likely to refer her clients to someone she knows will deal with them professionally, and who will provide them with the best service and loan product available. That's where you, as the mortgage originator, come in. As real estate agents have good experiences dealing with you, they can become an important source of referrals for growing your business.

You guide, instruct, and educate first-time homebuyers. They focus on finding the home of their dreams. They do not focus on the financing, but they want to make the right decision on both the house and the financing. Your job is to prepare them for the process and specifically and clearly communicate what they need to provide, and when, at each step. When they finally find that dream home, they will not want anything to jeopardize their ability to close the deal. Your job is to make sure that when they find the home they love, everything is in place to facilitate a smooth closing.

Moving from One Home to Another. A person already in a home who is moving into another is a slightly different story. People in this situation are concerned not only about financing a new home, they are usually also trying to sell their present home. The purchase of the new one may be contingent upon the sale of the present one. The sale of the present one may be contingent on the prospective buyer's ability to sell his present home, and so on.

People in this situation have been through the mortgage process and closing at least once before. If that experience was good, their expectations will be high for a repeat experience, and if they previously used you to get a mortgage, it makes good sense that they will use you again. Your job is always to keep your clients happy so that they keep coming back to you. If their prior experience was not good—things did not go smoothly, they were surprised by the numbers, costs, and so forth, then they will be on guard to prevent the things that went wrong the first time from happening again. Having been through the process, they may also assume that they know or understand certain issues but they may or may not, in fact, know and understand them correctly.

Timing is critical in these situations, as the proceeds from the sale of the present home will most likely be used to pay off the existing mortgage and provide the down-payment on the new home. There are mortgage and other *loan products*, for example, bridge loans, designed specifically to handle timing problems between closings.

For these borrowers, a lot is going on. They want to know that you know what you are doing, that you can be trusted with the details, and that everything is going to go smoothly on your end. Your problems are the least of their worries. Simple, straight, and to the point communication is crucial. But do not take shortcuts—it is important that you be certain that buyers know what to expect from you and what you need from them.

Major Cash Requirements

Home ownership is a long-term investment. *Property values* may rise or fall significantly due to economic conditions, changes in the surrounding homes and neighborhoods, natural disasters, supply and demand of houses for sale, interest rates, and many other reasons. Owners' equity in their homes—the value of the home minus the balance due on the mortgage note—is for many people the single largest asset in their financial portfolio. It is also a source of cash and/or credit for major purchases like a car, college education, investment opportunities, or to pay off or avoid other debt such as credit cards, medical bills, or home improvements.

Equity can be turned into cash by refinancing the home for a larger *principal* amount. Compared with other *lines of credit* and sources of cash, refinancing provides access to large sums payable over a long period, usually at significantly lower *rates of interest* than other credit such as credit cards.

When a homeowner cashes out equity, he incurs a *liability* in the form of the additional loan principal amount borrowed. This can be accomplished either by refinancing the home or by taking a *home equity loan* or *home equity line of credit*. Which product is the right one? It depends on how quickly the borrower intends to pay back the loan, and the impact it has on *cash flow*.

Jackie and Pete Hollister had a good life, raising their three sons, Tom 11, Matthew, 8 and Joseph, 6. When they bought their home 12 years earlier, there were only a few others in the neighborhood, which was being newly developed. Now, it was a highly desirable area of town, filling up with young families drawn to the neighborhood atmosphere and good nearby schools. Pete and Jackie didn't give too much thought to the impact of the steadily rising property values of the neighborhood. They liked living there and planned to remain at least until the boys were grown, if not longer.

Pete's parents, two married sisters, and brother all lived within a 35-mile radius. Holidays, birthdays, and other happy occasions brought them together to enjoy one another's company. Jackie's widowed mom lived alone in Ohio where Jackie had grown up, and her twice yearly visits with Jackie, Pete, and the boys were always special.

One winter, returning to Ohio after a holiday visit, Jackie's mom was hospitalized with pneumonia. Jackie flew home to tend to her mom and stayed for a few days. Over the next several weeks, she shuttled back and forth, taking care of mom, kids, and Pete. Beneath her cheery appearance, she was worried about her mom's long-term living situation, and the toll her absences were taking on Pete and the boys. Pete, sensing Jackie's concerns, started thinking about what he could do, and one evening, as they shared a few precious quiet moments together, he suggested moving Jackie's mom to live with them. Exhausted and touched, Jackie was grateful, but expressed her concern about the disruption adding another person to their just right house would be. The younger boys would have to share a bedroom to make room for mom, and the boy's bathroom, already a source of territorial contention, would have another person vying for its use. Pete assured Jackie that there was a way to make it work, and that he would start investigating.

On the recommendation of a neighbor for whom I had gotten a mortgage, Pete called me, explained his situation, and asked if I thought I could help. We talked for a while about what he wanted, and it became clear that he could either build out or look for a larger home, which neither he nor Jackie wanted to do. Clear that the goal was to finance a major home improvement, I started working on a solution for the Hollister family.

Twelve years into their 30-year fixed mortgage, they had paid off about $20,000 of the $125,000 they had originally borrowed, which along with a $25,000 down-payment had gotten them their home. In addition, similar homes in the neighborhood had recently sold for $300,000 to $325,000. They had plenty of equity. Next we looked at the pros and cons of a second mortgage versus refinancing a first, and could see that with interest rates presently lower than their current mortgage, for slightly more than they were now paying monthly on their mortgage, they would be able to take the equity out, refinance, and increase the resale value of their home.

In only three weeks Pete had the cash to begin construction on a beautiful mother-in-law suite, with private bath, bedroom, and sitting area. Jackie's mom, who after living alone for many years valued her privacy, had no concerns once she saw the plans. The boys, oblivious to the near loss of their private rooms and the prospect of more bathroom squabbles, looked forward to Grandma Sylvia watching their school plays and soccer games. Jackie, confident now that she could care for all her family, was much relieved.

Refinance. With a refinance, the equity converted to cash is added to the existing loan's outstanding principal, and the whole amount is extended over the *term* of a new loan. Interest rates for refinancing are typically lower than equity loans or lines of credit. If the equity value is used for a long-term commitment, for example, starting a business, it makes sense to extend the loan for the longest term at the lowest rates possible.

Second Mortgage. A home equity loan (or second mortgage) makes sense if the borrower wants to pay back the equity in a different period from that covering the remaining principal balance on the first mortgage. If there is a short term left on the first mortgage and the borrower wants to extend the repayment of the equity for a longer period, or if there is a long term remaining on the first mortgage and the borrower expects to pay back the equity sooner, then a home equity loan makes sense, leaving the primary mortgage intact.

HELOCS. A *home equity line of credit* (HELOC) allows the borrower to cash the equity as needed (for example, as college tuition becomes due), and to have the option to pay back only the interest on the loan until the home is sold or the principal repaid from another source. If the money is not needed all at once, or the money is only needed for a short period, then a HELOC makes sense.

Whether it is a matter of refinance, second mortgage, or HELOC, it is important for you to understand the need that is motivating borrowers, and to understand their current financial situation to be able to explain their options and the short-term and long-term benefits and shortcomings of each. By asking the right questions, you will be able to assist buyers in making decisions that best serve their short- and long-term needs.

Cash Flow

Many families have difficulty making ends meet from one month to the next. Interest rates and the term both impact the amount of cash that flows out each month to pay a mortgage. Refinancing is a widely used tool to accomplish changes in cash flow.

Income may fluctuate based on hours worked, overtime, commissions, tips, and so forth. Or expenses may rise sharply with the need for a new car, or college education, or the addition of a baby to the family. Changes in laws governing minimum payments on credit card balances have put some people in an even more difficult position, as higher monthly payments are required. And, of course, rising prices of gas, electricity and other essentials can squeeze what little cushion existed.

Over the life of a mortgage the owner's income may significantly increase (job promotion) or decrease (retirement, lay-off, or job loss), causing a change in the amount of cash available each month to cover basic living expenses. If income decreases, the owner looks at refinancing to reduce monthly mortgage payments, freeing up money to cover other monthly expenses. If income increases, some owners take advantage of the additional *discretionary income* to put a larger amount of monthly income toward paying off the mortgage. Or an owner may seek to shorten the term of the mortgage to repay it in 10 or 15 years instead of 30. In times of declining interest rates, people can also see an opportunity to free up cash on a monthly basis by refinancing at lower rates or by extending the remaining term and outstanding balance at their current rate.

People who are looking to refinance to solve cash flow problems are more concerned with dealing with their short-term problem than they are about the long-term impact of the solution. They want the best deal, now. The lowest monthly payment available may not be the best deal in the long run, and you will have to be able to explain the pros and cons so they can make an informed decision. Your job is to provide the best short-term solution for them, but also to look at their financial spending and earning habits to instruct them in ways to avoid being in the same short-term jam again in only a few years.

People who want to take advantage of an opportunity to improve their cash flow because of declining interest rates or higher earning power may be more interested in whether the short- and long-term benefits of refinancing are worth the cost and effort. Again, your job is to present them with options that balance long- and short-term advantages.

Changes that Create Risk

A homeowner may anticipate or be concerned about a future risk that could be avoided or reduced by taking cash out and/or changing the amount of monthly payments. People facing these types of situations look at refinancing as a way to position themselves financially for the future.

Roxanne had a good job managing a computer department for a major entertainment company. She made a very good living, complete with benefits and stock options. The great people working for her made her job easy. Life was good, and it was boring.

At 50 years old, after 30 years in the same career, she wanted a change—a big change. Opportunity presented itself. A close friend, who had invented a product that Roxanne believed strongly in, was looking for people to promote the product. Roxanne was intrigued. After discussing matters with her financial advisor, she began taking steps to restructure her finances to prepare for a period during which she anticipated little income until the new business started generating money.

She came to us wanting to minimize her monthly payments and secure as much credit as possible to sustain her until the business took off. She had two college-aged children, owned her own home, was making payments on a luxury car, but otherwise had no debt, and her credit was very good. She had accumulated several hundred thousand dollars in retirement assets, and her home had appreciated by about 50% in the six years she had owned it.

She tapped into some of the equity to pay off the luxury car and set aside college tuition for both kids for the next year, and about $10,000 to start the business. She was still able to reduce her monthly expenses by about $500. She refinanced at a lower fixed-rate mortgage for 30 years, and qualified for a HELOC on the balance of her equity.

About five months later she walked away from her job and started a new life, free to pursue her dream without financial concerns.

Anticipating the birth of a child, the care of a parent, starting a business, or the loss of a job are all situations that change a homeowner's ability to continue making current mortgage payments. Some mortgages have *adjustable interest rates* based on *economic indices*, and unfavorable economic forecasts (for example, rising interest rates) could cause concern that monthly payments will rise to unaffordable levels.

People concerned about a drop in income, whether it is permanent as with retirement, or temporary as with a change or loss of job or career, use refinancing to reduce their monthly payment either by reducing interest rates or extending the term of the loan. As with people who are looking to improve cash flow, these borrowers are looking for a balance between their anticipated short-term needs and the long-term impact their actions will have. People in this situation may also be looking to secure a line of credit against the equity in their home, so that should they need access to funds, they have it. Very often people will *piggy back* a refinanced first mortgage with a home equity line of credit so that they can feel securely situated should hard times befall them.

Refinancing a home can be an effective way to prepare for these events. *Adjustable-rate mortgages* (ARMs) have been very popular since the 1970s when interest rates were high. They initially provide a lower rate of interest that is fixed for the first few years of the loan, but is later adjusted based on one of several standard economic indices, like the *prime rate*. The popularity of these products continued even as interest rates reached all time lows, because their discounted rates in the first several years still look very attractive when compared to a higher interest fixed-rate loan. As interest rates rise, however, and the adjustment date approaches, many of these mortgage holders look for fixed-rate mortgages, betting that interest rates will continue to rise over the term of their loans. And for people who stretched their borrowing power on the basis of the low introductory rates on these ARMs, the prospect of higher monthly payments can be daunting. Folks in this situation are concerned about long-term stability and the cost of refinancing.

Regardless of motivation—new purchase, major cash requirements, cash flow, or reducing risk—the mortgage originator is the first point of contact for the prospective borrower. Your job is to understand clients' motivations, to prepare them for the options they will have to choose from, and to guide them through the loan process from application through closing. In order to do that, you must build and maintain trust at all times, so that they have the confidence to move forward at each decision point.

First Steps: Initiating Contact to Submitting the Application

Regardless of motivation—purchase, cash out, cash flow, or risk—the fundamentals of obtaining a mortgage are standard. The first leg in the process begins when prospective borrowers begin shopping for a loan. Their first point of contact is with a mortgage originator like you. After initial inquiries to find an originator, prospective borrowers complete a mortgage application and authorize a credit report. Based on an understanding of borrowers' needs and information contained in the application and credit report, the mortgage originator proposes a loan product for which he believes the borrower is qualified and which addresses the borrower's goals for the mortgage. Upon acceptance of the proposal by the borrower, the mortgage originator prepares the loan package for review and signature by the borrower, and then submits the package to a loan processor for the start of the second leg of the process.

Stephen had been a mortgage originator for only a few months when, following a direct mail campaign we had done for borrowers four+ years into 5/1 ARMs, he received an incoming call from George Durante. In less than six months the attractively low five-year fixed rate of the adjustable-rate mortgage would expire, and the rate for the remaining 25 years of the loan would go up significantly and was likely to increase annually after that. George was angry, and wanted someone to know it, and Stephen got an earful. He said he didn't believe we could do anything for him, and that the last time he listened to "one of you" he got suckered and now it looked as if he was going to have to sell his home.

As George vented, Stephen collected himself sufficiently to hear that underneath the anger was a man asking for help. He had been given poor advice from another mortgage originator who steered him toward a short-term solution without fully explaining the long-term risks that were now closing in on him. Stephen listened until George had finished, and then said, "I'm so sorry Mr. Durante, I can understand exactly how you feel, and if I were in your position I would feel the same way." He could hear George listening at the other end of the phone. He was straight with

George, and told him that he didn't know whether he could do anything to help him, but that if George was willing to work with him, he could count on Stephen to do everything possible to find options that made sense and present them fully. If the options made sense to George, they would move forward, or else Stephen would close the file and that would be the end of it. After a moment of silence, George conceded a gruff "fine," and Stephen had a customer.

As Stephen took George's application information, he learned that George had been married to his wife Gloria for 38 years, they lived in a modest house they bought when they started their family, and had raised two daughters, both married, and a son who was in college. George was a telephone repair technician—one of the guys who climbs the poles and rides the cherry pickers—and had been working for the local telephone company for 27 years. He liked the freedom his job gave him, away from the succession of the "suits" who had become his boss after numerous mergers and reorganizations of the huge company. Gloria answered the phones at the local community college, where their son Richard had just completed two years of study. Richard had earned a partial scholarship to the state university where he was now studying business administration. George and Stephen chuckled at the idea that Richard could be one of those suits George avoided in his job. Stephen also learned that four years earlier, Gloria's mother suffered a stroke, and George and Gloria refinanced their home to provide her with full-time care during her recovery. Now, the seductively low monthly payments they had enjoyed for the last four years were about to rise sharply, and George couldn't see how they could swing it, even with him and Gloria working overtime. The thought of losing his home made him sick. Stephen told George he'd pull the credit report and get back to him at 3:00 P.M. the next day. Based on the application they just completed, it appeared to Stephen that George and Gloria had some options, but until he saw the credit report he didn't want to get specific. George hung up the phone, hopeful.

George and Gloria's credit score, credit history and ratios made them good candidates for a variety of loans. The next day at exactly

3:00 P.M., Stephen called George who answered the phone with a gruff "yeah?" When Stephen identified himself, George remarked that he hadn't thought Stephen would call him back right away, let alone at 3:00 P.M. on the dot. Stephen laughed, and told George what he had found. Based on the information so far, it appeared that George and Gloria would have a number of options from which to choose. They reviewed the items on the credit report, including an old merchandise dispute that George thought was resolved. Stephen instructed George on what to do to have it removed from the credit report. He then explained that he would do some research and call some of the hundreds of lenders with which our brokerage firm does business, and present several options to both George and Gloria the next day at 7:00 P.M. If the proposal made sense, they would move forward and submit a loan for approval, which would require a refundable application fee. If the proposal didn't make sense to George and Gloria, Stephen would close the file and they would be done. George agreed, and remarked lightly that when the phone rang at 7:00 P.M. tomorrow he'd know it was Stephen, and he and Gloria would be ready to hear what he had to offer.

Stephen reviewed rate sheets, ran different scenarios through calculators and came up with two loan products that would keep George and Gloria's monthly payments close to their current rate. Stephen compared these two options to the do-nothing option, which was clearly not a smart choice for them. The next evening at exactly 7:00 P.M. when Stephen called, Gloria answered. George was heard in the background saying, "See, I told you it would be him." With both George and Gloria on the phone, Stephen reviewed what had taken place so far, and where the do-nothing strategy would take them. He went over two other proposals, one with no closing costs, and the other with higher closing costs but a lower monthly payment, and left the choice up to George and Gloria.

George and Gloria agreed they would rather keep some cash in reserve for emergencies, and to take a slightly higher monthly payment still within the range they knew they could carry. Stephen instructed them to gather pay stubs, bank statements, and tax returns for a meeting the

next evening at 7:30 P.M. at their home, where Stephen would go over all
the documents they would sign for the loan application, and they would
give Stephen the application fee.

At 7:30 the next evening, Stephen rang George and Gloria's door-
bell, and shook hands with George for the first time. The big grinning
George was hardly what Stephen imagined from their first phone call.
Stephen went over each document in the loan package and handed them
to Gloria and then George, giving them time to look over each one and
ask questions before they signed. At the end of the evening, Gloria and
George were satisfied, and Stephen had originated a loan.

From Initial Inquiry to Loan Application

Regardless of the borrower's motivation—purchase, cash out, cash flow,
or risk mitigation—the impression you make in your initial contact with
him is likely to determine whether he moves forward with you to complete
a loan application. You have just a few moments to convey knowledge,
professionalism, and a commitment to satisfying his needs. Your desired
outcome for each encounter with a prospective borrower is to take an
application.

How Borrowers Shop. Prospective borrowers actively seeking a
mortgage for a purchase, cash out, cash flow, or risk mitigation may research lenders, compare currently advertised rates, or ask friends or colleagues to recommend someone who can help them. A recent Internet
search engine query on "mortgage originator" turned up over a million
hits! Ultimately the choice to do business with you or with one of your
competitors will depend on whether you earn their trust and address their
needs and concerns in your first encounter. A good word on your behalf
from someone the borrower knows and trusts will carry much more weight
than any advertising or promotion you can do.

Contact between borrowers and mortgage originators can be initiated by either party. If you initiate the contact through marketing efforts
(outbound), it is up to you to engage prospects in conversations that grab

their attention and interest. If an individual is not actively seeking a mortgage, he may still be open to starting the mortgage process if you earn his trust and create for him the possibility of improving his financial status by obtaining a mortgage.

Purchases. When a homebuyer finds a home he wants and believes he can afford, he makes an *offer* to the seller for a specific price and gives the seller a small amount of money, or *binder*, which the seller applies toward the sale of the house or refunds if he declines the offer.

If the seller accepts the offer, the seller's real estate agent and/or lawyer prepares the legal *contract* of sale. When both buyer and seller sign the contract, the buyer places a deposit into an *escrow* account where it remains until closing. Then it is up to the buyer to secure the mortgage financing for the home within the period specified in the contract, usually 30 to 90 days. If a buyer fails to secure a *loan commitment* within that period, he risks losing the house of his dreams, so buyers, especially first-time homebuyers, can become very jittery during this period. That is why it is very important to be in communication with them even when you have nothing new to communicate.

Complete the Loan Application. The mortgage process officially begins by completing a mortgage application, which asks for information the lender uses to determine whether to commit to the loan, and if so, on what terms. Applications vary somewhat between lending institutions, but most lenders accept a Form 1003 (ten oh three), a Uniform Residential Loan Application. All applications ask questions about the value and price of the property, the borrower's ability to pay monthly living expenses, and the financial stability of the borrower based on *credit reports, employment history*, and in some cases, *tax returns* and other *documentation of assets*.

A mortgage originator helps the borrower fill out the application completely and accurately. The process can be as tedious and boring as . . . well, filling out a long, detailed form. Or it can be an opportunity for you to get to know your prospect, understand his needs, address his concerns and build a trusting relationship. Assuming the borrower has accurate knowledge of his data and has given it to you, the completed application provides enough information for you to understand his financial situation and motivation for seeking a mortgage, so you can begin looking for the right loan product.

At this stage the application information is not final—most of it will be verified by outside sources or official documents before submission to a lender. It is very important that, even at this early point, you now have the borrowers' trust. Without it, you'll be missing information you need to make a full and accurate analysis. For example, identity-theft headlines make people wary of revealing social security numbers over the phone or Internet, but the borrower's social security number (or resident alien ID number) is needed to move to the next step—obtaining the credit report.

Credit Report. Credit reports, obtained from at least one of three national *Credit Bureaus*, contain a *credit score* and details about amounts owed and to whom, late payments, and *judgments* or *liens* against the borrower. Registered mortgage originators can access credit reports over the Internet in a matter of minutes. In addition to the data credit reports provide, how well that data support the information already given by the borrower tells you a lot about his awareness, responsibility, and candor regarding his financial state. The credit report may be totally consistent with the information he provided. Or it may show problems that he did not mention, either because he did not know about them, didn't think they were important, or was hoping you wouldn't find out. In the next conversation you have with the borrower, you will review the credit report with him, learn the reason for discrepancies, and discuss what the report is likely to mean in terms of the products for which he qualifies.

Sometimes credit reports contain errors, so if there is a discrepancy between the credit report and the application, don't assume the credit report is correct. Ask the borrower about anything on the report that is potentially detrimental or that doesn't match up with the application. If he believes there are errors in the credit report, now is the time for him to correct them, either by contacting the credit bureau or the merchant who reported the erroneous information. If accurate facts are having a negative impact on the score, now is the time for the borrower to take corrective action in order to expand the loan options that will be available to him.

Even if a borrower has bad credit or no credit history at all, there are things that you can to do to assist in finding a lender. A serious borrower can improve, repair, or establish credit in a relatively short period in many cases.

As with completing the application, reviewing a credit report can be dry, boring, and uncomfortable, or it can be another opportunity to understand the borrower's motivation and commitment, and to build a trusting relationship.

Application to Proposal

When a loan application and credit report are complete and have been reviewed with the borrower, you can either research viable loan options or forward the application to a mortgage broker or lender to propose options. A mortgage originator must be associated with either a *mortgage broker* or a specific lender. The degree of your responsibility for finding a loan that meets the prospect's needs and for which he is likely to qualify depends on your experience and the policies of the company with which or for which you work.

Available Loan Products. An originator is at an advantage when working with a broker because a broker can shop a loan around among hundreds of *wholesale lenders* to find the best terms for the borrower. Dealing with lenders nationally, a mortgage broker has a wider choice of products than those offered by any one lender, like a bank. The broker knows what lenders will accept for *key ratios*, and can shop the application around for the best deal.

Most wholesale lenders provide *rate sheets* that lay out the terms of the loan products they offer, which mortgage brokers and their originators use to create proposals for prospective borrowers. *Retail lenders*, who lend directly to borrowers rather than through brokers, also have rate sheets for the originators working for them. Rate sheets provide timely information about which loan products are offered and at what rates and conditions.

A loan product is a set of terms and conditions under which the money will be lent and repayment of the loan will be made. The timing of payments, the duration (or term) of the loan, the amount of interest to be paid over what periods, when and by how much adjustments to interest rates will be made are some of the terms with which a mortgage originator must be familiar.

Loan products are constantly changing as regulations change, the economy changes, and lending becomes more competitive. Keeping abreast of new products like interest-only loans or reverse mortgages, and understanding the needs they serve is an important part of your job. Not only must you understand what is available to your prospects, but it is likely you will have to explain it to them as well.

Find Suitable Loan Products. Lenders, brokers, and mortgage origi-nators use the information on the mortgage application and credit reports to calculate key ratios, which allow them to assess quickly the risk asso-ciated with the loan. Lenders' guidelines for acceptable ratios vary, and reflect their ability and willingness to assume the financial risk of the loan. To know the loan products for which your prospect qualifies, you (or the broker or lender making the proposal) compute the key loan ratios to make a preliminary assessment as to whether the borrower is potentially viable.

It's important that you know your borrower's primary motivation for seeking a mortgage—purchase, cash out, cash flow, or risk—when you assess suitable loan products. Many factors come into play in your decision to propose a loan to a prospect. Low credit scores and unfavorable key ratios limit their choices. The mortgage with the lowest interest rate may not be the best one for a borrower, even though logically it seems to be the best loan for everyone. Focusing on the primary motivation the borrower has for seeking the mortgage directs you to the type of loan product that will best meet his short- and long-term needs.

Present a Proposal. As the main contact with customers, you are likely to present proposals to them so that they can see clearly the advantages of moving to the next steps in the mortgage process. Once again, the proposal can be a straight number-crunching exercise—or a good opportunity to reaffirm the prospect's goals and commitment, and continue to build the relationship and trust between you. The proposal highlights the key features of the loan, such as the monthly payment, the term of the loan, the rate of interest, whether the interest is fixed or adjustable, adjustment parameters, and points due on closing. It is a good idea to present more than one option to the borrower when you are making a proposal. At the very least, your recommendation compared to a do-nothing scenario highlights features and benefits of the loan you are proposing. At this critical decision point, it reminds the borrower of his goals, his reasons for having come this far, and why it makes sense to move forward. Assuming you do your job correctly and the prospect agrees to move forward with your proposed loan product, you are ready to prepare the loan package.

Proposal to Submission

The U.S. Department of Housing and Urban Development (HUD) issues statutory regulations regarding residential real estate transactions. The Real Estate Settlements Procedure Act (RESPA) is a HUD statute intended to protect consumers, particularly with regard to settlement or closing costs. It requires that at the time of the application, or within three days, the borrower receive a *Good Faith Estimate* of costs associated with the loan, and a *Mortgage Servicing Disclosure*, a statement of rights in the event that servicing rights to the loan are sold. These and other documents comprising the loan package are reviewed with the borrower prior to obtaining his signature. Upon completion the loan moves to the next leg of the process.

Assemble the Loan Package. The mortgage originator prepares the *loan package*, about two dozen forms and documents needing a borrower's signature and required by a lender to evaluate the loan. Whether you mail the package or present it in-person, you should review in detail the content of the package as each form is signed. At this step the borrower also provides standard verification documents such as pay stubs, W-2s and bank statements and a check for the application fee.

The Uniform Residential Loan Application (1003) is one of the loan package documents. Most of the other forms in the loan package document that you fully and accurately informed borrowers about the transaction, the process, and their rights. Many of the documents, including the Good Faith Estimate and Mortgage Servicing Disclosure, disclose fees and detail borrowers' rights during the mortgage process. Some documents authorize the lender to obtain information from the IRS or the borrower's employers and banks. Most states require additional forms, specific to transactions involving property within their borders. You may also devise your own forms to document that you informed the borrower of your policies and practices, for example, conditions under which you refund an *application fee*, if any.

Lock the Rate

Lock the Rate. Borrowers base their decision to move forward with the application on the terms you proposed. Lenders issue new rates frequently, sometimes changing rates several times in the same day. Unless you *lock in* the interest rate and points you proposed, you cannot guarantee the precise terms presented in the proposal. Locking in a rate insures, for a specific limited time, the interest rate and points on a fixed-rate mortgage, and the index and margin and rate cap on ARMs.

Rate locks are good for borrowers when interest rates are rising, or if they only marginally qualify for the proposed loan. On the other hand, if interest rates are dropping, it makes sense for the borrower to *float* the rate, betting that rates drop between the loan application and the closing. Some lenders offer *float-down* locks that protect borrowers against rising rates and retain the benefits of a float if rates drop. Nothing is for nothing;

it costs money to lock in a rate, and the longer the lock is in effect and the more it is to the borrower' advantage, the more it costs. A lock must be effective through the closing to protect the client fully. Extending a lock is expensive, and letting one expire could leave you unable to provide your client what you proposed. That is very expensive, indeed. It is up to you to monitor the expiration date and manage the process so that the loan closes within the period for which the lock is in effect.

The initial leg of the process is complete. Now you turn your attention to the mortgage brokers, lenders, and supporting players who process and approve the loan application.

Home Stretch: Processing, Underwriting, and Closing the Deal

When the loan package is complete the mortgage originator gives it to a *processor*, who is usually an employee of the lender or mortgage broker. The processor's job is to make sure the application and supporting documents are complete and accurate, and in compliance with laws and regulations before submitting the application package to an *underwriter* for evaluation and approval. Once approved, a closing is scheduled, completing the transaction.

Proposal to Underwriting

Regardless of whether you work with a broker or directly with a lender, the services of key people are needed to get approval for your clients' loans. Mortgage brokers can and do perform some of the functions described in this section prior to submitting the loan package to a lender, who will repeat the processes. By handling the package in much the same way the lender will, but prior to submission, the broker uncovers issues, problems, and discrepancies that must be resolved before a lender approves a loan. The broker works with you to resolve or explain these items, so that when the lender receives the package he can evaluate it quickly and efficiently.

Good relations between brokers and lenders mean good service for your customers.

Processing. The processor is the funnel for loan applications moving between originators and lenders. The processing department in a brokerage firm or a lending institution handles loans for all the originators affiliated with that institution. The processing department enforces quality and federal, state, and local legal conformance, arranges special services such as appraisals and title searches, tracks missing and pending items, obtains verifications, watches rate lock expirations, and keeps you informed. You are one of many originators for whom the processing department provides service. Your job is to make their jobs easy, so that they can provide the best service possible for you and your clients.

Upon receipt of the loan package, the processor checks it for completeness and accuracy. If there are errors, obvious discrepancies, or omissions, the processor may refuse the file. Don't let that happen. If you want to make a lot of money as an originator, you must be responsible for the quality of your work. If the package is acceptable, the processor records it for tracking and orders an appraisal and title search.

Security Interests. A mortgage is a *secured loan*, which means the borrower's promise to pay is backed up by giving the lender a legal interest in the ownership of the property. Because the property secures the loan, lenders are very interested in the value and condition of the property, especially compared to the amount of the loan. Lenders avoid situations where the amount owed on the mortgage is more than the property is worth, which can happen if property values decline. If the property is sold or the borrower fails to pay the mortgage, the lender, under the laws governing secured loans, can exercise its right to ownership of the property securing the loan. If other parties have legal claim to all or part of the property, it could interfere with the lender's ability to assert its security rights. Appraisals and title insurance protect the lender's security interest in the property.

Appraisal. The *appraisal* is an objective and professional valuation of the property, for securing the loan. The *appraiser*, usually a licensed professional, visits the property and compares it to other recently sold properties of similar age, size, style, condition, and location. Based on these *comparables* (*comps* for short) the appraiser assigns a value to the property and issues a written report, the appraisal.

Loan to Value (LTV), one of the key ratios mentioned previously, compares the amount of the loan to the appraised value of the property. Loan to Value measures the lender's security cushion should property values decline. Higher LTV means more risk to the lender, which translates into a more expensive loan for the borrower.

Title. Before the processor forwards a loan package to an underwriter for determination, he will order a *title search* from a title insurance company, or in some states, from an attorney or escrow agent. A title search establishes that every past transfer of the property occurred legally, and that there are no outstanding liens on the property now. Title insurance protects the lender up to the amount of the mortgage against any past claims on the property that the title search did not uncover. For a refinance, where no transfer occurs, a lender still requires a title search and title insurance to protect against any claims that arose since the time of the last title search. The cost of title searches and insurance is borne by the borrower, but the insurance does not protect the borrower's interest in the property, only the lender's. The borrower can, however, purchase separate owner's title insurance, if desired.

Insurance. The lender's security interest over the term of the loan depends on maintaining the value of the property, which is partly based on its condition. Damage to or destruction of the property reduces or destroys the lender's security, so lenders require the borrower to carry homeowner's insurance. In some cases the lender requires additional insurance against specific natural disasters, such as flood or earthquake. The borrower usually has the option to choose his own insurance carrier, but must provide proof of insurance before the loan package goes to the underwriter. If the borrower does not provide homeowner's insurance, the lender adds an insurance premium to the settlement costs at closing.

Verifications. The lender requires proof of key information provided by the borrower on the application. The processor sends out forms (the authorizations that are part of the loan package) to verify employment, balances on asset accounts like checking and savings, and other documents that prove the existence of assets or verify the borrower's ability to pay monthly expenses.

Underwriting and Approval

When all supporting materials are together, the package goes to an underwriter who reviews the application, credit report, and supporting documentation to determine whether the borrower qualifies for the loan product specified in the application. Lenders rely on established guidelines for key ratios to make the determination. The underwriter may request additional documentation or actions by the borrower before approving the loan.

With an approval, the lender bets that the borrower will be able to repay the loan. The security interest in the property, and in some cases *private mortgage insurance* (PMI), protect the lender if the borrower fails to pay, but the lender wants repayment, not to own the property. Lenders consider borrowers' income and credit to be key indicators of their ability to make the mortgage payments, and use them to calculate key ratios that help determine approval. Many lenders use automated underwriting systems that check for consistency of information, calculate key ratios, and compare borrower information to the established qualification guidelines.

The Secondary Market Influence. Most lenders like banks, mortgage companies, and finance companies (*primary lenders*) have access to limited (though very large) amounts of money with which to fund the mortgages they provide to consumers. Most of the profit is made early in the loan term, as most loans are structured to have the borrower pay most of the interest in the first years of the loan term. It is profitable for lenders to sell loans to the *secondary market*. The more often lenders turn over the money, the more profit they can make.

Three organizations sponsored by the U.S. federal government are predominant buyers of loans in the secondary market. These organizations,

Fannie Mae (Federal National Mortgage Association or FNMA), Freddie Mac (Federal Home Loan Mortgage Corporation or FHLMC), and Ginnie Mae (Government National Mortgage Association or GNMA) buy loans in bulk and then package them for sale on Wall Street as bonds. Because of the sponsored status of these organizations, these loans are less risky for investors, and hence earn investors less money than other investments. This allows the interest rates to borrowers to be lower for loans conforming to the requirements for sale to these organizations.

Fannie Mae and Freddie Mac provide guidelines to lenders for the loans they will buy. They also provide automated underwriting systems. They place limits on the amount of the loan and type of property, as well as specific values for key ratios. Loans that meet these requirements are called *conforming loans*. Loans that do not meet these requirements are call *nonconforming loans*, and generally carry higher rates of interest.

Ginnie Mae (Government National Mortgage Association) is a government organization that serves the same function as Fannie Mae and Freddie Mac, but for mortgage loans insured by the federal government. These federally insured loans are part of federal programs under the Federal Housing Administration and the Department of Veterans Affairs, and were created to facilitate home ownership for veterans.

Income. You will meet people in all sorts of income situations. You will find people of modest income who have large savings. You will find people who earn a lot of money and have no savings. You will find people steadily employed for decades with the same company and self-employed people who often do not know what their income will be, other than inconsistent. There's a mortgage for each of them!

The amount of a borrower's monthly income is not significant in its own right. I've gotten loan approvals for clients with very little income, and have had difficulty getting approvals for clients with very high incomes. Income is important only relative to the amount of the mortgage payment and other monthly household expenses, including the payment of other loans or debts. A lender wants assurance that monthly income is sufficient to cover these expenses, whatever the amounts.

When you think of income, you may think in terms of salary or wages from a job, but income from rental properties or other investments, interest and dividends, alimony and child support, commissions, tips, social security benefits, and other sources can all be considered.

In addition to income/expense ratios, lenders look at the borrower's income history to determine whether earnings are increasing, decreasing, or stable. Employment history and tax returns for the past two years are usually sufficient *income verification* for the lender to make an assessment regarding income.

Self-employed people pose a special challenge. Income may be erratic, and business deductions lower taxable income. The *stated income* or no-documentation loan is an option for people in those situations. The loans may have less favorable terms than an income-verified loan. Proof of self-employment is required, and the stated income must be an honest reflection of earnings, which can be documented if required.

Credit. Regardless of income or ability to pay, if a borrower has a history of late payments lenders take notice. The credit report verifies some of the information used to calculate monthly expenses—car payments, credit card payments, student loans, and so forth, are all shown. In addition, the credit report includes *payment history*. Given particular weight are payments made on the current mortgage or rent, and payments on installment loans (like car payments). If the report shows a history or pattern of late payments, the borrower represents a higher risk of failure to pay. Also, any *collection actions* taken against the borrower are a strike against them. Interestingly, too many *credit inquiries*, for example, requests for credit reports, also raise a red flag for the lender as a possible indicator of financial trouble. Another interesting fact is that even someone who recently declared *bankruptcy* can qualify for a mortgage! A lender may even consider it a good risk, since the law prohibits people from claiming bankruptcy more than once in ten years. Three credit bureaus collect this information and rate these factors and others into a credit score. Credit scores are one of the factors that determine whether a loan conforms to lending guidelines.

Approval to Closing

If the underwriter is satisfied that the appraised value of the property produces acceptable ratios and that the borrower is likely to be able to make the monthly payments on the loan, he notifies the borrower of approval with a commitment letter that details the terms of the loan. He may also specify conditions, such as providing additional documentation related to income, assets, or credit, which the borrower must satisfy before the closing. The transaction is completed at the closing.

Closing Agents and Documents. A closing agent prepares the *closing documents*, records them legally, and distributes the funds at the closing. Attorneys, *escrow agents*, and title companies can serve as closing agents, representing the lender in the closing transaction. Closing documents detail the terms of the transaction, disclose fees earned, costs associated with the closing itself, when payments begin, and so forth. RESPA requires a HUD-1 Settlement Statement of fees to be paid, commissions earned, how much money will be distributed to which parties at the time of closing, and other costs associated with the mortgage and closing process. The HUD-1 Settlement Statement should not be too far off the Good Faith Estimate provided to the borrower when the mortgage application was submitted. Other documents include a Truth in Lending Statement disclosing the mortgage terms, the loan note itself, the mortgage document establishing the lender's security interest in the property, and, in the case of a purchase, the deed to the property. Additional disclosures, affidavits, and statements will also be prepared for review and signature at the closing.

The Closing. The closing agent, representatives (lawyers) for the borrower, and in the case of a purchase, representatives for the seller attend the closing. The borrower (buyer in a purchase), real estate agents, seller, and others may also attend. The closing agent makes sure all documents are signed.

The closing is where the money changes hands, and it flows through the escrow agent. Typically on a new home purchase, the lender gives money to the buyer who gives it the seller who then uses it to pay off the balance of the mortgage he had on the property. On a refinance, the lender gives money to the borrower who uses all or part of it to pay off the previous mortgage and any other debts agreed to in the settlement documents. Brokers, attorneys, and agents generally receive payment at the closing as well. The mortgage or deed of trust is filed by the title company to become part of the public record.

Right of Rescission. For refinances, the funds are not actually released to the borrower for three business days after the closing. This period, mandated by RESPA, is called the rescission period, and during it a borrower may legally cancel or rescind the transaction and get a refund for any fees paid to obtain the loan. At the end of the rescission period, the escrow agent releases the funds to the refinancing borrower.

After the Close: Maintaining Relationships with Borrowers

While the mortgage transaction is complete at the closing, the mortgage itself goes on for years until the home is sold, the mortgage is paid off, or the home is refinanced. During this period the borrower makes payments to a loan servicing organization, which may be a department of the lending institution or which may be an independent organization that purchased the right to service the loan. The original lender may sell the loan on the secondary market as well. In addition, good business practices dictate that you remain in contact with your customers, who through their referrals can be a rich and cost-effective source of new business.

Servicing

Loan servicing involves the lender's logistics for receiving payment, record keeping, and communication with the borrower over the course of the loan. Some lenders service their own loans. Others sell the servicing rights to a third party specializing in the servicing business. The servicer is responsible not only for the collection, but for maintaining escrow accounts for real estate taxes and insurance if these are part of the monthly mortgage payment. By law servicers are required to provide statements to the borrower regarding their mortgage and escrow accounts. If a loan is being transferred between servicers, both are obligated to notify the borrower.

Customer Relations

Equally important as all the work you did to bring a loan to closing is the work you will do to keep in contact with your customers on a regular basis. Invite feedback. It is the best way to improve the service you provide, and it shows your respect for their opinion. If your customers have good things to say, ask them to write a short note, and keep it as a testimonial to your efforts. Stay in touch on a regular basis with letters, newsletters, postcards, and other material that remind them of their experience. A satisfied and happy customer who remembers you is the best advertising you can obtain, and it costs you next to nothing.

Key Points: Recapping the Highlights

You now have a big picture of the circumstances that motivate borrowers to seek a mortgage, the mortgage process, and the key players in it. The next chapter examines how you and other major players make money. Before we move on, here are some key points to remember:

- Mortgages are for purchases or refinancing.
- Borrowers seek mortgages for purchases, cash out, cash flow, or risk mitigation.
- Every interaction with a borrower is an opportunity to build relationship and trust.
- Milestones in the mortgage process are initial contact, application, proposal, loan package, processing, underwriting, and closing.

- The value of the property secures the loan.

- To be eligible for sale on the secondary market a loan must conform to standards established by Fannie Mae and Freddie Mac.

- Property value, income, and credit are the three main factors that are considered by lenders.

- The key players are the borrower(s), you the mortgage originator, mortgage brokers, processors, underwriters, and lenders.

- Supporting players include real estate brokers and agents, appraisers, title companies, escrow agents, servicing companies, secondary lenders, and attorneys.

- Your job is to generate leads, find the right loan for your client, and bring the transaction to closing.

CHAPTER THREE

Players: Defining Your Interests and Those of Borrowers, Lenders, and Brokers

Above all else, mortgage origination is a service business. Within the industry, everyone is competing for the same customers with essentially the same products. To differentiate yourself and to be highly successful as a mortgage originator, you must provide extraordinary service, and sell, sell, sell—not only to your customers whom you clearly serve, but also to those lenders, processors, underwriters, and others who provide service to you.

This chapter describes the roles, responsibilities, and motivations of the players previously introduced: Borrowers, originators, brokers, lenders, and some of the other supporting players in the mortgage process. Some of the information in this chapter may seem overwhelming, or difficult to get through unless you love numbers. It's not the sizzle of the business, and if you are itching to get going, this could be the hardest part of the book to get through, but it is important. By understanding the context in which others operate you will be able to respond to their needs, concerns, and motivations and provide what they want, need, and expect from you as a mortgage originator. Operating with an appreciation of their world gives you a tremendous advantage when you need their help to close a loan.

Borrowers: Seeking a Solution

People borrow money through mortgages for many reasons as previously discussed. Regardless of motivation, all borrowers have a real or perceived problem for which they are seeking a solution. They may or may not know it consciously. Some people know they need help and are open to your recommendations. For all the rest, it is important that you remember that they have a problem and you have the solution.

Why is this important for you to know? Because whether you are calling out to generate business or responding to an inbound inquiry, you have, at best, about 30 seconds to identify the borrower's need, convey your certainty that you have a solution, and demonstrate your integrity. The key to their success, and ultimately yours as well, is to build a trusting relationship.

Cindy, a seasoned mortgage originator, received a phone call from a brusque, cantankerous man, named Jerome, demanding a "cheap mortgage." He had unusual short-term circumstances regarding the purchase of a home from a family member, and had done a lot of research already. He knew exactly what he wanted: no points, no payments (!!@#!?!) and no prepayments. "What are you going to do?" he challenged.

Cindy says, "If I've learned anything over the years, it is that before you can give someone advice, you need their attention and they have to be interested in what you are going to say. When Jerome called, he was focused and interested only in getting his point across, not in hearing anything I had to say. Trying to talk to that is a waste of time. Yet here was a guy who clearly had a problem, and was motivated to do something about it. That made him worth listening to, at least for a few minutes."

Knowing that in a show-down about who was the expert Jerome was likely to hang up and go elsewhere, Cindy "surrendered," started asking questions, and listened with interest to everything he had to say. Cindy listened to everything he had done, and told him he had done a thorough job. She asked him if he was willing to share his information with her so that she could do some additional research for him and send it back to him. She says, "The minute I was willing to take information from him, he was willing to take information from me. Right there, in that moment, I changed in his eyes. I was no longer an adversary that he had to beat. We became partners in finding a solution to his problem." He never softened, but he listened, and with Cindy's assistance, Jerome and his wife found a loan that was right for their situation. And a few months later, Jerome referred a family member to Cindy.

Need. Most of the people who come to you need something. They may not know exactly what it is or even why they need it. Financial problems, concerns about ability to pay bills, upcoming major expenses, and questions about retirement conveniently and easily slip to the background as people go through their day-to-day business. They may not consciously know they need anything. They may be just curious. Not until circumstances push their way to the forefront do people pay attention to advertising, telemarketers, direct mail offers, and the host of other marketing messages barraging them daily. People don't talk to mortgage originators unless they need or want something. But unless they view their motivating circumstances in a positive light—*I'm buying a new home, I'm starting a business, I'm changing careers, my son is going to college*—they may be reluctant to reveal what has them speak to you.

Uncertainty. Everyone wants to make the right decision—about you, and about the loan you are offering. Is it the right thing for them? Could they do better elsewhere? Should they do it now or wait? Should they wait or forget the whole thing? Is there something else they should do instead? Should they get a second opinion either from another mortgage professional or from a friend, family member, or colleague who may know something about something?

People deal with the discomfort of uncertainty in a number of ways. They often respond with inaction. At the opposite end of the spectrum of responses, people exhaust themselves and those around them with questions, until they give up or circumstances force them into a decision. Some try to learn everything they can to understand and analyze the choices, and then may or may not make the decision. Some people (unconsciously) stall by being too busy, or by being confused. Some people abdicate responsibility for a decision—they let you make all the decisions for them. (Watch out—they are setting you up for a fall if anything goes awry).

Distrust. Nobody wants to be taken advantage of. Period. And when people don't know or understand their situation (for instance, don't know much about mortgages), their guard is more likely to be up. If you initiate contact with a prospect, assume you are not the first telemarketer, and possibly not even the first mortgage originator to call today. You may have to get past annoyance before you can even get to distrust. If someone they know referred you, they may give you the benefit of the doubt, but they will watch closely how you operate.

In the face of uncertainty and distrust, some people react with aggression and even hostility. They take and defend a position before you ever talk to them, and they already know that either no one can help them, or that they know best what they want and need. They want you to know they don't trust you, so you had better not try to con them. Often they ask questions like "what's your lowest rate on a 30-year fixed?" and counter your response with "I can do better elsewhere." It's not personal—it is only how they react to their own uncertainty and distrust. Some people don't express their distrust; they politely deny it, saying, "No, no, I trust you," but then don't move forward.

Regardless of how your prospects react to uncertainty and trust, trying to prove your trustworthiness by talking about it is a waste of time. If you've ever cringed when someone told you, "You can trust me," or "I am honest," you know that telling someone you are trustworthy is not only a waste of time; it actually raises a question about your trustworthiness. How do you build trust? Demonstrate it consistently. Do what you say you will do, when you say you will do it, the way it needs to be done, no matter what. Integrity is everything. And regardless of whether they place a mortgage with you, you will be empowered if you operate there.

You can't create lasting trust in one conversation; it takes some time in which to establish a consistent pattern of integrity and trustworthiness. The most successful mortgage originators do not push through an application to submission in one day, although it is possible to do that. The most successful mortgage originators take the time over several days to interact numerous times with their clients. The successful mortgage originators recognize each interaction as an opportunity to sell not only a mortgage, but themselves.

Conventional Wisdom. If you ask most people what a mortgage costs, they would probably say two things to you: rate and points. While these are factors in the cost of a mortgage they are not the only factors—just the most visible ones. Most people will tell you that a lower rate is better than a higher rate, and no points are better than any points. Unfortunately, mortgage pricing is a bit more complex, and rate and points are not separate factors in pricing, but are closely related, as you will soon see.

Investors: Defining the Market

To understand what drives prices in the mortgage industry, and hence how originators, brokers, and lenders make money, you must understand a bit about the mortgage-backed securities market, where lenders obtain funds and sell mortgages. This overview of the industry allows you to understand mortgage pricing and the factors that affect it.

Bond Market. Ultimately the money available for mortgages to homeowners comes from investors in the bond market. A bond is a loan and a promise by the issuer (borrower) to pay back the amount borrowed, plus interest (coupon), within a defined time frame, much like a mortgage. Mortgage-backed securities (MBS) are a special type of bond, bought and sold on the bond market. Just as a mortgage is secured by real property, a mortgage-backed security is secured by the mortgage itself—the payments of principal and interest that mortgagees make secure the bond. The mortgage industry therefore serves two customers with competing interests: investors who want the highest possible return on their MBS investments, and homeowners who want the lowest possible interest rates on their mortgages.

Bonds have a face value, an interest rate (coupon) and a price. A bond with a face value of $1000 and a coupon of 5% will pay $50 in interest. The price at which the bond sells may be different from its face value. The *yield* on a bond is the coupon value relative to the price. If the price of the bond is equal to its face value, the bond is said to be sold *at par*, and the yield is equal to the coupon, in this example 5%.

The bond market operates under the laws of supply and demand, much like the real estate market. If there is a large supply of money and hence large demand for investments like bonds, the price of a $1000 face value bond may rise to $1020. The interest the bond will pay, based on the coupon, remains fixed at $50. That means the yield to the investor is actually less than 5%—it is actually $50/$1020 = 4.9%. When bond prices go up, the cost of money as reflected in the yield declines, and mortgage interest rates generally drop.

What influences the supply of money in the bond market? Among other factors, actual and anticipated changes in inflation do. Inflation occurs when the demand for goods and services outstrips the supply, causing prices to rise. In periods of inflation the future purchasing power of the bond interest is diminished, causing the bond to be less valuable. Any economic indicators that imply pressure on the demand side of the economy—more money available in the financial markets, lower unemployment, rising retail sales—are all warning signals to which the bond market reacts negatively, meaning the price of bonds declines, and yields go up. Using the prior example of $1000 face value, 5% coupon bond, if the bond price drops to $960, the same $50 interest represents a yield of $50/$960 or 5.2%. Interest rates on mortgages are likely to rise.

Competition. Issuers of bonds compete with one another for investors' money. The U.S. Treasury is the largest issuer of bonds in the world, and considered one of the securest, as its bonds are backed by the *full faith and credit* of the U.S. government. Fannie Mae and Freddie Mac, created by legislation to promote home ownership particularly to low-, moderate-, and middle-income families, are *government-sponsored* *enterprises* (GSE) that issue mortgage-backed securities. Their status as GSEs implies that while not backed by the full faith and credit of the U.S. government, they have government support, which reduces the risk to investors of default on the bonds they issue. They guarantee their bonds, which are considered only slightly more risky than those issued by the U.S. Treasury, and which are safe investments for large institutional investors such as state and local governments, investment and pension funds, and which provide a steady source of capital for mortgage lenders. Most of the money for mortgages comes from this source, not from deposits in local banks.

Investors accept lesser yield in exchange for the relative safety of the investments. The 10-year U.S. Treasury note is the closest direct competitor with MBS investments. Because the MBS risk is slightly higher than treasury notes, the yield offered on MBS has to be slightly higher to attract investors. The average "spread" between rates on treasury bills and MBS is about 1.7%, although this varies depending on other forces that influence the money market.

For example, on one Thursday in mid-December 2006, a financial information web site quoted U.S. Treasury 10-year bonds with a coupon rate of 4.625% and a yield of 4.58, indicating that prices were up slightly over par. Thirty-year fixed-rate mortgages were quoted between 5% and 6.5%, with par pricing at about 6.250%, a spread of 1.625% over U.S. Treasury bonds.

Fannie Mae and Freddie Mac obtain the mortgages that secure the MBS by buying pools of mortgages from lenders. This makes more capital available to lenders for mortgage loans, which reduces the price of a mortgage, saving individual homeowners thousands in lower interest payments. The yield Fannie Mae and Freddie Mac offer to investors (also known as the pass-through rate) is slightly lower than the interest rate paid by homeowners. The difference is used by Fannie Mae and Freddie Mac to guarantee the payments to investors even if the mortgages underlying the MBS cannot support the payments, and for fees paid to servicers of the loans.

Beside MBS, Fannie Mae and Freddie Mac also issue debt on the stock market. Again, their low-risk status as GSEs allows them to borrow at lower interest rates than corporations. Funds are made available to mortgage lenders. Lenders watch Fannie Mae and Freddie Mac and the mortgage-backed securities market closely, and set rates daily based on a markup of the cost they pay for funds. Wholesale lenders post their rates with brokers who add another markup (interest rate and/or points) for their fees. Retail lenders build the additional markup into the rates they offer directly to borrowers.

Lenders: Playing the Market

Lenders make money in several ways: pricing loans above the cost of funds; sale of the loan paper in the secondary market; and loan servicing which they may do themselves for a fee, or which they may sell to a third party servicing company.

Pricing. Lenders issue rate sheets daily with several pricing options for each type of mortgage they offer. The basic information is interest rate and points. Table 3.1 shows excerpts from a rate sheet from a wholesale lender on a Wednesday, in mid-December 2006. The 15, 30, and 60 Day columns refer to the cost of a rate lock to be effective for the number of days indicated. The rate column is the interest rate on the mortgage. The other columns indicate the points added or (subtracted) at closing for the rate lock. As you can clearly see, the lowest interest rate available is 5.000.

TABLE 3.1   15-Year Fixed Conforming Program

15-Year Fixed Conforming Program			
Rate	15 Day	30 Day	60 Day
5.000	1.625	1.750	2.000
5.375	0.375	0.500	0.750
5.500	0	0.125	0.375
5.750	(0.875)	(0.750)	(0.500)

If the borrower wants the luxury of 60 days to close during which the rate is guaranteed, it will cost 2 percent of the amount of the loan (or $20.00 per thousand borrowed). If the borrower can close within 30 days, the cost is only $17.50 per thousand, a savings of $500 on a $200,000 mortgage.

Points are part of closing costs, and are the source of profit for lenders and brokers. Each point represents 1% of the amount of the loan. For each mortgage product, there is an interest rate priced with 0 points (or very close to it). This is called *par* and it serves as a baseline for other pricing options. In this table, the par pricing is 5.500, the rate with 0 points.

Below par pricing is an interest rate below par, plus points paid to the lender. The points *buy down* the interest rate, lowering the borrower's monthly payment in exchange for what is essentially a prepayment of interest at the time of closing. If the borrower wants a lower monthly payment at the 5.000 rate, it will cost a minimum of $16.25 per thousand (or $3250 on a $200,000 mortgage) in closing costs. The difference of the 1/2 percent in interest to the borrower (between 5.500 and 5.000) is $53.58 a month and is $9411.30 less interest paid to the bank over the course of the loan. For about $3250 up front at closing the borrower can save $6161 over 15 years.

Above par pricing is an interest rate above par, with points that the lender will pay as a rebate, usually to a broker or originator, in exchange for a higher monthly payment by the borrower over the life of the loan. In the same example, at 5.750, the monthly payment difference to the borrower compared to the 5.500 par price is only about $27 per month. In exchange, the closing costs/fees could be reduced by as much as $1750 (.875 on $200,000). To save the $1750 up front, it will cost the borrower an extra $6430 over the life of the loan.

Rate sheets also indicate charges (usually in points) for loan features that increase risk or reduce salability on the secondary market. You have already seen fees for rate locks (the longer the lock, the higher the fee). In addition, high loan to value, low credit scores, and low loan amount add to the cost of the loan, from .125 to 2 points.

Resale on Secondary Market. Most lenders sell their loans in the secondary market, thereby replenishing the funds they have available for new mortgages. To be highly salable in that market, loans must conform to risk guidelines set by Fannie Mae and Freddie Mac. The Federal Housing Finance Board surveys lenders monthly to compute the average price of homes, and annually adjusts conforming loan limits. In 2007, the conforming limit for a single-family home in most states was $417,000. You can find current limits and guidelines on the Fannie Mae web site at www.fanniemae.com. In addition, both Fannie Mae and Freddie Mac have automated underwriting programs that lenders or brokers can use to see if a proposed loan meets the conforming requirements.

Fannie Mae's automated underwriting system, Desktop Underwriter, uses information from credit reports and other factors, including key ratios, to determine eligibility. If a loan does not meet standards, it is referred back to the lender with suggestions. Ultimately the lender decides whether to fund a loan.

The credit report plays a key role in determining conformity. Desktop Underwriter weighs long-term credit patterns based on, among others factors, credit history, delinquencies, outstanding debt, and legal actions such as foreclosures and collections. Fannie Mae also considers other ratios and measures of income, credit, and equity. Because all these factors affect the lender's ability to sell the loan on the secondary market, the lender (via the underwriter) evaluates this information when you submit an application.

In addition to the MBS issued by Fannie Mae and Freddie Mac, there is a secondary market for nonconforming loans. Large loan amounts and poor credit are some of the reasons loans are not salable to Fannie Mae or Freddie Mac, and are therefore considered nonconforming. The lender's primary concern with a nonconforming loan is risk. The more risk, the more profit they want. The lender expects the broker and/or originator to sell a loan with higher interest, more points, or other conditions (or stipulations) that will either mitigate the risk or compensate the lender for the higher level of risk. It is your job to sell the loan by explaining the factors that make it more expensive. If appropriate, you can also identify specific actions to improve the borrower's circumstances and reduce the cost of the next loan.

Servicing Fees. Some lenders service the loans they make, whether they retain the loans or sell them on the secondary market. Fannie Mae and Freddie Mac pay a small percentage of the loan to the servicer. While the servicing income on any one loan is not large, servicing income on pools of loans can provide a sizable and steady source of cash. Since the money is made by doing a large volume of servicing, the efficiency with which a servicer handles the volume directly impacts profit, and keeping service costs down is key. Since it takes the same amount of work to service a $75,000 loan as it does to service a $750,000 loan, lenders may tack on a premium to the price of small loans.

Lenders can also sell the servicing rights to their loans to specialized servicing companies, usually for a percentage of the loan value.

What It Means to You. Knowing which factors lenders consider means you can do a better job proposing and selling loans to customers and preparing your loans for submission. With regard to any individual transaction, the lender's main concern is that the transaction go smoothly, both for the benefits of efficiency and for relations with the broker, originator, borrower, and others involved in the loan. Lenders expect originators and brokers to submit reasonable loans, work with them to negotiate terms that meet their needs and those of borrowers, and explain proposals to borrowers in a way that has them move forward to closing. Your relationships with brokers and lenders can affect your negotiations on behalf of clients, and have a direct impact on your ability to grow your business.

Brokers: Crafting the Transaction That Works for Everyone

Brokers have relationships with many wholesale banks. They make money like most others who buy wholesale and sell retail—they mark up wholesale lenders' prices. The difference between wholesale and retail pricing has to be enough to cover their costs of operations, plus provide a profit. In mortgages, the markup goes into points.

When pricing loans, brokers balance profit against the needs and expectations of borrowers. They look for the most profitable loan that clients will accept and lenders will fund. They combine rate, points, term, and other variables to provide a product that is both profitable for them and suitable for borrowers and lenders. They depend on originators' relationships with borrowers to negotiate mutually acceptable terms.

Markup and Points. As mentioned earlier, wholesale lenders issue rate sheets daily to brokers. Par pricing is the rate at which the wholesale lender will provide the mortgage with zero points. If the borrower wants an interest rate below par, it is available for an extra fee, in the form of discount points. If the broker can sell a higher interest rate, then the lender will pay a commission, or *yield spread premium*. In either case, a broker's margin is in points, or percentages of the principal amount being borrowed. The broker adjusts the rate sheet points by the amounts of the margins they seek. Depending on how they do it, points are paid by the borrower, or the lender, or a combination. Brokers disclose their profit on the HUD-1 Settlement Statement. Retail banks are not required to do so.

The below par points are referred to as discount fees, paid by the borrower to the lender at the time of closing in order to secure a lower rate of interest. When brokers sell loans below par, they tack on additional points to the discount points to cover their fees. For example, from Table 3.1, where par is 5.5% and 5.0% is priced with 1.625 discount points, if a broker wants a 2% markup, the price quoted to the borrower will be 5.0% plus 3.625 points. At the closing the borrower pays the lender 1.625 points for the lower rate and pays two points to the broker for his fee.

If a broker sells an above par loan, the lender pays the broker a *yield spread premium* (YSP) of points on the mortgage. The broker must disclose the YSP on the HUD-1 as a *cost outside of closing*. The broker may still charge the borrower points on the loan, if the rebate received from the lender doesn't completely cover the margin needed. So, from the table above, at 5.75% the lender's rebate is .875%. If the broker needs a 2%

margin, he quotes the borrower a cost of 1.125 points at 5.75%. In this case, the borrower pays a slightly higher rate of interest for lower closing costs. The broker gets a little more than half his fee from the closing costs paid by the borrower, and a little less than half his fee from the lender in the form of the .875 YSP rebate. The broker can also add a premium, called an overage, for special services, for example a particularly difficult loan to fund. A broker is free to use all or part of any earned YSP to pay off some of the closing costs the borrower may bear in connection with the loan.

By law, brokers are entitled to charge the borrower an *origination fee* on loans above par, and on various fees that cover the cost of overhead and administration of loans. The fee income is usually a flat rate, in the form of application fees or processing fees, so the number of applications and closings directly impacts revenue.

Building Relationships. For brokers, relationships with lenders, originators, and borrowers are very important. Borrowers are an important source of referrals, and a great relationship with a lender can grease the skids or sway a borderline deal one way or another. Sometimes a broker (or a lender), may place more importance on the long-term relationship than on the profitability of an individual loan. If a broker or originator is interested in building a business, the good word spread by a well-connected, satisfied customer can pay off many-fold compared with making a few extra bucks on one closing. Brokers who are in the game for the long run consider all these factors.

Expenses. To stay in business, it is critical for a brokerage firm to know how much it costs to generate a closing, including the cost of generating leads. Offsetting brokers' sources of income are the expenses of running a mortgage brokerage firm, such as overhead for office space, phones, electricity, and heating and air conditioning. Salaries and/or commissions paid to originators, processors, underwriters, and closers (folks who work directly with lenders to set up and prepare for the closing), bookkeeping staff, and so forth add to the expense. Marketing via direct mail, telemarketing, or advertising adds to the cost of doing business. All of these expenses determine how much income brokers must generate in loan volume and gross profit. Processing efficiency and cost controls impact brokers' profitability and their ability to expand.

What Does It Mean to You? Your relationship to a broker is important to your clients. If you establish yourself as reliable, efficient, and organized (well prepared for their processors), you may be able to leverage the goodwill you create to get even better service and pricing for your customers. That can translate into referrals for you as well!

Brokers are looking for you to be their eyes and ears with the borrower. They want to know that the borrower is fully informed and on board with the loan package you submit. They want to count on the loan package being complete and well organized so that they can process it efficiently. They want you to be accessible and responsive if questions arise or they need additional information from or about the borrower. They want to know that nothing will happen between submission and closing to cause the borrower to back out. And they want to know that you have all this handled for them!

Originators: Creating Opportunity

As a mortgage originator, you receive a commission from a broker or lender for the applications you submit that result in a closing. The commission may be a flat fee, a percentage of the profit on the loan, or a combination, and is paid after the loan closes. Depending on the company you work with or for, you may also earn money for preparing the loan file for processing by collecting and organizing documentation and getting required signatures. There may be minimum performance requirements and incentives for consistent performance and for performance above certain thresholds.

For example, there are three levels of loan originators in my mortgage company. Entry-level people, Application Specialists, only take applications. The applications come from leads they generate personally or from cold calls, from leads generated through the company's marketing efforts, and from prior customers. If they maintain minimum performance standards application specialists receive a flat fee for each closing resulting from an application they take. In addition, they receive another flat fee if they prepare a loan application package for submission to a processor by collecting signatures, documentation, and the application fee from the borrower.

Originators who maintain acceptable performance levels for several months are promoted to Loan Specialist Trainee, and become eligible to earn more money. They learn to interpret credit reports, read rate sheets, and suggest loan products. Commission rates rise with the number of closings, and bonuses are paid for closings from leads they generate. Loan specialist trainees are promoted to Loan Specialists when they demonstrate consistent acceptable performance over a period of several months. As loan specialists they have full responsibility for the customer and the closing. Their commissions are based on a higher sliding scale, and they receive an overage bonus on loans that exceed minimum profitability standards. In some firms, overages are at the discretion of the originator. In others, guidelines determine circumstances which warrant overages. As loan specialists demonstrate consistent performance they become eligible to train others, and earn additional commissions and bonuses based on their team's performance.

What It Means to You. It is very simple. As a commissioned originator, the more loans you sell, the more money you make. You determine your earnings by the number of loans you close. Your earning potential is virtually unlimited.

You are the gatekeeper. You are the person who opens the door for borrowers to access the money that enables them to fulfill their dreams and desires. You are the one who opens the door for lenders to market their commodity—money.

As a loan originator, your main concern is identifying leads, quickly qualifying them as serious prospects, selling them the best product, providing the best service, and moving them through the process with as little wasted time as possible. The more organized and efficient you are, the more time you have to generate new business, and the more money you can make.

There are opportunities to save people money, even in a rising interest rate market. This is the market in which the mortgage originators who are only order takers drop out, and the true salespeople rise to the top. Anyone can do the job when interest rates drop and remain low; the flow of applications is steady as people refinance to lower monthly payments. When the real estate market is hot, homebuyers seeking mortgages are plentiful. Anyone can make money in the mortgage business in these markets. But what happens when interest rates rise or the real estate market is slow? The high-income mortgage originator creates the need in the market, by creating the opportunity for borrowers and lenders. How do you do that?

You would be amazed at how many people have mortgages at rates that are higher than loans for which they qualify. Many people are not knowledgeable about mortgages and mortgage pricing. You have seen that brokers and lenders have a lot of flexibility to price a loan based on what the market will bear. I recently had an elderly couple who qualified for a much less expensive mortgage than they were currently in. I approached them as I do all prospects: "Let me take a look at your situation, and I may be able to save you money. If I can, and the loan makes sense, you'll move forward, and if I can't or it doesn't make sense to you, we'll close the file." This particular couple was glad they took my offer. They were able to refinance at a lower monthly rate and eliminate substantial credit card debt. The result was they had an extra $1500 in positive cash flow each month, making the difference between struggling to get by and living comfortably.

Not everyone is in a position where I can save him or her that much money every month. But for some people, even a savings of $100 a month means a lot to them. For those who turn up their noses at a $100 a month, I simply point out that I'd be glad to do the mortgage and pocket the $100 a month for the next 15 or 30 years if they don't want it. They usually get the point.

Start thinking about people who will be hurt by rising rates—the borrowers with ARMs, people with lots of revolving high-interest debt who can take equity out. These borrowers should be interested in what you have to say, whether they know it or not. It is up to you to get them to know it. Imagine and create the opportunities for people. The opportunities will not be obvious to everyone, so you have to get out there and start making people aware of the opportunities you see. This is a good time to cultivate your existing customer base. Check in with people, see how they are doing, and let them know you are still around and working for them.

Processors: Keep It Flowing

Loan processors are mission control for mortgage deals. They are the communications hub, quality assurance, the organizing and double-checking folks who keep things moving. Processors may get a fee based on the loans that go through them or more likely receive a salary from the brokerage firm or lender that employs them. They grease the skids so that underwriters, closing agents, and others have what they need to do their jobs without having to go back to the borrower or the originator for more information.

Processors are orderly and organized. They expect you to be the same. Accuracy and completeness are the watchwords of their trade. Good processors will teach you a lot about the ins and outs of the mortgage application and supporting documents, and they will make you a better salesperson. As a professional, you do things right the first time, both with your clients and with the processors and others who see your loan through to closing. The processor can be a great resource for you. Seek out his feedback. Show that you are eager to learn how to submit a loan package that is complete and well organized. Ask to have your mistakes pointed out to you so that you can learn from them. You will be astonished by what they know and their willingness to help you. And, as you become more proficient and your files approach perfection upon first submission, you may well find that your files are expedited—processors know your files will be quick and easy to deal with and will want to get them off their desk.

The requirements a loan processor places on a file's organization may seem unnecessarily rigid. You as a loan originator may handle a few dozen files in a week. Imagine the processor, handling files for 10 originators. Imagine each originator with a different "system" for filing the two dozen or more documents in the loan package. Without a well-defined and well-enforced method of file organization, the likelihood of misplacing or overlooking a needed document increases tremendously. Remember, the processor is all about flow. When you can pick up a file and flip immediately to the one document you need to reference, the process flows. When you repeatedly shuffle through papers to find what you need, it's a log jam.

Processors arrange the services of many of the supporting players in the mortgage industry, such as appraisers, title insurance, and closing attorneys. Every one of them values a file that is smooth. Every one of them, being human, procrastinates with the files that seem difficult or harder to complete. Don't let your file be the one that gets put on the Later pile. Learn to be complete and accurate. Learn to be professional, and to do it right the first time.

Files remain with originators or processors for a while, pending appraisals. When a written appraisal is received, the processor updates the affected items on the 1003 and verifies that the loan still meets the original Loan to Value and Debt to Income ratios that the rate was based upon. Good Faith Estimates and Truth in Lending forms may need adjustment as well. The processor also monitors rate lock expirations, but that does not absolve you of the responsibility to do the same. When all the paperwork is synchronized and up-to-date, the processor in a brokerage firm hands the file to an underwriter or to a closer for submission to a lender. In a lending institution, the processor forwards the file to an underwriter.

The more quickly a loan closes, the more quickly you get paid. Keep it flowing. Do it right the first time.

Underwriters: Assessing Risk and Reward

Underwriters decide whether the lender will take the risk on a loan. Underwriters are number crunchers, computing key ratios and assessing and weighing the information in the loan package. Underwriters make a decision based on three main considerations: Will the property's value be sufficient collateral against the loan? Does the borrower's financial situation—income, expenses, debt—leave him capable of meeting the mortgage payments? Does the borrower have a good credit track record?

Automated underwriting systems take a lot of the guesswork out of underwriting. Fannie Mae and Freddie Mac each provide automated underwriting programs that make quick decisions on whether the loan conforms to their requirements. What then is the underwriter's job? To interpret what a computer cannot about a borrower and the circumstances around the loan.

Just as you sell the borrower, at times you sell underwriters. The best ones are willing to work with you to find terms that are within tolerable risk parameters and solve the borrower's problem. Underwriting is as much an art as a science. Each underwriter is different, and while certain situations are black and white, within the grey areas it often comes down to the underwriter's opinion. That opinion can be influenced through conversations in which you as the originator can ask questions, explain situations, and in some cases, even negotiate with an underwriter to get a loan approved. In those cases, truly everyone wins.

Recently Dolores submitted a loan for Dennis G., who was buying a home following a divorce. His ex-wife remained in the house they had jointly owned, and had been making the mortgage payments on that house without assistance from Dennis for well over a year. At the time of Dennis' loan submission, that mortgage was still showing on his credit report, and the underwriter wanted a legal document releasing Dennis from the mortgage obligation. Dolores explained to the underwriter that no such legal document existed, and negotiated with the underwriter to accept proof that Dennis's ex-wife had been paying without his assistance for the past year. The underwriter agreed. Since Dennis and his "ex" were not on speaking terms, Dolores contacted the ex-wife and sold her on the idea of getting Dennis off her credit report, and providing copies of cancelled checks and deposits to show that she had funded the mortgage payments without Dennis's assistance. Then Dolores called the underwriter and sold her on accepting the documentation that the "ex" could provide.

Underwriters know that the company they work for only makes money on loans they fund. They are human—they want to do the right thing, and they want to please and to be liked. But they have to be sure—their jobs depend on it. If they are not sure, they may place conditions on the approval of the loan—things the borrower must provide before the closing for the lender to fund the loan. They will tell you what you need to provide in order for them to say yes. Provide it—in a timely fashion, and without a lot of talk about it. Just do it. And do it right the first time. The relationships you build with underwriters and lenders, based on the business you provide to them and the ease with which they can provide service to you can make the difference, in a close call, between a loan being approved or denied.

Supporting Players: Providing Assurances

Every loan you originate supports the businesses of dozens of people, each of whom should recognize that their success and yours are tied together. You depend on the goodwill and professionalism of appraisers, title companies, home inspectors, lawyers, underwriters, and processors to give your clients the best product and service available and a smooth closing. Nothing is more important to you than the satisfaction of your customers, as you will clearly see in the next chapter when we look at generating leads and prospects.

Appraisers. Appraisers are in the business of providing assurances about the security of the proposed loan by determining a value for the property. They are usually licensed independent contractors and may be self-employed or employed in a small firm. They depend on the real estate market and the mortgage business for their livelihood. Although appraisers depend on referrals, it is also critical that they remain independent—that the information they provide not appear to be influenced in any way by their relationships with referrers or with borrowers.

Appraisers interact with borrowers during the home visits when they inspect a borrower's home, and in some cases they collect a fee directly from the borrower. Appraisers research recent sales of comparable properties in close proximity to the subject property. Underwriters depend on the accuracy and reliability of the information provided by appraisers in the written appraisal report. Appraisers do this within a few days of being requested to, in order to build and maintain their relationships with the real estate agents, mortgage originators, and processors on whom they depend for referrals.

A Word About Real Estate Agents. With a purchase mortgage, other parties also have a stake and interest in the loan closing. A real estate broker or agent earns a commission only if the deal closes, and that is dependent on closing the financing. Consistently providing smooth, professional service for an agent's clients can lead to referrals that will help grow your business rapidly, especially in periods when real estate markets are strong.

Next Steps: Getting Up to Bat

You now have all the background information you need about the workings of the mortgage industry and the process you engage in as a mortgage originator. Be clear on your role: bring in the applications, sell the loans, and provide outstanding service to everyone with whom you do business. The more business you originate and close, the more money you make. It's that simple.

You are on the threshold of an exciting and rewarding career. The remainder of the book gives you the training and knowledge you need to be a high-income mortgage originator. Everything you need to be successful is here. Of course, you will learn everything you need to know about originating mortgages and getting loans approved and closed. And, you will learn an easy-to-remember five-step sales process that is effective whether you are selling a mortgage to a borrower or looking for help from others. Scripts, marketing materials, direct mailers, and other tools we use to generate leads, take applications, and sell loans are included in the book and are available on line at www.tomortgageservices.com for you to use as is or to tailor for your own use.

You aren't going to do things perfectly at first. That's okay. The important thing is to stay in action, and to keep track of what you do and the results you produce. If you don't get the results you want with the first actions you take, keep going anyway. If you implement the tools and strategies outlined in Part Two you quickly will learn the ropes and begin generating income. Follow the program, and you will develop the confidence to deal with any situation. If you have the knowledge, practice the sales techniques, and operate with integrity, you will generate a lot of income. It's time to get into action.

PART TWO

The Mortgage Selling Cycle

Step 1: Generating Leads, Prospecting, and Keeping Score

Well here you are, ready to begin your career as a mortgage originator. If you are waiting for the phone to ring so you can take your first application, you will be waiting a long time. *Originator*—that means it starts with you. Here's the little secret no one else tells you about being a mortgage originator: You have to market, and you have to sell.

The process described in Part One begins with taking an application. That's all well and good once you have a prospect for whom to complete the application, but where does that prospect come from? What is the process to get people to know about you, talk to you, and then agree to complete an application? It's basic common sense:

1. Call attention to your business and service. This can range from informal one-on-one conversations with people with whom you come into contact on a regular basis, to advertising or public speaking engagements.

2. Interest people in listening to what you have to say. It is not difficult to get people interested in what you are saying, especially when you are talking about them, not about you. When you understand what motivates people and the circumstances they deal with, it is not difficult to zero in on what is of interest to them.

3. Enroll people into completing an application. Your job is NOT to convince them or explain to them why they should complete an application. When people see a benefit for themselves, you don't have to push, convince, or manipulate them into taking action; they take action on their own. Your job is to have them see for themselves that it makes sense to complete the application.

Your target markets are limited only by your imagination and ingenuity. As new mortgage products come onto the market, and as economic factors affect interest rates and real estate values, it is important for you to know how to think about groups of people affected by similar circumstances and the messages that will interest them. It is not hard to do, and you will see that doing so makes sense, but the process does require some thinking on your part. There are many ways to reach prospects. There are many ways to deliver your message, including traditional mail (snail mail), telephone, e-mail, personal interactions, publicity, and advertising. Each of them has strengths and drawbacks.

When I started my mortgage company in 1984, I had no money but a lot of time on my hands. I went to the town clerk's office in my hometown of Waterbury, Connecticut, opened up the big books that contain the town's land records, and began copying the names and addresses of property owners and mortgage holders. Then I took my list back to my office and looked up the phone numbers in the telephone book, and started making calls offering them a free "mortgage check up." Fortunately, with today's technologies, you don't have to work that hard.

The first part of this chapter explores the pros and cons of different ways to define your markets and different methods to reach them. What do you need to know about choosing markets and delivery methods? How do you know which marketing strategy is the right one? You don't. You don't have to find the best way to market; just find one that works for you. And then another and another and another. How do you know if your marketing is working and is cost-effective? You measure and track, and you look at your numbers and use them to identify opportunities and actions for improvement.

Importance of Tracking. I cannot stress enough the importance of tracking your actions and results so you can see what is missing and needed in order for you to succeed. Most people resist the idea, and have good reasons for doing so—"it's hard," or "it takes too much time." But my experience has taught me two things that I know without a doubt—first, tracking your results tells you where there are opportunities for improvement, and second, you cannot grow your business or manage others unless you know the facts. This chapter contains tracking and measurement structures that clearly show your effectiveness and efficiency in generating leads and prospects, and then converting them to applications.

Ultimately, being a high-income mortgage originator is a numbers game, and you have to know your numbers to succeed. Not every application results in a closing. High-income mortgage originators know what it takes to generate a closing. By "what it takes" I mean how much it costs in terms of money and time or effort. Whether you are an independent contractor or employed by a broker or lender, if your income depends on commissions earned, the more you know about what it takes to create that dollar of commission, the more effectively you can use your time and the resources of those with whom you work.

If you receive, on average, a $500 commission for every closing, in order to earn a six-figure income you would have to close 200 loans a year. That comes out to about four loans a week. Where are they going to come from? It starts with the number of people who know about you, the number that are interested, and the number that complete applications. It is important for you to know the percentage of your applications that result in closings, so if you are shooting for 4 closings a week, you may need 40 applications. To get 40 applications you may have to speak with 160 people. And to speak with 160 people you may need to reach 4000.

Depending on whether you mail information, make phone calls, use the Internet, advertise, network, or use print media, TV or radio, there are different ways to measure the numbers and cost effectiveness of people who see your message, express interest, and complete an application. Always be able to answer these four questions, at a minimum:

1. How many people were informed of your business or service?
2. What was the response rate?
3. How many applications were generated?
4. How much did it cost to generate an application?

This chapter delivers all the tools you need to develop marketing campaigns and sales strategies to be successful. Warning! Do not be dismayed if at first you do not produce the results you expect or want. The secret to success and longevity in this business is to keep your name in front of many people, and do a great job for your customers, so that when they are ready for a mortgage they call you first. And when they call, you know how to prepare them to move forward. The second part of the chapter focuses on crafting a winning message that will move people into action and have you taking applications on your way to being a high-income mortgage originator.

Making Your Delivery Special

Technology has created a booming industry in mass communications to targeted markets. With electronic lists and word processors, it is easy to tailor a marketing message and sales presentation that looks as if it addresses the personal needs of the recipient. The bad news is that everyone is bombarded daily by junk mail, telemarketers, and spam, and it takes something to distinguish your message as one worth considering. The good news is that it can be done, and that you will learn how to do it. Whether you use direct mail, telemarketing, e-mail, or a combination, you will discover advantages and disadvantages to each method.

Lists. With the widespread use of computers today, information about consumers is now vast and instantaneously accessible over the Internet. Thousands of companies sell affordable electronic lists for phoning, mailing or e-mail. An Internet search on "mortgage mailing lists" turns up millions of results. How do you know which one is the best? You don't. You just need one that provides quality names at a price you can afford. You should shop around, then decide, and most important, measure and track.

With the sophisticated and easy to use search criteria now available, you can narrow your list to laser-like focus on people who meet very specific qualifications. You can find lists of people who meet almost any set of criteria you can imagine, including geography, age, gender, income, size and date of mortgage, loan terms, credit card balances, bankruptcies, credit scores, and virtually anything that involves financial transactions of any kind. One randomly selected list provider offers 17 selection criteria for demographic and spending pattern data including six categories of credit card purchase types, and 26 criteria for loan and property descriptive data.

Decide how you are going to use the list to determine which pieces of information you need reported and the presentation you want. I recommend that you use your first list for both direct mailing and follow-up phone calls. A mailing by itself is rarely as effective as a mailing with a follow-up phone call.

Not all lists come with phone numbers or e-mail addresses. Think about how you want to reach the people on the list, and be sure to specify all the information you need to deliver your message. If you are going to print labels or customize your message with the names or other information on the list, the presentation of the data comes into your decision. A list provided in all capital letters with heavily abbreviated addresses looks like junk mail and may not be opened. A list designed for merging with a customized letter, upper and lower case, with separate first and last names creates a much more personal-looking correspondence. Converting the former list for this use is possible but time consuming, so think first about what you are going to do with the list.

The data on purchased lists has a limited shelf life, meaning that it only remains fresh and valid for a limited period of time. The older the list the more likely that the information provided for any one name on the list is no longer valid—people move, refinance, change jobs, and so forth. The list provider may indicate an expiration date for the list. This is very important to know if you use the list for phoning in order to comply with federal Do Not Call (DNC) legislation.

If you are phoning, pick a list provider that scrubs the list to eliminate people who are included in the federal Do Not Call registry. Since the DNC legislation provides a limited grace period following new registrations, list providers must regularly rescrub their lists. This means that if you use that list after the expiration date and hit someone who is on the DNC list, you could be liable for a violation and a $10,000 fine—per incident! If you don't manage your lists properly, you could put yourself out of business and into real legal trouble in no time.

Because a list's shelf life is limited, it is also important that you size your lists based on what you are able to process and handle in a reasonably short period. You don't want to buy a six-month supply of names—buy what you will use within a few weeks, and then replace it with a new list when the first has been used or expires. List companies may also place restrictions on the number of times you can use a list. It can be as little as one-time only use up to unlimited use.

It is important to track the list's accuracy to compare list providers. It does you no good to get really cheap names if you get a high percentage of mail returns, out-of-service phone numbers, or bounced e-mails.

Prices depend on the size of the list and the number of selection criteria you use to extract the names from the general population. Lists are sold on a per name fee, and in general the more specific and restricting the selection criteria the fewer names you will get and the higher your per name costs will be. A specific search for expensive single-family dwellings and wealthy homeowners with high interest mortgages in Connecticut yielded about 1200 names with options ranging in price from 18 to 27 cents per name. By expanding the search to include all Connecticut homeowners with high interest mortgages, over 67,000 names were available with pricing options ranging from four to seven and a half cents per name. Strike a balance between cost and specificity of your target market.

Personal Lists. In addition to purchased lists, sources for leads and prospects are all around you. Every conversation you have, whether you think it is business related or not, is a conversation that could lead to a sale or to a referral.

Whether it is with others involved in the mortgage and related industries, or the clerk at your regularly visited coffee stop, if you don't let people know what you do, you don't have a shot at getting their business. Without much effort you can compile a list of hundreds of people on your own. If you are looking to establish yourself in your community, personal lists are a great way to do it.

Friends, family, and colleagues who know about your new business venture may be able to use you, or may know someone who is looking for a mortgage that they can refer to you. Begin making a list of the people you know. Don't waste any time thinking about whether to include or exclude someone. If you think of a name, add it to the list. Go through your check book and bills and add everyone for whom you are a customer.

There are many people you see on a regular basis whom you may not count among friends, family, or colleagues. These people, many of whom you recognize on sight but not by name, are potential customers and potential sources of referrals—but only if you tell them the nature of your business. Think about every person with whom you come into contact at least once a month. You may not know the name of the young man who sells you coffee every morning, but chances are he's either a renter or a homeowner, and either way, he's a potential customer. Ask his name (your daily coffee purchase experience will change), let him know yours and what you do. Offer your new business card; it is a relatively inexpensive way to market.

Collect business cards from everyone you meet and from places around town where people post their business cards—car washes, super markets, community bulletin boards. If you interact regularly with people who can refer others to you on a steady basis, you can offer to leave cards with them to give out to their customers. Local bulletin boards where you can post your cards are also an inexpensive way to get your name around town.

Associations often make their membership lists available to members. Chambers of Commerce, Jaycees, Rotary Club, Kiwanis, alumni associations, and trade associations are all good sources of people with whom you can establish relationships.

Many networking groups will make their member mailing lists available to members. But once again, the wisest way to spend your marketing and sales dollars is to target your message to a specific market.

Referrals are the most effective source of prospects available to you. They are free, and they carry with them the trust of relationships between the referrer and the referee. Your past customers (yes, you will have them!) are your best prospects, and a fertile source of referrals. When some relationship exists between you and a lead or prospect, however remote, it is harder for them to cut you off at the beginning. In many instances, your relationships open doors, but by themselves won't get you the sales.

Direct Mail. You aren't going to sell a mortgage with a letter alone. The purpose of a direct mail campaign is not to sell, but to generate leads—people who are interested. The outcome you want is an action the recipient takes that allows you to capture basic contact information, how they heard about you and what was of interest to them that had them take the action.

Think of offers that prompt someone to call, return an interest card, or visit a web site. Free offers are good action motivators, and are not necessarily expensive to produce or deliver. A well-done, self-produced, free three-panel brochure with information of general interest may be enough to generate a lead. Keep in mind that you are generating leads—people to talk to and make a presentation to. Then it is up to you to keep their attention and interest so you can present your proposition and close.

People receive such a large volume of junk mail that it is challenging to get your piece opened. Unless your envelope is compelling, there is a good chance that your mailing will get trashed before anyone actually reads your message. Notice the mail you receive, which envelopes you open and which letters you read. Then think about how to apply the effective techniques to your mail pieces.

Bulk mail may be cheaper than first class, but statistics show that bulk items are more likely to be discarded without opening than first class mail.

Postcards have the advantage of costing less in postage than first class letters. When designed well, they attract attention and are likely to be flipped over and glanced at. That means your postcard message has better odds of actually being read by the recipient than a first class letter. The U.S. Postal Service provides guidelines for postcard layouts at www.usps.com. Pay attention. When we added a web site address at the bottom of one of our postcards, we were dismayed to find out that the post office bar codes covered it completely. Moving it up 3/4 of an inch solved the problem.

The list provider we use also provides distribution services. I send them an electronic version of the letter I want mailed, and provide them with any specialized envelopes I am trying out. I tell them how many to send out against the list I've purchased. They print the letter, fold it, stuff it into the window envelope, seal the envelopes, apply first class postage and mail them. I pay them by the piece for the distribution services. I weigh that against the value of my time to do it myself. I will send out about 2000 pieces of a new mailing I am trying out, to see the response. I'll mail it a second time about two weeks later, and measure the response again. I may alter the envelope or the part of the letter that is visible in the envelope window to see if the response rate improves. And so on.

Average response rates on direct mail are not high—and a mailing of 1000 pieces is likely to result in a single closed loan. But do enough mailing, and you will get the responses you need to generate the business you want to become a high-income mortgage originator. By measuring and then altering one variable at a time, such as envelope color or design, you can begin to see what works best. It's important to keep in mind that it often takes more than one exposure for people to see or register the message, let alone to act on it. That is why we usually send out the same mailing to the same people at least twice before the verdict is in on the effectiveness of the campaign.

Mailing costs can seem expensive, but when coupled with follow-up phone calls, direct mail is an effective way to let your target market know that you are out there and ready to serve them.

As of this writing, there is no legislation proposed or in effect for Do Not Mail lists, which gives direct mail a marked advantage over phoning. Table 4.1 shows tracking for direct mail.

Timing of responses to direct mail is a bit tricky to measure. My experience has been that there is about a two week-lag time. By adding a unique piece of information to each mailing, I am able to match up the responses to it. I include it in the letter or postcard as an "offer code" that I ask the caller for at the beginning of the conversation. It tells me which mailing and which marketing message the caller is responding to. I use a coding scheme to come up with offer codes that allows me to know if the response was to the first or second mailing of the same piece, by altering one digit of the code. This particular mailing was a small trial run targeting recent bankruptcies in Connecticut for refinancing. I like to have the offer rate visible, so that when a call comes referencing the offer code, I know what the caller's expectation is. In this mailing I was trying a new envelope, blue with the words "important info" on the outside. Tracking the variations of envelopes allows me to see if the envelope produces a better result that is cost effective. The data source is the name of the file (in this case an Excel workbook) where the list names are stored. The cost per piece mailed includes the paper for the letter, the cost of the envelope, the price per name for the list, servicing cost per piece, and first class postage. Tracking the number of undeliverable mail pieces (Returns) gives me a track record for the list provider. One person called in (Response) referencing this offer code, which made this a successful trial campaign.

TABLE 4.1 Direct Mail Tracking

Date Ordered	Offer Code	Interest	Quantity	Description	Offer Rate	Envelope	Data Source	Cost	Returns	Response	Apps
10/24/05	347	CT Bankruptcy	250	refi	4.25	important info – blue	sep05_ct_bankrupt	0.55	2	1	

Telemarketing. Telemarketing is one of the most difficult things for new salespeople to do and provides the best training experiences that I can recommend. No one likes rejection. To survive in sales—any kind of sales—you come to the realization that rejections are not personal. While that is easy to understand on an intellectual level, it is not that easy to get free of the natural reaction you have when someone is rude or hangs up the phone abruptly. It's not personal. It has nothing to do with you, and it doesn't mean anything about you.

Telemarketing is the tool that toughens you. You learn to be sharp on your feet and not let anything that anyone says get to you. For many people, it takes practice just to sit down and dial the phone. I have only met a few people in all my years in business who have no hesitation about making cold calls. Most people are confronted by the prospect of speaking to strangers, and humiliated at the idea of being hung up on. (Think of how you have interacted with telemarketers—you know what they say about payback!)

I expect every mortgage originator who works for me to be on the phones at least an hour a day. I don't expect applications to come from the calls, although sometimes they do. I do expect originators to listen to themselves on tape and distinguish how their reactions and emotions influence their demeanor on the phones, and to practice not allowing the person on the other end of the phone to intimidate or disempower them. Everyone hates doing it at first. Many quit. But the ones who stick it out and work it through are unflappable and unstoppable, even with cantankerous callers.

You develop a thick skin when it comes to people saying no to you. And you will hear every reasonable objection to your presentation you can imagine (and a lot of unreasonable ones, too), and will develop ways to respond without being thrown by the questions. There is no better training.

The best way to develop mastery in the art of the cold call is to phone every day at the same time. It is essential that you set a time to make the calls—and make them at that time. It creates a habit. Set a target for yourself—something you can measure—for example, how long you will be on the phone, or how many numbers you will dial—then do it just that way. When you get past all the excuses and reasons and circumstances that prevent you from making the calls when you say you will, and make the calls regardless of your feelings or the circumstances, you will have a sense of control and power over your future that comes from confronting your fears and concerns. The power you develop by doing what you say you will do, without compromise, is the foundation for the confidence and enthusiasm that you need to exude to turn a dry script into an engaging conversation that results in a sale.

What I've learned in more than 30 years of selling is that it matters less what you say than how you present yourself in the saying of it. The exact same script, word for word, when delivered by a wimp will be very different from when delivered by a dynamic leader. Which one are you going to be?

An effective telephone script has to grab attention and interest in the first few seconds. Your "Hello _____, this is _____" has to catch the other person's attention long enough for you to introduce yourself and the purpose of your call. In one sentence you must enroll the person at the other end of the receiver into staying on the phone long enough to hear your proposition.

We begin each phone script with

"Hello, Mr./Ms. _____. My name is _____ and I'm from Mortgage Services. I am calling about your mortgage. The reason for the call is that there is a possibility we could save you money on your mortgage. My job is to get in touch with you to see if you might be able to qualify. Do you have a few minutes now?"

The words, by themselves, will not get someone's interest unless they are already in the market. In the next chapter you will see how to train

TABLE 4.2   Call Tracking

Date	Source	Start	End	Dials	Contacts	Presentations	Apps	No Apps	Comments
10/30/2005	sep05_ct_ bankrupt	3:00p	3:50p	30	10	3	1	2	

yourself to deliver the message with the conviction, with such certainty, that the receiver has to take notice and listen. Again, I cannot stress enough that the best sales presentation in the world cannot compensate for a weak or poor delivery. And all it takes is practice.

Legislation at the state and federal level restricts telemarketers from calling those who have registered their names on the federal Do Not Call (DNC) list, and the laws impose strict penalties on violators. It is important for you to stay abreast of the law, which you can find at www.dnc.gov. Your state may have additional restrictions of which you must be aware. The web site will tell you what days and hours you can call, and what relationships are exempt from the restrictions. Know the laws and abide by them, since fines for violations could put you out of business.

Table 4.2 shows what to track for calling.

Recording the start and end times for the calling session is important to determine your "distractibility." Thirty dials in an hour is not difficult to do. A contact is a live person answering the phone. The call counts as a presentation if you get far enough in the script to ask, "Do you have a few minutes now?" If you don't get that far (usually because people hang up), it counts as a contact but not a presentation. If you take an application while on the call, it counts as an "App," and if you make the presentation but don't take the app, it counts in "No Apps." The comments column holds information about follow-up activities.

E-mail. General guidelines for constructing an enrolling e-mail message are no different from those for letters or phone scripts. Your subject line has to generate enough attention and interest for the recipient to open the message before deleting it. Use the first two lines of the body to nail down the attention and interest—that is often all that will be seen in the mail preview mode. Keep it short. Clicking on a hyperlink in the message is a very effective close for e-mail. It is convenient, easy, immediate, and free. Often I will click without reading the details of the message, and will then browse the destination to see if I am interested enough to read.

E-mail is cheap, fast, and effective. It is also so abused and overused, that you stand a good chance of being automatically directed to a spam or junk folder, or of being deleted in bulk with other unsolicited messages.

Antispam legislation is gaining momentum at the federal and state level. As with the Do Not Call laws, it is important for you to remain abreast of the law and of current guidelines for good Internet etiquette. Always give people an option to remove themselves from your list.

Table 4.3 shows tracking information for e-mail campaigns.

E-mail distribution services provide the statistical tracking of "clicks" for our e-mail campaigns. We track the date, count, and content of the message, including the offer code, rate, and subject line. In this case we also have a per message cost for the service. They track and report back to us the number of bounced (undeliverable) e-mail messages, the number that were deleted by the recipient without opening, the number that were opened by the recipient, the number of recipients who requested removal from the mailing list, and the number who clicked on the hyperlink contained in the e-mail message.

Networking. Some people swear by networking events. If you are a naturally gregarious and outgoing person (I am not), you may have great success meeting people who can help you grow your business. Just keep in mind that most people who attend these events are looking for the same thing; they want to know how you can help them grow their businesses.

Obviously you are not going to reach the same numbers of people as you will with other delivery methods, but you will have a better chance of actually having an enrollment conversation with someone who could become a source of referrals for you, if not a customer. While it doesn't cost much relative to other attention-getting methods, networking does

TABLE 4.3 E-mail Tracking

Date	Offer Code	Interest	Quantity	Text	Offer Rate	Subject	Data Source	Cost	Bounce	Delete	Open	Opt Out	Clicks	Apps
10/24/05	947	CT Bankruptcy	1000	bankrupt.doc	4.25	important info	sep05_ct_bankrupt	0.05	25	112	50	1	5	1

take time, so you want to make sure that the groups with whom you mingle are highly qualified and motivated.

Attending the weekly meeting of your local Chamber of Commerce may be a good way to meet fellow business people, but spending the same hour at a well attended real estate open house can yield better results. If the local Chamber of Commerce is willing to sponsor a first-time homebuyers workshop at which you are the featured speaker, that will yield even more.

If you have an opportunity to be a featured speaker at one of these events, you can establish yourself as a professional among a large group of people, at little or no cost.

If you are going to network, commit yourself to following through with the people you meet. That means phone calls, e-mails, and so forth.

Viral Marketing—Best of Two Worlds. Done right, the Internet can be an incredibly fast way to reach an incredibly huge number of people. "Viral" marketing—a kind of grass-roots wildfire—combines the ease and cost effectiveness of e-mail with the subtle endorsement of a referral. A viral marketing campaign spreads when people forward a message to their contacts, and they forward it to their contacts, and so on. A catchy message with the right motivation (something free) for the sender and an easy way to send it can generate a ton of leads over the Internet. Generally the call to action is to visit a web site, click on a link, fill out an e-contact form, and so forth. As with any lead-generation tool, if you don't have the process to handle the incoming leads, your efforts are wasted.

There are services available online for tracking viral marketing campaigns. Statistics include the basics for e-mail marketing, adding details about the timing of peak activity for downloading and passing your message, and pass-around rates, which measure the percentage of people who send your message to others. The important thing for you to consider is the offer code, which allows you to identify the number of applications received as a result of that campaign.

Advertising. Where target marketing identifies people with common needs, advertising reaches masses of people, some of whom will be interested, and many of whom will not. While it can be an effective way to build name recognition over time, it is relatively expensive, especially when you first start out.

Available at the local, regional, and national levels, media such as newspapers, magazines, trade journals, billboards, television, and radio can reach huge numbers of people (millions) at once. These media tradition-ally describe their audiences in terms of age and gender, with occasional income or ethnic descriptions. In the case of a newspaper, magazine, or trade journal marketed to a target audience (for example, a trade journal for realtors), you can find more detailed reader information that may be important to you.

Pricing for all these delivery methods is based on the size of the audience reached, the size or duration of the message, the number of times the message is presented, and competition for most desirable position or placement (rotation, in TV and radio lingo) of the message.

Most media will offer you discounted prices if you are willing to give them flexibility regarding the time of day and day of week your ad will appear. The more leeway you give them, the cheaper the rate and the more *unqualified* people will see your ad. Repetition is important in print and broadcast media as well, so a more specific targeting of an audience may result in a higher number of viewers or listeners getting the message multiple times.

For example, certain parts of magazines and newspapers (front cover, back cover, inside cover, inside back cover, centerfold) are prime adver-tising territory and command higher prices. TV ads in prime time (usually 7:00 to 11:00 P.M.) will cost a lot more than those airing between 3:00 and 6:00 A.M.

Production costs for advertising can be very expensive. The design of your ad should be professional, and developing a consistent look may cost you plenty. On the other hand, many publications have sections where your business card can be the ad. Usually that costs less, but you are competing for attention with possibly dozens of other ads on the page. With print, outdoor advertising, and television, the visual display you create must command attention and create interest as much, if not more than the words. When Cingular wireless phone service first launched, it lined the highways in Connecticut with billboards that had nothing but their stick figure orange logo and the name Cingular. For weeks I wondered what it was. By the time they revealed what they were selling, I was eager to learn.

On the other hand, we were enticed to try our hand at advertising on local cable television a few years ago. We hired professionals to develop a classy 30-second ad for us, complete with logo, music, graphics—the works. We bought air time spread throughout the day and aired the commercial over several months. We spent over $30,000, and got not one response. It was an expensive lesson. This doesn't mean that TV advertising doesn't work. It didn't work for us and for the type of service we provide.

Table 4.4 shows tracking for print ads in the local newspaper.

The information you track for TV or radio is very similar. In place of "Publication" you would indicate the stations on which the ads air. Markets for advertising are local, regional, and national. Circulation (print) or audience (TV and radio) tell you the potential number of people who will see your message. With print advertising, the type indicates the size of the ad, or in the case of the first item, the fact that it was a flyer inserted into the paper. Radio ads can be live or recorded, and vary in length. TV ads also vary in length. The cost includes the production cost of the commercial or advertisement as well as the cost of running the ad one or more times. Cost per thousand (CPM) divides the audience or circulation figures by the cost of the ad to tell you how much it costs to reach a thousand people. It is a standard measure that allows you to compare different advertising media. Again, tracking offer codes is important to knowing how effective the campaign is in generating a response and applications.

It's a Numbers Game—Know the Score

The purpose of tracking is to inform you. Don't give up if the results are disappointing at first. It takes practice to develop methods that produce results. A 1% response rate on a mailing is successful. Most people don't

TABLE 4.4 Print Ad Tracking

Date	Publication	Market	Circulation	Type	Cost	CPM	Offer Code	Interest	Offer Rate	Response	Apps
4/2/2006	Our Metro Reporter	Local	26034	inserts	989.00	38.00	537	Purchase	4.25		
4/5/2006	Our Metro Reporter	Local	26034	full page	4,224.00	162.00	537	Purchase	4.25		
4/7/2006	Our Metro Reporter	Local	26034	half page	2,537.60	97.47	537	Purchase	4.25		

take action the first time they come upon something. This reaction is not personal, it is only human nature.

As I said, I believe that cold calling is the best training you can give yourself. Your numbers tell volumes about your salesmanship, and ultimately about what you need to work on to become a high-income mortgage originator.

The first thing you want to ask yourself is "Am I making the calls when I said I would, and am I doing what I said I would in each calling session?" If you are not doing that, you have some work to do to come to terms with whether you are willing to do what it takes to be successful in this business. To be successful, 80 to 90% of your time will involve marketing and selling. Put structures in place to support you in doing what you say. Make a list of the things that get in the way and clear them out of the way, one by one. Ask someone who wants you to succeed to support you in making the calls. Once you can count on yourself to do what you say you will do, you will have a new sense of power, and the phone calls will not be so daunting.

The next thing to look at is the number of dials you make in the time you allow. When you become seasoned, you will be able to make 30 dials in an hour without any trouble. Let the phone ring four times. If no one answers, hang up and move on to the next number. This is a numbers game. Keep dialing! At the beginning you will not make anything near 30 dials an hour. Look at what is in the way. Where do you dawdle or waste time? How can you eliminate distractions to increase the number of calls you make in the allotted time?

I can tell in two hours whether a new hire is going to make it or not, just by how they handle cold calls. We train them and give them instructions for what to do and say. We get them on the phones, making cold calls on their first day. Most of them are *very* uncomfortable. The ones that follow the instructions, make the dials, repeat the script, and keep at it in spite of their discomfort and in spite of no success are the keepers. Especially at the beginning, know that you will not be successful. Consider cold calling your boot camp, and know that you will be a better salesperson for the training, much as you may dislike going through it.

The number of contacts and presentations tell you if your confidence and enthusiasm and conviction are coming across effectively in your opening line. If the ratios are less than 3 presentations out of 10 contacts, practice your delivery. Buy a tape recorder. Deliver your opening remarks and listen to them. You will hear why people are not willing to listen. Make the necessary adjustments and practice, practice, practice.

The number of presentations and sales (at this stage, apps) tell you how effectively you are addressing the needs and concerns of your market. You should sell at least one out of every four people to whom you deliver a presentation (that's average). If you are not closing 25% or more, tape and then listen to yourself. Are you confident—or pushy or arrogant? Do you give people the impression that they would be nuts not to move forward with you, or do you leave a question in their minds? Once you are satisfied that your delivery is solid, then if your closing ratio is still not where it should be, you can begin to look at the message and the proposition, and try different things. Again, keeping statistics is very important as you make adjustments so that you can learn what changes are effective.

What Makes an Effective Sales Presentation?

How do you get people to take what you are offering—whether it is more information, a free mortgage checkup, or a $300,000 loan? What causes them to be interested in what you offer? And when they are, how do you move them to the next step, whether it is completing an application, approving a proposal, or closing a loan? I will share with you a simple system that I have mastered, and you can, too. It is a system that makes it almost impossible for people to say no to you.

At the heart of any effective communication to a prospective borrower (or any sales prospect for that matter) is something of interest and importance to them. People will not act on things that do not interest them. When they are interested, they usually are willing to take some action—especially if little or no risk is involved. What you say about mortgages and yourself as a mortgage originator is of no interest to anyone (except perhaps your mother) unless people can relate what you are saying to themselves. The biggest mistake salespeople make is to sell features—flexible payments, low rates, and so forth. People want the benefits that the features provide, not the feature. Security, peace of mind, freedom from creditors—those are of interest to potential borrowers. Your job is to have them see the benefit, and to sell them on the benefits they will get. If you sell them on the benefit to them, they want what you offer. If you don't spell out the benefit to them, your proposition is not of interest. Unless the prospect can see a clear benefit, you are wasting your time. With a little thinking and practice, you will learn to create messages that arouse interest and compel people to take action.

I recommend you read sales books night and day. Consider it part of your training as a professional. One of the best books written on the mechanics of selling, is *The Five Great Rules of Selling* by Percy H. Whiting (it is no longer in print, but used copies are available online). The five great rules of selling are *attention, interest, conviction, desire,* and *close.* This fundamental structure for any sales presentation has proven very successful for me, and I know it will for you as well, if you keep it in mind as you develop your marketing and sales strategies. It is simple, easy to remember, and very effective, and I am grateful for having discovered it early in my sales career, before entering the mortgage business.

Five-Step Overview. Before you can sell anything, you must get people's attention. They have to be interested, or become interested, in what you are saying. Without their attention and interest, your letters, phone messages, and personal entreaties are a waste of time. Once you have their attention and interest, describe the benefits *to them* of the product's features. Next, paint a word picture of them enjoying the benefits you have them wanting, for example, what they could do or have with the money the mortgage will provide. And finally, invite them to take the needed action to make that picture a reality for them—whether it is to call for more information, complete an application, or write a check to close a loan.

The following letter is part of marketing and sales materials developed for a successful direct mail campaign to promote mortgages for first-time homebuyers. We bought a list of people whose rent payments were roughly equivalent to a monthly mortgage payment on a moderately priced home. As you read this letter, see if you can identify each of the five elements of sales: attention, interest, conviction, desire, and close.

Special Government Program Helps Renters Become Homeowners!

Great news! The government is offering a special program for those *with limited incomes and cash for a down-payment*. Many renters do not understand that the government will help them purchase homes.
This special program helps by—

- *Allowing for the least amount of cash possible.* Zero down-payment programs are now available.
- *Qualification guidelines are quite liberal* with a lower amount of income necessary to qualify for the monthly payment.

With today's *low interest rates*, you can have a payment, after taxes, below your current rent payment. At the same time you will put ***an end to rent increases*** and you will ***be building up equity*** in a home you can own forever.

Call today for a **Free Analysis**

(800) 987-6543

Offer Code: 210

State of Connecticut Banking Department License #0909900

In this example, the opening headline conveys breaking news that attracts your attention and interests you enough to continue reading if you are a renter, or if someone close to you is a renter. Questions, provocative statements, and even silence can all be attention getters. Look around at advertising and marketing materials. What catches your attention and interest?

Think about the interest, needs, and concerns of the people you are reaching. What can you provide that satisfies that interest, takes care of the need or addresses the concern? In this case, the target market is renters. Renters may be concerned that they cannot afford a home or that they cannot save enough money for a down-payment. The first paragraph continues to hold the reader's attention and spark interest, especially if the reader has those concerns. The prospect of government assistance to purchase a home also piques interest.

The "conviction" part of the sales presentation is about the facts and features of your product, and more importantly, the benefits they provide to the interested (and attentive) reader or listener. In the example above, "zero down-payment programs are now available" is a feature. The benefit to the reader is that this allows "for the least amount of cash possible." Another fact/feature is that qualification guidelines are liberal. The benefit is that the reader can qualify even with low income. *Fact*: Today's interest rates are low. *Benefit*: The reader could pay less for a mortgage, after taxes, than she now pays for rent.

Tailoring the Message. Taking the reasons people seek mortgages, tailor the interest and conviction steps to address a particular benefit that the target prospect will enjoy, or a need that the mortgage will fill. For example, a person with high credit card balances feels the weight of large minimum payments that seem endless. An opener like "Are your credit card balances pushing you to the limit? Now you can do something to push back," will get his attention and interest enough to keep reading.

Building on the *interest* and moving into *conviction*, you again want to let the prospect know that you understand her problem and that you have a solution. You describe a *feature and benefit* of what you are selling.

For example, "refinancing your mortgage can give you a fresh start and relieve the pressure of high interest rates." Come up with two or three facts or features and two or three benefits for each that are of interest to the market you are targeting.

The *desire* step paints a word picture describing the effects of the product or what it would be like if the reader were enjoying the benefits of the product. For first-time homebuyers, phrases like "putting an end to rent increases" and "building up equity in a home you can own forever" paint a picture of the difference buying a home (and the mortgage that comes with it) would make for readers. They can put themselves in that picture, and it looks pretty good!

The *conviction* step also anticipates and addresses reasons the prospect might give not to buy the product or not to buy it from you. We always anticipate a "too good to be true?" skepticism and questions or concerns about the legitimacy of our business or our reputation. We include our state license number and a "20 Years in Business" seal to address those anticipated concerns indirectly, before they arise. As you experience the objections that prospects express, you develop your presentation to incorporate a response and convert it to a fact/benefit that works for you, not against you.

The *close* step is a call to immediate action. It could ask prospects to request additional information, visit a web site, or buy something. We want the reader to call us, and we offer a free analysis as incentive to move them into action. Providing something of value for free is a good way to establish trust, which is a key element to your success. Adding limits—time limits, expiration dates, exclusivity, or limited quantities available—to the offer will often move people to immediate action.

Attention: Targeting Needs, Providing Solutions

No matter what books you read or what systems you follow, there is no substitute for thoughtful consideration and common sense thinking. The first part of the book gave you the background to understand what motivates borrowers—events and circumstances that lead them to inquire into a mortgage. Now it is time to apply that understanding to distinguish what is of interest to borrowers in each situation so that your sales message is effective in generating leads, converting leads to prospects, and prospects to applications.

We're going to think about borrowers in different situations, and through an inquiry generate ideas for lead sources, and what would be of specific interest to them such that they would contact you. Get into the habit of asking these kinds of questions. New loan products are developed and marketed constantly, and the successful mortgage originator can identify the best-served market, address its specific needs, and creatively describe the benefits to the borrower.

In Part One, we talked about different goals that refinancing a home can help a homeowner to accomplish. Turn equity into cash or credit to pay for major expenses. Or, reduce monthly living expenses to improve cash flow. Or a mortgage can provide a safety net in risky situations. By looking at each of these general categories we can create a list of different target markets and craft sales messages that address their needs and concerns. A marketing message or sales presentation that understands and addresses the specific needs of the consumer will yield better results (read more sales!) than a shotgun approach.

Renters. Where do people live before they buy a home? Most likely they rent. Renters are great potential first-time homebuyers. With a little encouragement and information, you can show them that owning a home is within their reach, when they may not realize it. By completing an application they have an opportunity for you to determine whether owning a home is feasible for them. If it is, you can help make it a reality. If it is not feasible, you can recommend actions they can take so it becomes feasible, and when it is, you can help make their dream of home ownership a reality.

Homebuyers/Sellers. People looking for a new home are also potential customers, whether they presently rent or own. Who knows people who are looking for a home? Real estate brokers and agents! What do people who are looking for a home often do about the same time as they buy? Sell their present home. Again, real estate agents and brokers can be a great source of referrals. And today many homes for sale are part of the Multiple Listing Services (MLS) which are available online or through a subscription. What is of interest to buyers and sellers? Preapprovals, quick closings, and no hassles.

Cash Out. One feature of a mortgage is that it can convert equity into cash or credit for major purchases or expenses. What would be a major purchase or expense? How do you identify people who have or are about to incur that kind of expense? Who else do those folks come into contact with who could make a difference for your business?

One of the largest expenses faced today is the cost of a college education. Annual tuitions of $30,000 to $40,000 are not uncommon among private institutions, and even state schools can run into the tens of thousands of dollars, placing a financial strain on most households. How would you identify homeowners with college-age children? What problems are they facing that a mortgage with cash out or a HELOC would solve? What can you offer them that would entice them to pick up the phone to call you for more information? Who else provides services or does business with people in this market? Why would they want to help you?

Another major expense people incur is the purchase of an automobile. Leasing has become a very popular, low-up-front cost way of financing an automobile. At the end of a lease (three, four, or five years typically), the car owner is faced with either a lump-sum payment on the present car, or buying or leasing a new one. By refinancing their home to pay for a car, people are able to spread the payments out over 15 or 30 years rather than three to five. And in an appreciating real estate market the car could end up costing little more than the interest by the time the property is sold.

Again, the questions to ask are these: How do you identify people who are about to buy a new car? What problem are they facing that a mortgage with cash out or a HELOC would solve? What can you offer them that would interest them enough to pick up the phone to call you for more information? Who else provides services or does business with people in this market? Why would they want to help you?

Another major expenditure and reason for taking cash out is home improvement. Whether it is adding a bedroom or garage, updating the décor, or modernizing a kitchen or bath, renovations are expensive. How do you identify people who are making home improvements? What problems are they facing that a mortgage with cash out or a HELOC would solve? What can you offer them that would move them to pick up the phone to call you for more information? Who else provides services or does business with people in this market? Why would they want to help you?

Sometimes in sales you create a need and then fill it. In the cases above, the need existed based on identified expenditures. How about people who have a lot of equity in their homes but aren't doing anything with it? If they turned that equity into cash, what could they do with it? By drawing attention to the value people have stored in their homes, you can create interest in tapping into that for other things. Especially in rising real estate markets, tapping into equity gives people the opportunity to do things they have been putting off—like home improvements, a new car, or a vacation, or that medical procedure they've been putting off, or finishing their education. How do you identify people who have built up a lot of equity in their homes? When you are creating a need, rather than ask what problem can a mortgage solve, ask what opportunity can a mortgage create? What can you offer them that would entice them to pick up the phone to call you for more information and complete an application? Who else provides services or does business with people in this market? Why would they want to help you?

Cash Flow. According to the Federal Reserve Board's 2004 Survey of Consumer Finances, 46.2% of families carry a credit card balance, with the median balance at $2200. With recent changes in banking laws, minimum payments have increased to include at least 1% of the outstanding balance, in addition to finance charges which are now commonly around 20 to 24%. That is a lot of money going out each month.

Refinancing a home is a way for people who are in some financial difficulty to reduce their monthly outflow of cash. That extra cash can go into savings, investments, or purchases that avoid new debt. By consolidating all outstanding debt with the mortgage, homeowners take advantage of lower interest rates, a longer term, and tax deductions.

Who else is in trouble financially? People who have filed bankruptcy. People with low credit scores who are stuck in subprime mortgages. What problem can a mortgage solve? What opportunity can a mortgage create? What can you offer them that would motivate them to pick up the phone to call you for more information and complete an application? Who else provides services or does business with people in this market? Why would they want to help you?

Risk Mitigation. What kinds of life changes shake up financial stability? Retirement, layoffs, new business start-ups. How would you identify people in these categories? Age, unemployment benefits, new business registrations—all of these conditions leave a financial trail that you can zero in on with a little imagination and creative thinking. What benefit would a mortgage provide? Do you think peace of mind and freedom to pursue your dreams would be of interest?

Mortgage Type. There are two other groups of people who become good target markets when interest rates rise and real estate values begin to decline: Holders of adjustable-rate mortgages should be frightened enough in times of rising interest rates to pay attention to compelling offers like yours. And people who have little equity in their homes (due to heavy mortgage financing), do not want to be in an upside down situation, where the sale of their home will not yield enough to cover the repayment of their mortgage. By creating an attention-getting message with benefits specific to people in each of these situations, you can start the phones ringing.

You Don't Have to Start from Scratch

All of this may seem like a lot of work. It is. As I said, people starting out in this business, or any other for that matter, should expect that marketing and sales will consume 80 to 90% of their time. Fortunately for you, however, there are plenty of brokers and lenders who have marketing and sales programs in place, so that you can begin taking applications quickly. When you interview companies to work with or for, you would be wise to ask about their marketing programs and sales resources. By working with an established company, you can begin earning quickly while you are still learning and perfecting the art of salesmanship, and you can concentrate on learning the fine points of mortgage lending at the beginning. It is not an easy business, but the rewards are outstanding if you are willing to do the work. Later, the marketing programs you implement and the business you generate will enhance your earning power and increase your value to those with whom you work. That is how you become a high-income mortgage originator.

CHAPTER FIVE

Step 2: Moving a Lead to a Prospect

Whether you are calling out or responding to incoming calls, the impression you make when you first connect with prospective buyers establishes your relationship and determines whether they will move forward with you. Trust is key. Remember, the product you sell is not unique. Your many competitors are selling the same rates, terms, and loan products. That can work for you, or it can work against you. On the one hand, you can offer the best products available on the market. On the other hand, you have to create a reason for a buyer to select you over your competition. If you sell product you will achieve some success, but to be a high-income mortgage originator, sell what no one else has—you, your expertise, and your commitment to do the best thing for the customer.

People want to be certain they are doing the right thing. Obtaining a mortgage is a major financial step. Most prospects begin interacting with you with their guard up. They don't know the intricacies of mortgage financing, and they depend on you to deal with them honestly and fairly. They don't want to be taken advantage of, so they may not be open with you. So they say things that put them in a safe position, trying to see if there is anything you can really do for them. They tell you what they think is the right thing to say, for example: "I want the lowest rate."

Be very clear about what people do—how they operate. As human beings, they all do the same thing, although when you first start selling, you may think they are all different. They all do the same thing; they just do it in different ways. They don't tell you the truth, and sometimes they don't even realize they are not telling you the truth! They call and talk to you for a reason, and, whether they realize it or not, it is often not the reason they tell you. For example, they don't really want the lower interest rate, but they don't even realize it; they want what the lower interest rate will provide for them: more cash each month to pay the bills or to invest, for example. A lower interest rate may be only one of several ways you can provide what they are truly looking for.

They are concerned about you selling them, and they do not want to be sold. They want to protect themselves against pressure or being manipulated into doing something they really don't want to do. They want what they want. They want you to give them what they want. They want you to give it to them on their terms. Know what they are trying to accomplish, or you will not be able to make a difference for them. They have a problem, and your job is to figure out what it is and how to solve it.

With so many competitors to choose from, the mortgage originator in whom they have the most confidence, and the one that they feel has their best interests in mind, is the one who wins their business. Your job is to get them to see that in spite of what they are telling you, you know something they don't (it's the cash they want, not the rate). Then you can get them to see what that is, and that you can provide it to them.

After all your diligent marketing efforts, the phone rings or a live person answers your call. In the next 30 seconds, you set the stage for a loan, or you lose a sale. You have one goal—to take an application. You have about a half minute to do two things to succeed. The first is to establish yourself as the expert who is on their side and can solve their problem. The second is to figure out what they want to accomplish, regardless of what they tell you.

There is no right script. There are no right responses. No script and no amount of memorization can prepare you for every interaction. But you have to start somewhere. Practice your scripts until they are second nature to you. Scripts are like training wheels on a bicycle. They are good to get you moving in relative safety, and you won't get hurt if you get too far off balance. But the big guys—the pros—don't need them anymore. If you have never been in sales before, I strongly recommend that you read as much as you can, and study sales to become a professional.

Think of sales as a game involving two worlds. There is your world, the world of the mortgage professional, with the experience of dealing with people in all kinds of circumstances. And there is the prospects' world, where they want what they want and believe that the circumstances with which they deal are unique to them. The objective of the game is to get them to cross over willingly from their world into yours and to see your view of what is in their best interest to do. Here are a few rules and game winning strategies and tips:

- Know that their world and yours are different. Theirs is real—to them.
- You can't pressure, coerce, bribe, lie, or cheat or make promises you can't keep to get them to come into your world.
- You can't tell them your perspective; they have to see it for themselves.
- They have to trust you, or they won't come over.
- They have to believe there is a benefit to them, or they won't come over.

Develop and practice your own conversation snippets. Make a list of points you want to cover, and know the conversation for each point. Then let it rip. You don't have to be eloquent to be successful. At one point in my career, a manager told me that I didn't speak well enough for a sales job. I went on to become highly successful at selling many things, including mortgages. Nothing gets in my way when I am selling.

Be clear about the value you offer, and what your intended outcome for the call is—an application. It matters less what you say than it does where you come from when you say it. I believe 100% in what I am selling, and you should believe 100% in what you are selling. I am 100% for my customers and doing what is best for them, even if that is not what they initially say they want.

Be involved in an inquiry with them. When you are willing to be involved, your sales presentation is transformed into a conversation between you and the prospect. Come from that place to be extraordinarily effective in sales. When I am having a conversation with a prospect, I know where I want the conversation to go. It looks like an open conversation—I am asking questions, but I know that no matter what answer they give me, I am going to take them where I want the conversation to go. I do not pressure anyone to do anything. My job is to make them see for themselves what is best for them, as I see it, so they want and choose freely what I am giving them.

This chapter gives you tools to field questions and responses you are likely to encounter, whether during outbound or inbound calling. The chapter provides a structure to classify prospects' readiness to move to the next step, and a system to interact with them in a way that gets them ready.

Eight Rookie Sales Mistakes and How to Avoid Them

It has taken me 40 years of selling to learn these lessons. I know these are mistakes—I've made them all. I'm giving them to you, knowing that you are still likely to make them. But my goal is that once you've made the mistake, these words will allow you to see clearly what didn't work, so that you can avoid making the mistake again. And again. And again. And so that it won't take you 40 years to master the art of salesmanship, or to become a high-income mortgage originator.

Mistake 1: Focusing on the Feature, Not the Customer. I love car salesmen as a group. They provide so many great examples of what people hate about being sold. They love to spout features, and then leave it to you to either assume the benefits or feel like an idiot for not knowing what they are. A product feature means nothing to me, until you, as a salesperson, get it to mean something to me.

How many times have you heard this car feature: "From 0 to 60 in 2.5 seconds." Unless I am into fast cars or drag racing as opposed to economy or family-oriented cars, it's nice to know, but it won't sell me on the car. In fact, if safety is of primary interest to me, that fact by itself might put me off, as if the car were more of a hot rod than I want or need. If, rather than leaving it up to me, you give me a conversation about benefits I can relate to, I'll see it as a feature I wouldn't want to be without.

You know how it is if you are passing a truck with oncoming traffic, and you want to get by it in a hurry. Especially if you have your family with you, you can get out of the way of danger quick and fast. When you push your foot down on that gas pedal, you want to know the car is going to go. So you see, safety is so important.

In the end, people are sold on the benefit, not the product. Focus on the customer, not the product. Sell the benefit, not the feature.

Mistake 2: Over-Selling Things That Are Not Important. Another mistakes rookies make is to pile on feature after feature after feature, hoping that if they pile on enough, something will stick with the customer. With apologies to the good, professional car salespeople out there, if I'm spending $30,000, or $50,000 or $100,000 on a new car, the cup holders are not going to make or break the sale. Neither is the radio, for that matter. Or the automatic locking gas cap. Or the cigarette lighter, or the coin holder, or the map light. Know what is important to customers. And everything you say has to be important to them, or don't say it.

After they are sold, if you want to point out these goodies to make them feel even better about their decision, go ahead. But until you've sold them, focus on the big ticket benefits.

Many new salespeople think that when they are in a sales presentation they have to talk all the time. No you don't. When you've made a good point, and you know it is a good point, let the prospect sit with what you have said. Be silent. If you wait, they usually will say something because they are uncomfortable with the silence. They will usually say they can see your point, at which time you can come back with "I'm glad you can see that." If they don't say anything after a few moments, you can ask, "You can see that, can't you?" In either case, they acknowledge your point without you trying to convince them.

Mistake 3: Using Words That Create Doubt and Separation. Small words make a big difference, not so much in the content, but in the underlying message they subtly communicate. Here are two ways of presenting essentially the same content. The impact is strikingly different in each case:

> **1.** *What we want to do is look to see whether or not we can make a difference for you and let you know what you need to know to make an intelligent decision.*
>
> **2.** *Let's see what's going to make the biggest difference for you, so we can come up with an intelligent decision about what is the right thing at this point.*

In the first statement, "whether or not" raises doubt about your capability to make a difference. "Let you know" has you doing something and then turning it over to the customer to make the intelligent decision. The second statement implies that a difference will be made—the only question is how big. And you and the customer are in partnership to arrive at an intelligent decision. The first statement has a sales-presentation quality to it. Notice that the second statement is more conversational, and more of an inquiry in which you and the customer are partners.

Mistake 4: Not Willing to Get "Up Close and Personal." Generalities don't sell, and most explanations are general in nature and not significant at the personal level. If you are talking to someone in generalities about biweekly mortgage payments versus monthly payments, you would say they reduce the interest you pay over the life of the loan, and shorten the term by X number of years. Nice to know, but what difference does it make to me? As the salesperson, you want to be very clear on why you are giving me the information, and what difference it makes to me.

> *Just by making automatic biweekly payments instead of one monthly payment, you'll save $40,000 over the life of your loan. And you'll pay it off seven years sooner. It would be like the bank giving you back your mortgage payment when you get to the 23rd year. Wouldn't you like that? That's what we're talking about here.*
>
> *And by the way, before I went to the accelerated payments, I was rushing around every month, worrying that things might slip through the cracks, but now, it's automatic, and I don't even think about it. How's that for peace of mind?*

Now you have my attention and interest, I'm glad to know about biweekly payments, and I get a sense of you as a human being, not a mechanical fact giver.

Mistake 5: Confusing Precision with Honesty. New salespeople think being honest and being precise are the same thing. Don't use qualifiers unless you want to purposefully raise the question. Qualifying words like "some" automatically bring up "not all," and raise a question about the ones that aren't. Being too precise can hurt you by weakening your declarative statements and creating doubt. I can say, "The bank looks at three things when they consider a mortgage." Or I can say, "Anyone doing a mortgage for you is going to look at three things." The first one, by mentioning "bank," raises the question "Why not go directly to a bank for a mortgage?" The second statement closes the door on that question. Both statements are true and honest.

Be conscious of your word choices and the subtle messages you communicate. I've been in situations where a salesman has gone through an entire presentation, and it is all logical and makes sense, and I'm agreeing all the way through it—but at the end, when it comes time for the decision, I'm not willing to go forward. It is the little things that leave the impression about you and your commitment. Practice listening closely to yourself and others, and choose your words consciously.

Mistake 6: Responding to What They Say. People tell you they want the lowest interest rate. Don't respond to what they say; respond to why they say what they say. If a customer tells you he can get a better rate elsewhere, and you know your rates are as low as anyone else's, responding to the rates can only lead you down a path of defending yourself. You can only say, "You can't get that, they probably don't have all your information," or something to that effect, which leaves everything open to question. Again, why is the customer saying this to you? The customer wants to make sure he isn't going to get taken advantage of. Here's one way to respond to his reason for saying what he said, not what he said:

> *Everyone gets their money at the same place. Interest rates represent the cost of money and everyone is paying the same price. If I lock in the rate today, it is going to be the lowest rate available to you. There is no incentive for me to give you a higher rate—I get paid the same amount from the lender.*

If they argue back, a little facetiousness and humor can head off an argument in which both you and the prospect lose.

> *Who said that? When did you talk to them? I'm going to go down and get a job there if you can get that rate there. Who is the guy you talked to down there. I want to see, because I want you to know something, this company has been in business over 20 years. I've been with this company for five years. Do you know what I know? This company is a phenomenal company, and nobody can beat our prices because we all get our money from the same place with the same cost of funds. We guarantee the lowest*

rate—my best incentive is to get you the lowest rate, and I guarantee no one can do better. So, if you've got something, I want to know. I want to go down and talk to them. Because if they are beating us, that's who I want to work for.

If your company won't make that guarantee, find another place to work.

I'm going to use whatever they give me to sell them. I leave them with "no way—you must have misunderstood or what they are telling you is not what you are going to get," without actually saying that. I turn their question about me into a question about the competition—that's salesmanship. If you, as a salesperson, are not willing to play there with people shopping for a mortgage, this is not the business for you. Get out now because you are going to work hard, and aren't going to be successful.

When you sell, know exactly where you are going with a customer. There should be no doubt in your mind. If you want to close 90% of the people you talk to, learn to maneuver the conversation to turn out the way you say it will. When I sell, customers get what I want to give them. It looks as if they are telling me, but in the end, I give them what I know is the best thing for them. Salesmanship is getting them to want what I have and what I know is best for them, and getting them to believe that is what they want as well. In the end, the choice is a foregone conclusion. They have been sold, but never feel they "were sold."

Mistake 7: Closing Without Knowing It's a "Yes." Most new salespeople are afraid to ask for the sale because they don't know whether they will get a yes. If you do trial closes (opinion questions) to nail down points throughout your conversation, you will know exactly where your customer is, so that by the time you get to the closing, decision-making question, you know they will say yes. That makes sense, doesn't it? (By the way, that was an opinion question, not a close.)

Mistake 8: Telling, Not Selling. Facts are just facts. Facts don't sell. If you are going to make a point with a fact, be very clear that it is important to the customer. And know why you are making the point. Then sell the point, do not just tell it. Here's an example. *Fact:* There are three credit reporting agencies. Here are two ways to communicate a benefit—the first one tells, the second one sells:

- *It's good for you because if one of them makes a mistake it won't ruin your credit across the board. There is accuracy because of verification.*

- *Three credit agencies are competing to make sure the information is accurate. That allows you to question anything that is on a credit report, so if there is anything inappropriate, we can challenge it. When you have only one credit agency, they don't have a tendency to do anything, but with three they have a tendency to correct the bad information. So if there is anything bad on your credit report that we know shouldn't be there, we can have it removed for you.*

Both responses deal with the same fact and benefit: having three credit agencies means accuracy. But the first conversation leaves the customer with a concern about mistakes. The second conversation puts you on the customer's side providing a service to take care of him if there are any mistakes. The first conversation tells the customer the fact and benefit. The second uses the fact and benefit to sell the value you provide.

From Lead to Prospect—Getting the Go Ahead for the Application

How to do convey trustworthiness? If you have ever had a salesperson tell you that you can trust him, you know that your warning sensors immediately get activated. Telling someone she can trust you doesn't work. You demonstrate trustworthiness, and the demonstration is in the small things. Our sales presentation is designed to do three things. First, it establishes our legitimacy and integrity through our longevity, licensing, and experience. Second it sets expectations—both what customers can expect and what we expect in return. Finally, it sets up a specific agreed-upon time for the next step. Setting up the next step creates an opportunity for us to demonstrate integrity (by doing what we say for the next step) and another opportunity to build the relationship with the customer. Here is a sample script for inbound calls that leads to an application:

> *Good morning/afternoon, this is* _____, *how may I help you?*
>
> (Response: he is calling about a letter that mentioned a low interest rate.)
>
> *Okay. At the bottom of the letter, under the phone number where it says, "Mortgage Services Since 1986," right underneath our state license number there is an offer code. What is that number, please?*

This one exchange establishes the legitimacy of the company, which you can safely assume is always of some concern to the caller. It tells them we have been in business a long time, that we have experience. By using our state license number as a reference, we point out that we are reputable without having to say it. The offer code identifies the marketing campaign that generated the call, which tells us what interested the caller, regardless of what they say.

> *Thank you. Let me bring it up on my computer screen, <repeat the offer code number> Yes. Ok, may I have your name so I can pull up your file, please? Could you spell that for me, please?*

Taking the time to spell the name out shows that we are accurate, not sloppy. We are not rushing anyone. We are verifying that we are dealing with the right person. We establish a professional relationship and establish ourselves as professional people. Now we can start the conversation.

> *Thank you. What we do is simple, fast, and easy! Our goal is to have you save money each month and improve your financial position. We also know that we can't do that for everyone, but to be sure, it is important that the information we have on you is up-to-date and accurate. Is your address still* _____?

We've now given them a reason to continue to give us information—saving money. By stating that we know we can't help everyone, we are honest. And we create exclusivity which automatically has them listening to find out how they can be one of the lucky ones for whom we will make a difference.

> *I want you to know, we are licensed with the state banking department as a lender and a broker and have been in business for over twenty years. We work with over 300 wholesale lenders nationally, allowing us to secure the best mortgage programs available.*

We continue to communicate honesty, professionalism, and experience. We establish ourselves as a substantial business, with a track record and a national reach.

> *After we update your information, which will take about 8 to 10 minutes, one of our senior mortgage underwriters will process your information through our national network of wholesale lenders/bankers. We'll see if there is a mortgage program that can better benefit you, and if we can beat the rate we are offering you in the letter we sent you, which is <interest rate>.*

If there was any concern about a bait and switch to a more expensive product, this conversation puts it to rest by offering the hope of an even better deal. It establishes that we are on the prospect's side, not taking advantage of him. And referring prospects to a senior underwriter tells customers they are important.

> *My primary job is to update your file and make sure it is accurate. I will then call you back and go over your information and your credit report and propose some options. I'm going to explain everything to you. You are going to have all the information you need to have, so if you decide to go shopping you'll have what you need to make a smart, intelligent decision. And by the way, we don't charge you for any of this. Does that make sense?*

What you are communicating is "I'm not trying to sell you anything. No pressure. I'm here to do a good job for you." While I leave the door open for them to shop around (which I assume they have considered anyway), I fully expect and assume that when I do my job, they will not feel the need to shop around because they see that what I am proposing is the smart, intelligent, right thing for them to do.

"Does that make sense?" is a "trial close" and is one of the most important questions you can ask during a sales presentation. It tells you where the prospect is in the conversation, and whether you have sold the point. If the prospect agrees, you can move on. If not, sell the point again before moving on.

> So let's see what's going to make the biggest difference for you, so we can come up with an intelligent decision about what is the right thing for you to do at this point. Do you have any questions? Okay, great, let's get started.

I am in the interaction with them. I am not just talking. I've established that we are in this together, that a difference will be made, and that the decision will be theirs, intelligent and the right thing for them to do.

If prospects have a question or concern at this point, do not react to it. Never answer a question with an explanation. It will spawn more questions. A question means there is a point you didn't sell. Respond by reselling the point. For example, if they come back with something like "I just want the rate you said in the letter," you didn't get across the point that you are on their side, working to get them the best rates possible, maybe even better than the rate in the letter. Have a conversation that goes something like this:

> I'm glad you want that rate. That is my job. My job is to get you that low interest rate. That is what I am here to do. And we might even be able to get you a lower rate than what we have published. I'm not going to promise, but I will do everything in my power to get you that—it would be fantastic wouldn't it—we're not able to do that with everyone. But for

me to do that for you, we need to get some information together so our senior underwriter can look at which of our hundreds of wholesale lenders has the program that will make the biggest difference for you. Then, when we go over it together, you'll have all the information you need to make a smart, intelligent decision. That makes sense, doesn't it?

Respond but don't react to the question or comment. I went over every point I needed to make in that response, taking the prospect where I know she needs to go, ending with a trial close to gauge where she is before closing.

If you deliver the presentation and ask for the go ahead and don't get it, regardless of the reason the prospect gives you for the no, you did not establish the necessary relationship and trust for the prospect to move forward. This is very important: Responding to objections is a waste of time. You will address one, and three more will spring up in its place. The key to success is to understand why the objection is being expressed and to address the underlying cause. In most cases it will be a trust issue.

Objections Are Opportunities. Why, after listening to your whole presentation, don't people go ahead with the application? Here are some of the most common reasons they give: "I'm all set." "I don't have time now." "I don't have any information available." "I need to check with my spouse." "I don't give out my social security number." If you have established trust and created opportunities for them, not one of these objections is legitimate, nor is any one of them cause for killing off the prospect. Each of them is an opportunity to engage in another conversation to establish trust and create an opening for action. If they think they are all set, create a benefit they would enjoy if you can do something, and that if you can't, you'll close the file. If they don't have time, then set up a time, and make sure you call when you say. If they don't have any information now, offer up two or three things they can gather together, set a time for a follow-up call and get a social security number so that in the meanwhile you can pull a credit report. If they need to check with their spouse, set a time for a follow-up call when both they and their spouse are available, and make sure you call on time. If they don't give out their social security number over the phone, give them a way to check you out and schedule a follow-up call if still necessary.

Rating Commitment

This three-tier classification system was created to establish a common understanding of prospect readiness and commitment so that we can conduct the appropriate conversations at the right time to increase conversion ratios. The system provides three ratings for commitment: "eager and ready," "cautious but open," and "prove it to me first." This classification system helps all mortgage originators clearly understand what it takes to help a prospect move into action. You can use it during your initial conversation with the prospect, as a way of guiding you to the appropriate conversations that will be effective in moving them forward to an application. Throughout the loan process, using this classification system keeps you consciously checking in with the prospect or customer, to know that he is still enrolled in moving forward to reap the benefits of the mortgage.

There is no right place for a borrower to be in terms of commitment. It doesn't matter where she is. It matters that you know where she is, so you can have the appropriate conversations to move her into action.

Rating your prospects' commitment is important for you and important for them. Do not waste time with people who are not likely to move forward, no matter how good the product or service you propose is. By rating their commitment you can take actions and have conversations that remove their concerns and allow them to move forward with this important financial decision.

Commitment is a prospect attribute to evaluate at each step in the process before you move on to the next. If you misjudge commitment, you are likely to take your prospects down a path that at some point before closing they will decide they are no longer willing to travel with you.

That leaves you having done a lot of work for nothing, and leaves them without a solution to the problems or issues that had them start the process initially.

It is very important for you to know how committed your prospect is to having a mortgage. It is a very good indicator of the level of cooperation you will receive in getting the information and documents you need—when you need them. The level of commitment also indicates the amount of work you will have to do to build trust and sell the proposal. When you check the prospect's level of commitment at each step, it is easy to know whether you need to do more work with the prospect before moving ahead. This assessment is based strictly on your interactions with prospects and how they respond to you. Their attitude is more important than what they say about their commitment.

Level 1—Ready for Anything, on the Edge of Their Seat. These folks have a pressing need or have already determined that they want to do something with regard to a mortgage. They are the easiest people to work with. You can tell by their voices, by the questions they ask, and by the way they interact with you that they are ready to move forward. Having already decided to do something, they are looking for the right thing to do and the right person to do it with. Establishing, building, and maintaining trust are keys to moving a Level 1 to the next step in the process.

Level 2—Listening and Open. Sometimes if you approach people about a mortgage, or even if they respond to a marketing piece, they may be interested and curious, but not convinced they should go ahead. Level 2 prospects are open to what you are saying, but are a bit cautious about making decisions. While there doesn't appear to be anything specific in the way of moving forward, they aren't quite there. They evaluate the impact the proposed mortgage will have on their short- and long-term goals, and they listen to you when you talk (as opposed to arguing with you). As long as they are open and listening, willing to look at what works and what might not work for them, these folks can move to the next step in the process. You have to continue to build trust, and are likely to want to explain pros and cons of different options so they can make an informed choice. They may be looking to you to make a recommendation, but they will want to understand the reasoning behind your choices. These folks are not quite convinced you are on their side. You need to keep demonstrating that you are.

Level 3—Show Me, Prove to Me, Not Open. Some people you contact through your outreach or who respond to a marketing campaign are skeptical and are at least partially convinced that you will not be able to do anything for them. They are right. Unless you can get them to be open to the possibility that you can solve their problem or improve their situation, you are not going to be able to do anything with them or for them. They have taken a position that you have to prove something to them before they move ahead. Sometimes these people can come across as belligerent, even as they ask for your help. How do you know a Level 3? They aren't really listening to you, they already have all the answers, they think they know more than you do, they are negative about anything you propose without offering anything constructive or productive to move things forward, and can rattle off all the reasons you are not going to be able to do anything for them.

Here is a typical Level 3 exchange for an initial call:

Good morning/afternoon, this is _____, *how may I help you?*
I want your lowest rate (4.75%).

I'm glad you want that rate. That is my job. My job is to get you that low interest rate. And I'm glad you want that rate. What do you have right now?
5.2

Not bad. At 4.75 you'll save a little bit, it will add up over time—are you planning to stay in that house any length of time?
Yes

Good. If I were able to get you the 4.75 what difference would it make other than lowering your payment—is there something else you want to do with that discretionary income?

Just lower the payment.
What are you going to do with this extra cash?
I haven't thought about it.
Okay, are you having a problem meeting your payments now?
No.

I know at this point that there is something else going on beside what is being said or not being said in the conversation. If I tell you it is my job to get you that interest rate, what else can you say? Often Level 3s don't believe you can help them, and are betting that you can't. Be willing to address suspicion and mistrust, and engage in a conversation with them. You can't chase them for the conversation. Get them coming toward you.

Ok good. Because we have a program if you were having a problem paying your bills, but I'm not even going to get into that with you. Ok, so you want 4.75.

I've just held up something they are not going to get unless they engage with me. If they are serious, they will start moving in my direction.

My job really is to get you that lower interest rate. That is what I am here to do. And we might even be able to get you a lower rate than what we have published. I'm not going to promise, but I will do everything in my power to get you that—it would be fantastic wouldn't it—we're not able to do that with everyone. The people who are very wealthy usually get the better rates because they have great credit scores. Do you know what your credit score is?

Interact with them and get them to talk to you. Don't give them a presentation. Let's have a conversation, let's talk and see if there is anything we can do for you. There may be or not. If they are giving me a lot of resistance and attitude, I will hold out the "maybe" rather than the certainty of a yes to get them moving toward me again.

We're not going to do anything that doesn't make a difference for you—you are smart enough to make your decisions based on the facts I'm going to give you. You aren't going to do something that is going to hurt you, are you?

At this point, they can't say much. Unless you can move the Level 3 to at least a Level 2—someone who is cautious but open—you are wasting your time. You will learn that sometimes it is better to walk away from a deal than it is to talk to a stone. And sometimes it is just that willingness to walk away that shifts the prospect to be open to hear what you have to say. Be willing to be in an inquiry, but not in order to get them. If they called you, know that you already have them.

If you are dealing with people who are at Level 3, you cannot do anything until you shift them to at least Level 2. If they can't hear what you say with an open mind, you are wasting your time. Sometimes you have to get tough with these people in order for them to hear you. When you do that, you take a risk that they will end the conversation there and then. While this may sting at first, over time you will come to realize that it is not personal. The key is for you to speak knowing that you are there to make a difference for them, and that it matters more to them than it does to you whether they go forward or not.

These folks will confront you with challenges to your knowledge, your integrity, your honesty, and your commitment to make a difference for them. They may be cynical or nasty. You can't take it personally. Remember that you have what they want and need—money. And that while they are free to shop around with your competition, they won't find a better deal or a better person to take care of them than you. As with trustworthiness, telling them will not convey the message, but how you say whatever you say will. The key to being able to do this is to be willing to walk away from the deal. If you put this choice in the prospect's hands, it does two things. First it eliminates any question of whether you are just trying to get him or snooker him into a loan for your own selfish purposes, and second, it puts the responsibility for refusing help squarely on his shoulders. If he doesn't get what he needs, it isn't because you were unwilling to give it to him; it was because he was unwilling to do what was necessary for you to help him.

As you classify prospects, it is important to know what their spouse's or partner's attitude and commitment is. It is very important that both parties agree about moving forward. Each partner may have different ideas about refinancing or what their priorities are, or even whether to buy or change homes at this time. Include your prospect's significant other in the process to discover what goals and objectives excite and motivate both of them. Classify each partner, and notice and respond to any differences between the partners. This will help you identify the appropriate conversations you need to have with them for them to move forward in agreement with one another. It is only when both partners are comfortable with you, that both like what you are proposing, and that both can see how your proposal fits into their short- and long-term goals that they will move forward with you.

Integrity

Integrity is key. A person at Level 3 or even Level 2 is looking for a reason to hang up or walk out. It is your job not to provide that excuse. Do whatever you say you will do, when you say you will do it, and do it the way it should be done.

The single most important factor in your success will be the relationships you develop with your prospects. Your relationship with your prospect is the foundation that gives you the best chance of closing a loan; this is even more important than the interest rate. While you offer great programs at competitive rates, most of your competition can offer the same, since brokers get their rates from the same sources. People do business with people they like, trust, and have faith in, unless they are desperate and have no choice. By establishing a strong relationship with your prospects, they will listen to you as a professional. As the professional, your function is to support them to take actions that have a positive impact on their lives and the lives of the people most important to them—their family. They will move into action with people they respect and trust.

I cannot stress enough the importance of integrity to build the relationship and trust between you and your prospects. It is the single most important factor in your success. With integrity, you will convert the majority of people you talk with to closings. Without it you will spend a lot of time on deals that go nowhere, as people drop out during the process. It is not hard, but it does take practice and discipline.

The most important tool you have in your arsenal is your word. That means doing what you say, when you say, the way it needs to be done, without compromise and without excuses. When you tell a prospect that you will call at a specific time, you call promptly at that time. If you say you are going to call back at 3:00 P.M. tomorrow, call them back promptly at 3:00 P.M. tomorrow. If you say you will call back at 3:00 and you don't call or you call at 3:10 or 4:00 or 5:00, what else do you expect them to think other than you only operate "in the ball park" or what you say is "about accurate." Even if they are not home at 3:00, by leaving a message that you called as you said you would, they see that you do what you say—in other words, they can count on you. If you don't do what you say you will do, you invalidate the main advantage you have over your competition—your integrity. Whether your prospect keeps his word to you by being available at the specified time and place is secondary to your keeping your word, even if you don't have all the information you need when you call him. Building a business as a high-income mortgage originator is easy when you are your word.

Along with integrity, straight talk is essential in building trust. This means, especially at the initial stages, that you not make promises that you are not certain you can keep. Until you process an application and credit report, you really don't know how you can help someone. We never promise people that we can get them the lowest rates or a better loan than they already have. We do, however, promise to do everything in our power to make the biggest difference for them. We also lay out for them that if we cannot help them we will let them know that, and then close the file. But if we are able to help them, that we expect them to move to the next step.

Keeping Track

It is essential that you keep track of the number of presentations you make and the number of applications that result from them. Aim for one out of four or five at the beginning. If you are not able to do that, practice your delivery. And make more calls. The more you make, the more at ease you will be with people. It is also useful to know how you classified the people who both did and didn't go on to complete applications. This information may point to weaknesses in your responses to questions, qualifications, or assessing the attitudes of prospects. Once these problems are identified, you can then begin to look at corrective action.

It is very important to receive sales training and develop the art of salesmanship. If the company you work for does not provide it, change companies. As a company owner, I know that my staff is only as good as the training we provide them, and training is a prerequisite for success. Make sure you are trained.

CHAPTER SIX

Step 3: Facts and Forms: Taking the Mortgage Application

Congratulations! You've gotten past the cold calls, the mailings, the hang ups, and the "no thank you's"; you've enrolled a prospect into filling out the mortgage application with you. Good job. You've completed the first step of many on the way to having a satisfied customer. The good news is you already have the fundamental skills you need to take the next steps with the prospect. You will use the basic skills of enrollment and sales—attention, interest, conviction, desire, close—and the classification system you learned in the previous chapter to assess where the prospect is at each critical point through the closing and follow up.

The next step is to begin completing the Uniform Residential Loan Application, or Form 1003 (ten oh three). This form is published by Fannie Mae (as Form 1003) and by Freddie Mac (as Form 65) and is available to originators online for completion either directly with Fannie Mae or via specialized mortgage origination software packages.

Anyone can fill in a form. A pro (that's you) uses it as a selling tool. Is the 1003 a long, detailed, required form? Yes. It looks formidable to the uninitiated. But in the right hands (yours), it is an effective sales tool that can be used to learn what is of interest and value to the prospect. With that knowledge, you have what you need to engage effectively in the facts and benefits conversations covered in the previous chapter. As long as you always have in mind what is of value to them, prospects will move forward from application to proposal to closing to glowing referrals. That is the winning strategy to become a high-income mortgage originator.

In this first interaction with a prospect, you don't need every piece of information asked for on the 1003 form. As mentioned in Part One of the book, you will gather some basic information, pull a credit report, and make a proposal for a loan product based on the information you gather. Before the loan is submitted for approval, the information on the 1003 must be complete and accurate, but right now your goal is to gather enough information to pull a credit report and, with its additional information, compute the key ratios that give you a good idea of the types of loan products for which this borrower qualifies.

There is no "right way" to complete an application. Eventually all information on the 1003 must be completed. The application experience is better all around if, during the completion of the form, you get to know the applicant as a person, not simply as a source of data.

This chapter begins by explaining the basic information needed and how to use it to qualify the prospect. It defines key ratios—Loan to Value (LTV), Debt to Income (DTI or Back End Ratio), and Expense to Income (Front End Ratio)—and discusses how income, employment, and property information impact a loan's approval. We cover a basic, vanilla scenario first—single owner, employed at a job, single-family residence—and then delve into variations of importance in each section of the 1003. At the end of this section you will know what information to collect on this first call, why you are asking for it, and where to put it on the form. You will be able to complete each section of the 1003 with clarity and confidence.

The second part of the chapter provides a conversational script in which to collect the necessary information and get to know the applicant. At the end of the conversation you will set up the next steps in the process, the credit call. Building a relationship and setting up next steps are the two most important building blocks to ensure that an applicant moves forward and that your efforts result in a closing—and that means income to you.

The chapter concludes with structures to track your results. If you set up and use these structures from the beginning, they will provide tremendous value to you. You will be able to see clearly which parts of the process you have mastered and which parts still require practice. You will be able to identify the areas in which to focus your time and effort on your way to becoming a high-income mortgage originator.

Why Do You Ask?

The primary objective of the application call is to gather sufficient data to formulate a proposal for the prospect. You need personal information about the borrower: income and employment history, debt and credit history, and property value. You need the basic information you collect on this initial phone call to pull a credit report and calculate LTV, DTI, and Housing Ratio. Doing so gives you a sense for which loan products prospects may qualify, and what they want to accomplish with the loan. You will be able to develop a picture of borrowers' qualifications and financial history to formulate proposals that makes sense. And you will assess borrowers' commitment and need.

The three most important things lenders look at when making a decision on a loan are credit, property value, and income. The credit report contains most of the necessary credit information, but preliminary information about property value and income come from the borrower in the process of completing the application. Each of the following sections begins with a vanilla example of a borrower who is employed at a job and is seeking a mortgage for his or her primary residence, which we will assume, unless otherwise stated, is a single-family home. Other situations that affect the information you collect at this stage are discussed as subsections.

I. Type of Mortgage and Terms of Loan

Use the first section of the 1003, shown in Figure 6.1, to record the amount of the loan requested in the "Amount" box. If the borrower inquires about

Borrower		Co-Borrower				
I. TYPE OF MORTGAGE AND TERMS OF LOAN						
Mortgage Applied for:	☐ VA ☐ FHA	☐ Conventional ☐ USDA/Rural Housing Service	☐ Other (explain):		Agency Case Number	Lender Case Number
Amount $	Interest Rate %	No. of Months	**Amortization Type:**	☐ Fixed Rate ☐ GPM	☐ Other (explain): ☐ ARM (type):	

FIGURE 6.1   1003 Section I Type of Mortgage and Terms of Loan

a specific type of loan product, record the loan term (in months) in the "No. of Months" box, and check "Fixed" or "ARM" in the Amortization section. Prior to submitting the loan application, you will use this section to record the description of the loan for which you are seeking approval, but it is not necessary at this point.

II. Property Information and Purpose of the Loan

Since the loan is secured by the property, the value of the property is important to a lender when making a decision to approve or deny a loan. Lenders want a cushion between the mortgage amount and the value of the property, so that if property values drop, their interest is still secured. Figure 6.2 shows Section II, which holds the property information.

II. PROPERTY INFORMATION AND PURPOSE OF LOAN						
Subject Property Address (street, city, state & ZIP)						No. of Units
Legal Description of Subject Property (attach description if necessary)						Year Built
Purpose of Loan	☐ Purchase ☐ Refinance	☐ Construction ☐ Construction-Permanent	☐ Other (explain):	Property will be: ☐ Primary Residence ☐ Secondary Residence ☐ Investment		
Complete this line if construction or construction-permanent loan.						
Year Lot Acquired	Original Cost $	Amount Existing Liens $	(a) Present Value of Lot $	(b) Cost of Improvements $	Total (a + b) $ 0.00	
Complete this line if this is a refinance loan.						
Year Acquired	Original Cost $	Amount Existing Liens $	Purpose of Refinance	Describe Improvements ☐ made ☐ to be made Cost: $		
Title will be held in what Name(s)			Manner in which Title will be held		Estate will be held in: ☐ Fee Simple	
Source of Down Payment, Settlement Charges, and/or Subordinate Financing (explain)					☐ Leasehold (show expiration date)	

FIGURE 6.2   1003 Section II Property Information and Purpose of Loan

Subject Property Address. Record the full mailing address of the property for which the mortgage will apply in "Subject Property Address."

Occupancy by Owner. One of the risk factors that underwriters consider is whether the owner of the property will reside there or whether the property will be occupied by others. Lenders consider a property owner who lives in the property more likely to pay the mortgage than one who lives elsewhere. Also, people who own the homes they live in are more likely than renters or lessees to maintain the property to retain its value. Select one item in the "Property will be" group, consisting of primary residence (the borrower is going to live in the home all or most of the year), secondary residence (the borrower will live in the home part of the year), or investment (the borrower will not live in the home, or the property contains more than four housing units).

Loan Purpose. Select one item from "Purpose of Loan," purchase, refinance, construction, construction to permanent, or other. Second mortgages, home equity loans, and home equity lines of credit are either "refinance with cash out" or "other." If the loan is a refinance, enter the principal amount owed on the existing mortgage(s) and equity lines in the box labeled "Amount of Existing Liens," and indicate in "purpose of refinance" either cash out, debt consolidation, and so forth.

III. Borrower Information

In order to pull a credit report, you need a social security number (in "Social Security Number"—see Figure 6.3) and authorization by the prospect. Some credit agencies require date of birth ("DOB") as additional identity verification. You should have the borrower's correctly spelled full name (in "Borrower's Name"). The information you record here when the application is submitted for approval will become the name as it appears on the mortgage note and all supporting and related documents.

Contact Information. You will follow up with the borrower after you review the credit report. Ask for "Home Phone" and make a note of the best phone number and time to reach him. Verify home address ("Present

Borrower	III. BORROWER INFORMATION		Co-Borrower	
Borrower's Name (include Jr. or Sr if applicable)		Co-Borrower's Name (include Jr. or Sr. if applicable)		

Social Security Number	Home Phone (incl. area code)	DOB (mm/dd/yyyy)	Yrs. School	Social Security Number	Home Phone (incl. area code)	DOB (mm/dd/yyyy)	Yrs. School
☐ Married ☐ Unmarried (include ☐ Separated single, divorced, widowed)	Dependents (not listed by Co-Borrower) no. ages			☐ Married ☐ Unmarried (include ☐ Separated single, divorced, widowed)	Dependents (not listed by Borrower) no. ages		
Present Address (street, city, state, ZIP) ☐ Own ☐ Rent____No. Yrs.				Present Address (street, city, state, ZIP) ☐ Own ☐ Rent____No. Yrs.			
Mailing Address, if different from Present Address				Mailing Address, if different from Present Address			
If residing at present address for less then two years, complete the following:							
Former Address (street, city, state, ZIP) ☐ Own ☐ Rent____No. Yrs.				Former Address (street, city, state, ZIP) ☐ Own ☐ Rent____No. Yrs.			

FIGURE 6.3   1003 Section III Borrower Information

Address"), and mailing address, if different. A post office box address is only acceptable as a mailing address. Indicate whether he owns or rents the property he lives in and how long he has lived there.

If he has not been at his current address for at least two years, ask for previous addresses so that you have two complete years of residence history. This information is useful to identify complete mortgage and rent payment history for the borrower on the credit report, and lenders require two years of history on these items. This information is also useful in determining whether the borrower is eligible for first-time homebuyer programs.

Family Information. Knowing a borrower's age, marital status, and the ages of dependent children gives you a quick picture of the borrower's short- and long-term financial needs and considerations. If you are working with a person who is married, whether or not the spouse is listed as a co-borrower, part of your job is to get the spouse on board with your proposal before you submit the loan. The same is true for an unmarried co-borrower.

A borrower's marital status, dependents, and age tell a lot about what stage of life he is at, and, as a result, what financial circumstances he is likely to have in the past, present, and future. A young couple without children has different financial concerns from a family with teenagers approaching college age, or older people looking toward retirement. Fill in "Age," "Marital Status," and number and ages of "Dependents." Learning about someone's family is also a great way to relate to him. Getting a prospect to open up about himself establishes rapport and trust. (See Figure 6.3.)

Co-Borrowers: A paragraph at the top of the 1003 indicates that co-borrower information must be included in the application

A. If income or assets other than the borrower's will be used to qualify the loan,

or

B. If there is another party (whose income and assets are not being used to qualify the loan) who has community property rights

and

1. the borrower lives in a community property state, or
2. the property is in a community property state, or
3. property held in a community property state is being relied upon for repayment of the loan.

In the case of B, while you are not required to include the income or assets of the other for qualification, you must include the liabilities of the other. Community property states are currently Arizona, California, Idaho, Louisiana, Nevada, New Mexico, Texas, Washington, and Wisconsin; and community property rights are conferred upon present and former spouses. For detailed information, refer to the IRS publication "Community Property" at http://www.irs.gov/pub/irs-pdf/p555.pdf.

Co-borrowers who are not legally married to one another must file separate loan applications, including separate credit reports. Married (to each other) co-borrowers may file a single application. Complete all sections of the application that provide space for co-borrower information for both the borrower and co-borrower if you submit a single application.

Foreigners. Resident aliens do not have social security numbers. They do have resident alien identification numbers, which they must provide in place of a social security number. Persons who are not in this country legally do not have a number, and are not likely to qualify for a mortgage through licensed lenders.

IV. Employment Information

One of the things that lenders look at to determine if a borrower is a good risk is employment history. Steady employment means steady income, which lenders interpret as continued and reliable ability to pay the mortgage and other expenses. If the borrower has been in the same field of work for a long time, an underwriter will consider it a mitigating factor, even if the current job is newer than two years.

A minimum of two years of employment history is required, including monthly income earned while at prior jobs. Lenders look at the earnings trend over the two years, and obviously increases are less risky than decreases. Lots of job changes or little experience in the present line of work are negative factors to an underwriter, and indicate a higher likelihood of interrupted income streams, jeopardizing prompt payment. Being new to the job (and therefore having least seniority in case of cut backs) is also negative, but is offset by lots of experience in the same line of work or profession. Talking to prospects about their work is a good way to learn more about them, and to relate to them. You also get a sense of whether they are looking to change jobs, which may impact their motivation and goals, and their ability to retain a steady source of sufficient income.

At this stage, for "Name & Address of Employer," the name, city, and state of the employer are sufficient if street address is not known. Be sure to get "Yrs on this job" to know if you need to ask for additional employment history. Ask for the "Business Phone" so that you have a way of contacting the borrower during business hours, if necessary. "Yrs in this line of work/profession" is an important income stability indicator. "Position Title/Type of Business" is interesting for getting to know the borrower. (See Figure 6.4.)

At This Job Less Than Two Years. Be sure to get employer information, as well as the dates when the borrower worked there, and

Borrower		IV. EMPLOYMENT INFORMATION		Co-Borrower
Name & Address of Employer	☐ Self Employed	Yrs. on this job	Name & Address of Employer　☐ Self Employed	Yrs. on this job
		Yrs. employed in this line of work/profession		Yrs. employed in this line of work/profession
Position/Title/Type of Business	Business Phone (incl. area code)		Position/Title/Type of Business	Business Phone (incl. area code)

If employed in current position for less than two years or if currently employed in more than one position, complete the following:

FIGURE 6.4　1003 Section IV Employment Information

approximate monthly income. If the borrower only remembers approximately how much he earned on an annual basis, use what he tells you, and convert annual earnings to monthly by dividing by 12.

Self-Employed. If the borrower owns his or her own business, is self-employed, or employed strictly as a 1099 independent contractor, check this box. This borrower faces certain challenges when it comes to income information. For now just check the box, and then watch for the special case of the self-employed borrower when we get to the next section of the application. If you are collecting prior employment history, note whether the borrower was self-employed during the period in question. Underwriters interpret moves from employed to self-employed or from self-employed to employed in different ways. Income trend (rising, declining) further informs the underwriter as to the reliability of the borrower's income stream (and related risk).

V. Monthly Income and Combined Housing Expense Information

Underwriters use information in the Monthly Income and Combined Housing Expense section of the application to calculate Debt to Income (DTI or Back End Ratio) and Expense to Income ratios (Housing to Income, or Front End Ratio), which play a large role in determining the borrower's qualification and if qualified, how much the loan will cost relative to par. Figure 6.5 shows this section of the 1003 is to be completed for both borrower and co-borrower, if applicable. The left side of the table identifies sources of income, while the right side itemizes housing expenses. The absolute amounts, whether high or low, are not as significant to an underwriter as the ratio between income and expenses. It indicates the financial cushion a borrower has for paying housing and directly related expenses, both presently and with the proposed loan. Right now you only need to gather information about the borrower's current income and expenses.

Gross Monthly Income. For most people who have a job, monthly income consists only of wages. At this application stage, the borrower

V. MONTHLY INCOME AND COMBINED HOUSING EXPENSE INFORMATION						
Gross Monthly Income	Borrower	Co-Borrower	Total	Combined Monthly Housing Expense	Present	Proposed
Base Empl. Income*	$	$	$ 0.00	Rent	$	
Overtime			0.00	First Mortgage (P&I)		$
Bonuses			0.00	Other Financing (P&I)		
Commissions			0.00	Hazard Insurance		
Dividends/Interest			0.00	Real Estate Taxes		
Net Rental Income			0.00	Mortgage Insurance		
Other (before completing see the notice in "describe other income," below)			0.00	Homeowner Assn. Dues Other:		
Total	$ 0.00	$ 0.00	$ 0.00	Total	$ 0.00	$ 0.00

     * Self Employed Borrower(s) may be required to provide additional documentation such as tax returns and financial statements.

Describe Other Income   *Notice:* Alimony, child support, or separate maintenance income need not be revealed
                                         if the Borrower (B) or Co-Borrower (C) does not choose to have it considered
                                         for repaying this loan.   Monthly Amount

B/C $

FIGURE 6.5   1003 Section V Monthly Income and Combined Housing
Expense Information

can approximate annual before tax earnings. If the borrower gives you an
annual salary, divide it by 12 to come up with the monthly amount. If the
borrower reads you the information from a pay stub, find out how often
he or she is paid in order to calculate the monthly amount. Use Table 6.1
to compute monthly income from Gross Wages from a pay stub.

     Overtime, Bonuses, and Commissions. Annual commissions, over-
time, and bonuses are averaged over the last two years and divided by 12
to derive an estimated monthly value. For example, say Josh earns $60,000
a year in regular base pay at his job. And, when he generates business,
he receives a commission. Last year he only earned $2000 in commission,

TABLE 6.1   Monthly Base Pay Calculations

Pay Method	Number of paychecks per year	Annual Salary	Monthly Base Empl Income
Biweekly, also known as "every two weeks" or" every other week"	26	= Gross wages × 26	= (Gross wages × 26)/12 = Gross wages × 2.17
Semi-monthly, also known as "twice a month"	24	= Gross wages × 24	= (Gross wages × 24)/12 = Gross wages × 2
Monthly	12	= Gross wages × 12	= Gross wages

but this year he has done very well and earned $6000 in June and another $4000 in October. Josh's annual average commission calculation is:

$$($2000 + $6,000 + $4,000)/2 = $6000.$$

His average monthly commission is $6000/12 months = $500 per month. Compute bonuses and overtime the same way.

Other Income. Unless a large portion of the borrower's income comes from interest, dividends, income from rental properties, public assistance, alimony, or child support, you do not need details at this stage. If these other sources of income are not significant relative to wages, commissions, bonuses, and overtime, then it is not necessary to include them at all on the application. If, after analysis, your borrower's ratios need to be improved, you can include these other sources of income, but if included, documentation will be required before the loan can be submitted for approval.

Self-Employed Income. Self-employed borrowers often are hard-pressed to estimate sufficient steady income. Earnings may be erratic and inconsistent. I know independent real estate agents who go months without income, and can score over $100,000 in commissions in one or two closings. In addition, small business owners and self-employed people are able to avail themselves of tax deductions that reduce the amount of their taxable income, which is the income figure that lenders use for self-employed applicants.

While there are challenges to obtaining a loan for self-employed borrowers, their ability to show other assets or fund a large down-payment can mitigate the risk for the lender. In most cases lenders will require additional income verification documentation, including tax returns and profit and loss statements for the business.

Small business failures are common, especially in the first five years of operation, so unless the borrower has been in business at least two years, a mortgage will be very expensive. However, if the borrower started a business in the same field in which he or she was employed for many years, or if the borrower completed an educational degree in that field to start the business, lenders look favorably upon those circumstances.

At this stage in the application process, you do not have to get into too many details with self-employed prospects. Use the income they tell you for initial evaluation (two-year average, divided by 12), and later, if necessary, look more closely.

Remember, if a lender is going to assume the higher risk of a loan for a self-employed borrower who is unable to qualify on the basis of taxable income, the lender will charge more money for the loan. "Stated income" or "no documentation" ("no-doc") loans are available for those who have been self-employed for at least two years.

Combined Monthly Housing Expense. The information requested on the right side of Section V of the 1003 gives the lender a picture of the basic cost of shelter, and the cost of protecting the bank's security interest on the future loan. For renters it includes monthly rent and renter's insurance, and for homeowners, mortgage principal plus interest payments, real estate taxes, homeowner's, mortgage, and hazard insurance, and any fees paid to condominium or homeowner associations. Use the "Present" column to record the information. If the borrower has a mortgage, a recent mortgage statement will provide exact amounts for Principal and Interest. It also shows escrowed funds for real estate taxes and private mortgage insurance (PMI), homeowner's insurance, and hazard insurance premiums, if applicable. If the refinance is for a condominium, then include the Home Owner's Association (HOA) dues.

If the borrower's taxes and insurance do not appear on the mortgage statement, ask specifically for those monthly amounts. Estimates are fine at this point, but make a note to ask the prospect for exact amounts before you present a proposal. Other documents and sources will verify much of the information before you submit the application.

VI. Assets and Liabilities

As a lender, the value of the property securing the loan is of critical importance. For refinances, this information is recorded in Section VI, Assets and Liabilities, as shown in Figure 6.6. (On a purchase, the value of the new property is in Section II, Property Description).

VI. ASSETS AND LIABILITIES

This Statement and any applicable supporting schedules may be completed jointly by both married and unmarried Co-Borrowers if their assets and liabilities are sufficiently joined so that the Statement can be meaningfully and fairly presented on a combined basis; otherwise, separate Statements and Schedules are required. If the Co-Borrower section was completed about a non-applicant spouse or other person, this Statement and supporting schedules must be completed about that spouse or other person also.

Completed ☐ Jointly ☐ Not Jointly

ASSETS Description	Cash or Market Value	Liabilities and Pledged Assets. List the creditor's name, address, and account number for all outstanding debts, including automobile loans, revolving charge accounts, real estate loans, alimony, child support, stock pledges, etc. Use continuation sheet, if necessary. Indicate by (*) those liabilities, which will be satisfied upon sale of real estate owned or upon refinancing of the subject property.		
Cash deposit toward purchase held by:	$			
List checking and savings accounts below		LIABILITIES	Monthly Payment & Months Left to Pay	Unpaid Balance
Name and address of Bank, S&L, or Credit Union		Name and address of Company	$ Payment/Months	$
Acct. no.	$	Acct. no.		
Name and address of Bank, S&L, or Credit Union		Name and address of Company	$ Payment/Months	$
Acct. no.	$	Acct. no.		
Name and address of Bank, S&L, or Credit Union		Name and address of Company	$ Payment/Months	$
Acct. no.	$	Acct. no.		

VI. ASSETS AND LIABILITIES (cont'd)

Name and address of Bank, S&L, or Credit Union		Name and address of Company	$ Payment/Months	$
Acct. no.	$	Acct. no.		
Stocks & Bonds (Company name/number & description)	$	Name and address of Company	$ Payment/Months	$
		Acct. no.		
Life insurance net cash value Face amount $	$	Name and address of Company	$ Payment/Months	$
Subtotal Liquid Assets	$			
Real estate owned (enter market value from schedule of real estate owned)	$			
Vested interest in retirement fund	$			
Net worth of business(es) owned (attach financial statement)	$	Acct. no.		
Automobiles owned (make and year)	$	Alimony/Child Support/Separate Maintenance Payments Owed to:	$	
Other Assets (itemize)	$	Job-Related Expense (child care, union dues, etc.)	$	
		Total Monthly Payments	$	
Total Assets a.	$	Net Worth (a minus b) ▶	$	**Total Liabilities b.** $

Schedule of Real Estate Owned (If additional properties are owned, use continuation sheet.)

Property Address (enter S if sold, PS if pending sale or R if rental being held for income) ▼	Type of Property	Present Market Value	Amount of Mortgages & Liens	Gross Rental Income	Mortgage Payments	Insurance, Maintenance, Taxes & Misc.	Net Rental Income
		$	$	$	$	$	$
Totals		$	$	$	$	$	$

List any additional names under which credit has previously been received and indicate appropriate creditor name(s) and account number(s):

Alternate Name	Creditor Name	Account Number

FIGURE 6.6   1003 Section VI Assets and Liabilities

The left columns of the 1003 Section VI record assets, while the right side is used for liabilities. In your initial conversation with the borrower to complete the application, focus on the assets, as the credit report will provide you with most of the pertinent liability information.

Lenders are interested in the financial reserves, in the form of savings, retirement plans, and so forth, that a borrower can fall back on if circumstances interfere with income. This information also gives you a picture of the borrower's savings and spending habits. Lenders look at the reserve of assets in terms of how many months of principal, interest, taxes, and insurance expenses (PITI) it can safeguard. For borrowers with good credit, two months reserves are sufficient. Borrowers with lower credit may qualify for better loans if they can show six months of assets in reserve.

Checking and Savings Accounts. Ask the borrower at which bank they have checking accounts and savings accounts. Record the name of the bank or credit union, or investment firm, and the estimated amount in each account. List each account's information in a separate row.

Value of Real Estate. At this stage, if the mortgage is a refinance, you may rely on the borrower's best guess about the value of the home, knowing that the LTV will be reevaluated when a more reliable number is available. Before the loan is submitted, an appraisal will determine the value and what numbers the lender will use to calculate Loan to Value ratio. If an appraisal was done within the last 120 days, that value can be considered reliable. The borrower's best guess as to the value of their home can come from a recent appraisal, an evaluation by a real estate agent, real estate tax assessments (usually a percentage of the value, which varies from state to state), recent sales of neighboring homes, or just plain thin air. Use the best number you can get, knowing that in the end, it is the appraisal and the sale price, in the case of a purchase, that will determine value.

Retirement Funds. If the borrower has an Individual Retirement Account, pension plan, or 401(k) or other retirement account, put the estimated vested interest in those accounts in the box marked "Vested interest in retirement fund." Only 70% of the value of retirement assets can be used to calculate reserves.

Self-Employed Borrowers. If the borrower owns a business, ask him to estimate what the business is worth, and record that information in "Net worth of businesses owned." If needed to qualify, this information will be verified through the financial statements of the business later in the process.

Purchases. In addition to having an interest in a borrower's financial reserves, lenders want to know how the down-payment on a home purchase will be funded. Because it is usually a substantial amount of money, if the down-payment is coming from savings, the remaining reserves may fall short of optimum levels. If the money for a down-payment will be borrowed from a family member or financed through another debt, it is considered a liability even though it may not appear on a credit report.

Record the source of the down-payment in "Cash deposit toward purchase held by," and the amount of the down-payment in the box to the right.

Schedule of Real Estate Owned. Use this section to record information about the value of the borrower's current home, whether for a new purchase or a refinance transaction. Assuming a primary residence, enter the property address, the borrower's estimate of its current market value, the remaining balances on the first mortgage, and any other liens, for example a second mortgage or home equity loan. The information in the next boxes is the same, in most cases, as the Housing Expense information gathered in Section V. Record the amount of the monthly principal and interest payment in "Mortgage Payments" and record insurance, taxes, and so forth in the box so labeled to the right.

Rental Income. If the borrower seeks qualification based on the inclusion of income from rental properties, record that information in the Schedule of Real Estate Owned. List each property separately. Gross rental income is the monthly rental receipts before payment of any expenses. Net rental income is the difference between 75% of the gross rental income and the combination of principal, interest, taxes, and insurance (PITI) on the rental property.

For example, if the property rents for $1000 per month, and the PITI is $500 per month, then compute net rental income as follows:

$$\text{Net rental income} = (\text{Gross rental income} \times .75) - \text{PITI}$$
$$= (\$1000 \times .75) - \$500$$
$$= (\$750) - \$500$$
$$= \$250$$

VII Transaction Details

For a purchase transaction, record the purchase price of the home in "a. Purchase Price" and the down-payment amount in "e. Estimated Prepaid Items." On a refinance, enter the amount of the loan request in "d. Refinance." You will complete the rest of this section later in the process based on the terms of the loan for which the application is submitted. (See Figure 6.7.)

VIII. Declarations

The declarations section of the 1003 (Figure 6.8) uncovers any legal issues that could interfere with the lender's security interest (questions a, d, f, g, h, and i), or the ability of the lender to obtain judgment in case of default (questions b, c, e, j, k). Questions l and m address owner occupancy and qualification for first-time homebuyer programs.

Each declaration is a "yes/no" question. Both borrower and co-borrower must answer all questions, and if any answer is "yes" ask for and make note of the circumstances and particulars on a continuation sheet to attach to the application.

IX. Acknowledgement and Agreement

Section 9 (Figure 6.9) will be signed by the borrower when the loan package is prepared.

VII. DETAILS OF TRANSACTION	
a. Purchase price	$
b. Alterations, improvements, repairs	
c. Land (if acquired separately)	
d. Refinance (incl. debts to be paid off)	
e. Estimated prepaid items	
f. Estimated closing costs	
g. PMI, MIP, Funding Fee	
h. Discount (if Borrower will pay)	
i. Total costs (add items a through h)	

VII. DETAILS OF TRANSACTION	
j. Subordinate financing	
k. Borrower's closing costs paid by Seller	
l. Other Credits (explain)	
m. Loan amount (exclude PMI, MIP, Funding Fee financed)	
n. PMI, MIP, Funding Fee financed	
o. Loan amount (add m & n)	
p. Cash from/to Borrower (subtract j, k, l & o from i)	

FIGURE 6.7   1003 Section VII Details of Transaction

X. Information for Government Monitoring Purposes

You can complete most of the information in Section 10 (Figure 6.10) later in the process, prior to submission of the package, but fill in the following information now: "The application was taken by"—select all that apply: face to face interview, mail, telephone or Internet. Enter your name and today's date in "Interviewer's name."

VIII. DECLARATIONS

If you answer "Yes" to any questions a through i, please use continuation sheet for explanation.	Borrower Yes	No	Co-Borrower Yes	No
a. Are there any outstanding judgments against you?	☐	☐	☐	☐
b. Have you been declared bankrupt within the past 7 years?	☐	☐	☐	☐
c. Have you had property foreclosed upon or given title or deed in lieu thereof in the last 7 years?	☐	☐	☐	☐
d. Are you a party to a lawsuit?	☐	☐	☐	☐
e. Have you directly or indirectly been obligated on any loan which resulted in foreclosure, transfer of title in lieu of foreclosure, or judgment?	☐	☐	☐	☐

(This would include such loans as home mortgage loans, SBA loans, home improvement loans, educational loans, manufactured (mobile) home loans, any mortgage, financial obligation, bond, or loan guarantee. If "Yes," provide details, including date, name, and address of Lender, FHA or VA case number, if any, and reasons for the action.)

VIII. DECLARATIONS

If you answer "Yes" to any questions a through i, please use continuation sheet for explanation.	Borrower Yes	No	Co-Borrower Yes	No
f. Are you presently delinquent or in default on any Federal debt or any other loan, mortgage, financial obligation, bond, or loan guarantee? If "Yes," give details as described in the preceding question.	☐	☐	☐	☐
g. Are you obligated to pay alimony, child support, or separate maintenance?	☐	☐	☐	☐
h. Is any part of the down payment borrowed?	☐	☐	☐	☐
i. Are you a co-maker or endorser on a note?	☐	☐	☐	☐
j. Are you a U.S. citizen?	☐	☐	☐	☐
k. Are you a permanent resident alien?	☐	☐	☐	☐
l. Do you intend to occupy the property as your primary residence? If "Yes," complete question m below.	☐	☐	☐	☐
m. Have you had an ownership interest in a property in the last three years?	☐	☐	☐	☐
(1) What type of property did you own—principal residence (PR), second home (SH), or investment property (IP)?	_____		_____	
(2) How did you hold title to the home—solely by yourself (S), jointly with your spouse (SP), or jointly with another person (O)?	_____		_____	

FIGURE 6.8   1003 Section VIII Declarations

IX. ACKNOWLEDGEMENT AND AGREEMENT

Each of the undersigned specifically represents to Lender and to Lender's actual or potential agents, brokers, processors, attorneys, insurers, servicers, successors and assigns and agrees and acknowledges that; (1) the information provided in this application is true and correct as of the date set forth opposite my signature and that any intentional or negligent misrepresentation of this information contained in this application may result in civil liability, including monetary damages, to any person who may suffer any loss due to reliance upon any misrepresentation that I have made on this application, and/or in criminal penalties including, but not limited to, fine or imprisonment or both under the provisions of Title 18, United States Code, Sec. 1001, et seq.; (2) the loan requested pursuant to this application (the "Loan") will be secured by a mortgage or deed of trust on the property described in this application; (3) the property will not be used for any illegal or prohibited purpose or use; (4) all statements made in this application are made for the purpose of obtaining a residential mortgage loan; (5) the property will be occupied as indicated in this application; (6) the Lender, its servicers, successors or assigns may retain the original and/or an electronic record of this application, whether or not the Loan is approved; (7) the Lender and its agents, brokers, insurers, servicers, successors, and assigns may continuously rely on the information contained in the application, and I am obligated to amend and/or supplement the information provided in this application if any of the material facts that I have represented herein should change prior to closing of the Loan; (8) in the event that my payments on the Loan become delinquent, the Lender, its servicers, successors or assigns may, in addition to any other rights and remedies that it may have relating to such delinquency, report my name and account information to one or more consumer reporting agencies; (9) ownership of the Loan and/or administration of the Loan account may be transferred with such notice as may be required by law; (10) neither Lender nor its agents, brokers, insurers, servicers, successors or assigns has made any representation or warranty, express or implied, to me regarding the property or the condition or value of the property; and (11) my transmission of this application as an "electronic record" containing my "electronic signature," as those terms are defined in applicable federal and/or state laws (excluding audio and video recordings), or my facsimile transmission of this application containing a facsimile of my signature, shall be as effective, enforceable and valid as if a paper version of this application were delivered containing my original written signature.

<u>Acknowledgement.</u> Each of the undersigned hereby acknowledges that any owner of the Loan, its servicers, successors and assigns, may verify or reverify any information contained in this application or obtain any information or data relating to the Loan, for any legitimate business purpose through any source, including a source named in this application or a consumer reporting agency.

Borrower's Signature X	Date	Co-Borrower's Signature X	Date

FIGURE 6.9 1003 Section IX Acknowledgement and Agreement

Let's Talk

Don't fill out the application—talk to prospects. In the conversation, they sense you are interested in them—and you are getting the information you need. You should already have the proper spelling of their name, and their

---

X. INFORMATION FOR GOVERNMENT MONITORING PURPOSES

The following information is requested by the Federal Government for certain types of loans related to a dwelling in order to monitor the lender's compliance with equal credit opportunity, fair housing and home mortgage disclosure laws. You are not required to furnish this information, but are encouraged to do so. The law provides that a lender may not discriminate either on the basis of this information, or on whether you choose to furnish it. If you furnish the information, please provide both ethnicity and race, For race, you may check more than one designation. If you do not furnish ethnicity, race, or sex, under Federal regulations, this lender is required to note the information on the basis of visual observation and surname if you have made this application in person. If you do not wish to furnish the information, please check the box below. (Lender must review the above material to assure that the disclosures satisfy all requirements to which the lender is subject under applicable state law for the particular type of loan applied for.)

BORROWER ☐ I do not wish to furnish this information		**CO-BORROWER** ☐ I do not wish to furnish this information	
Ethnicity: ☐ Hispanic or Latino ☐ Not Hispanic or Latino		**Ethnicity:** ☐ Hispanic or Latino ☐ Not Hispanic or Latino	
Race: ☐ American Indian or ☐ Asian ☐ Black or African Alaska Native American ☐ Native Hawaiian or ☐ White Other Pacific Islander		**Race:** ☐ American Indian or ☐ Asian ☐ Black or African Alaska Native American ☐ Native Hawaiian or ☐ White Other Pacific Islander	
Sex: ☐ Female ☐ Male		**Sex:** ☐ Female ☐ Male	
To be Completed by Interviewer This application was taken by: ☐ Face-to-face interview ☐ Mail ☐ Telephone ☐ Internet	Interviewer's Name (print or type)		Name and Address of Interviewer's Employer
	Interviewer's Signature Date		
	Interviewer's Phone Number (incl. area code)		

FIGURE 6.10 1003 Section X Information for Government Monitoring Purposes

address, if you followed the call script in the previous chapter. If not, this is a chance to establish your accuracy and attention to detail. (See Figures 6.11 to 6.17.)

Okay, let me get the correct spelling of your first and last name.

Do you use a middle initial or a middle name? Okay, we want to make sure we get the paperwork drawn up correctly. Is that how it appears on your mortgage statement?

Borrower	III. BORROWER INFORMATION	Co-Borrower
Borrower's Name (include Jr. or Sr. if applicable)		Co-Borrower's Name (include Jr. or Sr. if applicable)

FIGURE 6.11   1003 Section III Borrower Information

Okay, and the property you want the mortgage for, is that your primary residence now? [Or if a purchase,] will that be your primary residence?) And that's a single family house, correct?

Okay, good.

II. PROPERTY INFORMATION AND PURPOSE OF LOAN	
Subject Property Address (street, city, state & ZIP)	No. of Units

Purpose of Loan ☐ Purchase ☐ Construction ☐ Other (explain): ☐ Refinance ☐ Construction-Permanent	Property will be: ☐ Primary Residence ☐ Secondary Residence ☐ Investment

FIGURE 6.12   1003 Section II Property Information and Purpose of Loan

Here's what we are going to do—I'm going to take a quick question-naire, which will give me a snapshot of where you are. Then I will get to work to see what is available to you. If there is something available, then we will put it into our system and check it out with the 300 lenders. That makes sense, right?

I know you have been in your house awhile, how long have you been there?

(Repeat their answer, Oh, seven years).

Was the house new when you bought it? Do you know when it was built?

Okay, is that the first house you own, or the second?

Complete this line if this is a refinance loan.				
Year Acquired	Original Cost	Amount Existing Liens	Purpose of Refinance	Describe Improvements ☐ made ☐ to be made
	$	$		Cost: $

FIGURE 6.13 1003 Section II Refinance Information

(Oh, the first house!) And how much did you pay for the house? And do you know what it is worth now? That's great.

VI. ASSETS AND LIABILITIES

Real estate owned (enter market value from schedule of real estate owned)	$

FIGURE 6.14 1003 Section VI Assets and Liabilities

When you bought the house what kind of mortgage did you take? Was it a fixed or variable? 30-year? And how much did you borrow?

II. PROPERTY INFORMATION AND PURPOSE OF LOAN

Complete this line if this is a refinance loan.				
Year Acquired	Original Cost	Amount Existing Liens	Purpose of Refinance	Describe Improvements ☐ made ☐ to be made
	$	$		Cost: $

FIGURE 6.15 1003 Section II Property Information and Purpose of Loan

You tell me you have been in your house a year. Where did you live before that? For how long? Why did you buy your house?

Get two years of residence information. The question about why they bought their home has no bearing on the loan, but does open a relationship-building dialogue.

You know as well as I do, the equity builds up in your home. Most people could never save as much as the equity in their house. What if we

could save you another couple of hundred a month that could be "blow money," while you still are building the equity in your house. Doesn't that make sense?

That's why I want to know how much you owe on your mortgage right now.

You have enough room there so that if you did want to take some of that out as cash, we'll be able to come up with a program that will let you do that with the best rates that are available to you. Are you thinking of taking any money out, maybe to consolidate some bills, or a vacation, or some work around the house? What would you be using it for? And do you know the interest rate? Okay, great.

Okay, and who lives with you? Are you married? What is your husband's/wife's name. Same last name? Okay. And will <<name>> be listed on the title as well? Okay, good.

Borrower			III. BORROWER INFORMATION		Co-Borrower	
☐ Married ☐ Separated	☐ Unmarried (include single, divorced, widowed)	Dependents (not listed by Co-Borrower) no.	ages	☐ Married ☐ Separated	☐ Unmarried (include single, divorced, widowed)	Dependents (not listed by Borrower) no.	ages

FIGURE 6.16 1003 Section III Borrower Information

And what is your birth date? And your social security number? And your wife's birth date? And social security number? Okay.

Do you have any kids? (No kids!) How old are they? Boy or girl. That's a great/tough/wonderful age.

How long do you plan on staying in this house? 5-10 years— Forever—you must love it there! How nice for you.

The reason I'm asking is that most people stay in their house an average of seven years, and we look not only at now, but at what you want to do for the future. My job is to look at the long term and the short term and explain the options to you so you can make an intelligent and informed decision. That makes sense, doesn't it?

That is the other thing, if you are going to be moving, why go with a 30-year mortgage—you might be better off with a 15-year or a variable. So those are the things we check and look out for.

How long have you/ has your husband been at his job? Ten years! What does he do there? Who does he work for? And where is that located?

Borrower	IV. EMPLOYMENT INFORMATION		Co-Borrower	
Name & Address of Employer ☐ Self Employed	Yrs. on this job	Name & Address of Employer ☐ Self Employed	Yrs. on this job	
	Yrs. employed in this line of work/profession		Yrs. employed in this line of work/profession	
Position/Title/Type of Business	Business Phone (incl. area code)	Position/Title/Type of Business	Business Phone (incl. area code)	

If employed in current position for less than two years or if currently employed in more than one position, complete the following:

FIGURE 6.17   1003 Section IV Employment Information

Some of these questions, for example, how long your clients plan to stay in their home, have no box on the 1003 but still provide useful insights into the right mortgage product for the borrower. Use every opportunity to sell your services and what you provide, and to get related to the prospect. This is the time to build up the confidence and trust the prospect has in you.

Cindy, a Senior Loan Specialist says, "I love asking questions about family and job. These are usually the most important aspects of a person's life, and the easiest to relate to. No matter what line of business the borrower is in, I'm always curious. If they are new to a job or industry I ask them how they like it. If they've been at it for a long time, I'm impressed. If it is an unusual line of work, I ask them what they do. I can always ask whether they like what they do. If they do, they'll usually say so. If they don't, I always ask what they would like to be doing—when you get someone in touch with what they dream of doing, you never know where the conversation will lead. And whenever I have a borrower with kids, I use the opportunity to let them know I am a grandmother. I know that makes me nonthreatening to them, and makes it harder for them to say no. When they talk about themselves, I'm always listening for their level of interest and commitment. The way they answer the questions gives me a pretty good indication of how they will be to deal with as the loan progresses. If they answer the questions without doubt, I know I've got someone who is probably well organized and committed. If there is hesitation with some of the answers, I know they may not trust me enough yet to feel comfortable, and then I'll ask a question or offer something personal to build relationship. If they can't answer basic income and expense questions, I know that I most likely have someone who has not been responsible financially, and will want to begin preparing them for the realities from the beginning—and using it as an opportunity to sell myself as the person they need on their side. If I can get them talking to me, I know I've got them. If not, I know I still have some work to do in the trust department."

At this point, if you had the conversation recommended in the previous chapter, you have already accomplished the following objectives:

Established yourself and the company as professional, reputable, and honest.

Set expectations for a follow up call from an underwriter.

As I said earlier, I'll review this information and get back to you tomorrow. The first thing we will cover is your credit. What time should I call you tomorrow?

As Soon as You Get Off the Phone

1. Sign and date the application in Section X (Figure 6.18) and check the appropriate box for how you took the application.
2. Mark your calendar with the call-back time, phone number, and file number, so you have all that information handy when the time comes to make the call.
3. Log your application and update your statistics. Congratulations. You have converted a call into an application. (See Table 6.4 at the end of this chapter.)

X. INFORMATION FOR GOVERNMENT MONITORING PURPOSES		

The following information is requested by the Federal Government for certain types of loans related to a dwelling in order to monitor the lender's compliance with equal credit opportunity, fair housing and home mortgage disclosure laws. You are not required to furnish this information, but are encouraged to do so. The law provides that a lender may not discriminate either on the basis of this information, or on whether you choose to furnish it. If you furnish the information, please provide both ethnicity and race. For race, you may check more than one designation. If you do not furnish ethnicity, race, or sex, under Federal regulation, this lender is required to note the information on the basis of visual observation and surname if you have made this application in person. If you do not wish to furnish the information, please check the box below. (Lender must review the above material to assure that the disclosures satisfy all requirements to which the lender is subject under applicable state law for the particular type of loan applied for.)

BORROWER ☐ I do not wish to furnish this information	**CO-BORROWER** ☐ I do not wish to furnish this information
Ethnicity: ☐ Hispanic or Latino ☐ Not Hispanic or Latino	**Ethnicity:** ☐ Hispanic or Latino ☐ Not Hispanic or Latino
Race: ☐ American Indian or ☐ Asian ☐ Black or African Alaska Native American ☐ Native Hawaiian or ☐ White Other Pacific Islander	**Race:** ☐ American Indian or ☐ Asian ☐ Black or African Alaska Native American ☐ Native Hawaiian or ☐ White Other Pacific Islander
Sex: ☐ Female ☐ Male	**Sex:** ☐ Female ☐ Male

To be Completed by Interviewer This application was taken by: ☐ Face-to-face interview ☐ Mail ☐ Telephone ☐ Internet	Interviewer's Name (print or type)	Name and Address of Interviewer's Employer
	Interviewer's Signature Date	
	Interviewer's Phone Number (incl. area code)	

FIGURE 6.18   1003 Section X Information for Government Monitoring Purposes

4. Rate the prospects' commitment level. Are they Level 1, ready to go? Level 2, open but cautious? Or Level 3, doubtful, obstinate, and waiting for you to prove something to them?

5. Pull the credit report.

Credit Reports

The credit report is a picture of how your prospects pay their bills, and, when obtaining a mortgage, dictates what lenders will be willing to risk with a borrower. The higher the credit score, the better the programs for which your borrowers will qualify. Scores range from 350 to 850. A high score means that the borrower will pay less for the mortgage, both in terms of interest and points, than a person with a low score will pay.

Three credit bureaus collect and report information about borrowers. They are Trans Union, Experian, and Equifax. Credit agencies provide a combined report, called a *tri-merged report*. Banks will generally use the middle score, although in some cases score averaging is accepted. If there is a co-borrower on the loan application, the credit report must be a combined report for the two parties. Separate details will be provided for each, combined on a single report.

Credit agencies provide reporting services that combine information from the three credit bureaus to give you a comprehensive picture of borrowers' credit history and outstanding debt. Most will turn out the report in a few minutes, so once you get off the phone with the prospect, you can get to work completing the data gathering.

The combined credit report is divided into several sections: Identification Information, Residence, Public Records, Credit Inquiries, Credit Scores, Credit History, and Creditor Information. Agencies offer additional services, at additional cost, to discover other identification (maiden name, for example), any fraudulent activities, and other information to alert you to possible identity theft issues.

Identification and Residence Information

In order to request a combined credit report, you must provide the credit agency with sufficient information to properly identity the borrower. This usually consists of a social security number, name, date of birth and address for verification. (See Table 6.2.)

Public Records

This section of the credit report (Figure 6.19) lists and briefly describes bankruptcies, foreclosures, law suits, judgments, and other matters of

TABLE 6.2   Credit Report Identification and Residence Information

```
BORROWER'S INFORMATION            CO-BORROWER'S INFORMATION
  NAME: xxxxxxx xxxxxxxxx           NAME:
  SSN:                   AGE: 43    SSN:                  AGE:
  CURRENT ADDRESS: 12 STREET ADDRESS  ANYTOWN CT 06999

  OWN/RENT:                         SINCE:
  NUMBER OF DEPENDENTS:             MARITAL STATUS:
```

Public Records					
Bankruptcy	BQ1 BX1 BU1	**Chapter 7 Bankruptcy**	Docket # 0987654- DSP-01/02	Liabilities $	Status **Discharged in bankruptcy**
		Court name **Us Bkpt Ct St Anytown**	Filed 09/01/2001	Assets $	Status date 01/02
		Comments **Attorney: JOHN C LEGAL**			

Judgment	BQ1 BX1	**Judgment**	Docket # SCAW 123456	Amount $1672	Status **Judgment**
		Court name **Anytown Small Claims**	Filed 06/01/2001		Status date 06/01
		Comments **Plaintiff: CREDITORS INC.** **Defendant: BORROWER'S NAME**			

FIGURE 6.19   Credit Report Public Records

public record. Each item has a date, a description, and a status. Any recent or active items require explanation on the loan application. Cross-check this information with the responses the borrower gave you for the Declarations Section of the 1003, and make a note of any discrepancies so that you can discuss them with the borrower on the next phone call.

Inquiries

This section of the credit report shows the date on which credit inquiries were made and by whom and in some cases, for what purpose (in cryptic abbreviations which you will get used to). Unless the applicant's credit score was affected negatively by excessive inquiries (you'll know in the next section of the credit report), you do not need to know much about the details in this section, but they will alert you to the fact that the borrower has been shopping around. If the applicant's scores dropped because of the

Inquiry Information	
01/03/2007 FACTL DTA (BQ1)	11/14/2006 KROLL FACTUAL DATA/060 (BX1)
12/14/2006 CREDSTAR (BQ1)	10/31/2006 CSC CREDIT SERVICES (BX1)
11/14/2006 FACTL DTA (BQ1)	
10/31/2006 CSC (BQ1)	
10/30/2006 CBCINNOVIS (BQ1 BX1 BU1)	01/15/2007 FDC (BU1)
	01/03/2007 FDC (BU1)
01/03/2007 KROLL FACTUAL DATA/060 (BX1)	12/14/2006 CHASE CREDIT (BU1)
	11/14/2006 FDC (BU1)
12/14/2006 FISERV CREDSTAR (BX1)	10/31/2006 CSC MTG (BU1)

FIGURE 6.20   Credit Report Inquiry Information

number of inquiries, make a note to ask the applicant about it on the next call (Figure 6.20).

Credit Score(s)

A credit score is a computer-generated number that weights different credit factors according to mathematical and statistical models based on experience with millions of consumers. Credit scoring is relatively new, and its purpose is to predict the likelihood that the borrower will repay a new loan on time.

Each credit bureau has its own mathematical model for computing credit scores. All of them take into account factors such as the ratio of credit card balances to credit limits, when accounts were established, how many accounts have balances, delinquencies (how many, how late, and how long ago), and the number of credit score inquiries made in the last 12 months. Scores range from 350 to 850. High scores (over 700) mean that the borrower will be eligible for the most loan products at the best prices. Moderate scores (620 to 700) are still eligible for conforming loans through Fannie Mae and Freddie Mac, but scores below 580 indicate that

Credit Score Information						
	Repository **Trans Union**	Brand **Classic 04**	Type **FICO**	**987-65-4321**	**BORROWER NAME**	**BU1**
612	038 – Serious delinquency, and public record or collection filed 016 – Lack of recent revolving account information 018 – Number of accounts with delinquency 013 – Time since delinquency is too recent or unknown					
	FACTA: Inquiries impacted the credit score.					
	Repository **Experian**	Brand **Fair Isaac**	Type **FICO**	**987-65-4321**	**BORROWER NAME**	**BX1**
605	38 – Serious delinquency and public record or collection field 18 – Number of accounts delinquent 20 – Length of time since legal item filed or collection item reported 16 – Insufficient or lack of revolving account information					
	FACTA: TOO MANY INQUIRIES LAST 12 MONTHS					
	Repository **Equifax**	Brand **BEACON 5**	Type **FICO**	**987-65-4321**	**BORROWER NAME**	**BQ1**
593	38 – Serious delinquency, and derogatory public record or collection filed 18 – Number of accounts with delinquency 14 – Length of time accounts have been established 16 – Lack of recent revolving account information					
	FACTA: Inquiries impacted this score.					

FIGURE 6.21   Credit Report Credit Score Information

the borrower, if able to qualify at all, is likely to pay high interest rates and/or points to obtain a loan. People with scores below 500 are generally unqualified for loans.

In addition to the score, each reporting bureau indicates reasons (with their own coding numbers) that the score was negatively impacted. See Figure 6.21 for examples of reasons for scoring deductions. Note all these items for discussion with the borrower on the credit call.

Credit History

The credit history section of the credit report shows detailed information about secured and revolving debt and loans, current, and past. The history

TABLE 6.3   Credit Report Credit History

```
      CREDIT GRANTOR       DATE    LAST DT       HIGH    BALANCE CURR
HISTORY
      ACCOUNT NUMBER       OPENED  REPORTD       CREDIT       OWING RATE
30 60 90

  1  FLAGSTAR BANK      12/2004 08/2006      270000       264592 M1
0  0  0
     987654321098
TERMS=360M1554
     MR=11  ECOA=I  B / XPN=01,EFX=01,TU=01
     PP START DT= 08/2006 PP=111111111111
     TYPE OF LOAN: CONVENTIONAL REAL ESTATE
MORTGAGE
     TRANSFER; CURRENT ACCOUNT; FANNIE MAE ACCOUNT; REAL ESTATE
MORTGAGE

  2  CHASE               06/2006 08/2006      15000         9007 R1
0  0  0
     1234567890123456
               TERMS=REV180
     MR=2   ECOA=I  B / XPN=01,EFX=01,TU=01
     PP START DT= 08/2006 PP=11
     TYPE OF LOAN: CREDIT CARD / CHARGE
ACCOUNT
     CURRENT ACCOUNT; CREDIT CARD; AMT IN HIGH CREDIT IS CREDIT
LIMIT

  3  SOVEREIGN BANK     11/2002 01/2005      55000            0 I1
2  0  0
     2468013579246801
TERMS=60M1059
     MR=26  ECOA=I  B / XPN=01,EFX=01,TU=01
      DEL DATES=04/2004
     PP START DT= 01/2005 PP=X111111111121111111111111
     TYPE OF LOAN:
AUTO
     ACCOUNT AUTO
```

can go back 10 years or more, even for closed accounts. Mortgages, student loans, automobile leases, credit cards, store charge cards, and second mortgages are all included. (See Table 6.3.)

Creditor and Account Information. All accounts, whether owned individually or jointly, are reported. The creditor name (credit grantor) and the account number appear. The date the account was opened shows lender's "depth" of credit. The older the account, the better. "Last date reported" is important if there are derogatory items, and tells the lender how far in the past those items are. More recent history is given more weight in many instances. "High credit" shows maximum balances or credit limits for credit cards. "Balance owing" is self-explanatory, but consider it in light of last date reported. The next item, under current rate is actually the type of account (M for mortgage, R for revolving credit, and I for installment loan). "Terms" shows the number of months and monthly payment amount. In the example above, the Flagstar mortgage terms are "360M1554" meaning a 360-month loan (30 years) with a monthly payment of $1554.

This information is necessary to complete the 1003 Liabilities column in Section VI (Figure 6.22).

Liabilities and Pledged Assets. List the creditor's name, address, and account number for all outstanding debts, including automobile loans, revolving charge accounts, real estate loans, alimony, child support, stock pledges, etc. Use continuation sheet, if necessary, Indicate by (*) those liabilities, which will be satisfied upon sale of real estate owned or upon refinancing of the subject property.

LIABILITIES	Monthly Payment & Months Left to Pay	Unpaid Balance
Name and address of company	$ Payment/Months	$
Acct. no.		
Name and address of company	$ Payment/Months	$
Acct. no.		
Name and address of company	$ Payment/Months	$
Acct. no.		

FIGURE 6.22   1003 Section VI Liabilities

V. MONTHLY INCOME AND COMBINED HOUSING EXPENSE INFORMATION					
Co-Borrower	Total	Combined Monthly Housing Expense	Present	Proposed	
$	$	Rent	$		
		First Mortgage (P&I)		$	
		Other Financing (P&I)			
		Hazard Insurance			
		Real Estate Taxes			
		Mortgage Insurance			
		Homeowner Assn. Dues			
		Other:			
$	$	Total	$	$	

FIGURE 6.23   1003 Section V Monthly Income and Combined Housing Expense Information

Use minimum monthly payments from the credit report to calculate debt to income ratios and net worth. First mortgage and second mortgages are reported in the same area of the credit report as other debt. Identify those items, and record them in Section V Monthly Income and Combined Housing Expense in the boxes for Current First Mortgage P & I and Other Financing P & I. Be sure when you add up the total liabilities in Section VI that you are not counting the mortgages again. (See Figure 6.23.)

Payment History. In Table 6.3 the payments begin with "PP=" followed by a string of up to 24 numbers or X's. X's indicate no activity, 1's mean on time payment, and 2's mean late payments (30 days past due or more). In this example, mortgage payments to Flagstar were on time. Payments on the installment loan for the automobile show one late payment, and "DEL DATES=04/2004" tells you when it occurred.

Verify and Update Current Mortgage Information. Compare any items that appear to be for current mortgages or equity loans to the information the borrower gave you regarding:

Original amount of loan: (See the Credit Account section, look for "mortgage" as type of loan, and the original amount will be in the "high credit" slot). In the Table 6.3 example, the Flagstar mortgage was for $270,000.

Term: In the Table 6.3 example, the term is 360 months or 30 years.

Monthly payment: In the Table 6.3 example, the payment is $1554. You cannot tell from the credit report if this amount is principal and interest only, or whether it includes taxes and insurance.

Balance due: In the Table 6.3 example the balance due is shown under Balance Owing, and is $264,592.

Make a note of any discrepancies or omissions so that you can discuss them with the borrower on the credit call.

Keeping Score

The number of applications you take is one of the major gauges of your success. It is the point of origination, the beginning of the pipeline of activity that will lead eventually to loan closings—and your income. Keeping statistics regarding calls out, calls in, applications taken, and loan packages submitted will do two very important things for you. First, the numbers will tell you where you need to practice. If you are making a lot of calls, or receiving a lot of incoming calls with very few applications taken, you know that you need to work on your initial contact scripts from Chapters 4 and 5. A high-income mortgage originator will take an application almost 100% of the time on incoming calls. Stats for cold calls will be less, of course.

If your ratio of applications to calls is acceptable, the next place to focus is the conversion ratio—the number of applications taken for which you submit loan packages to lenders. There are several steps between the application and the submission of the loan package, each addressed in a chapter later in this section of the book. For now, just remember that if, when you get to the point of tracking submissions, you find that your conversion ratios are not as high as you like, come back to this chapter to practice the conversations to build relationships that begin with the application (Table 6.4).

This New Application Log will become your record of performance going forward. Think of it as a navigational tool. If you use it fully, you

TABLE 6.4 New Application Log

NEW APPLICATION LOG

X = NEW PURCHASE

Rep:

Last Name, First	Date Taken	Source	Credit Call	Proposal Call	F/Up 1	F/Up 2	F/Up 3	Loan Pack	Submit Dt	Final Status Dt	Outcome
1											
2											
3											
4											
5											
6											
7											
8											
9											
10											
11											
12											
13											
14											
15											
16											
17											
18											
19											
20											
21											
22											

will know what direction and action to take to improve your performance to become a high-income mortgage originator. Coupled with your marketing statistics, you will know how much effort it takes to generate an application and how many applications you need to generate to close the number of loans you need to make a six-figure income. It will also provide valuable information regarding how long it takes to move a prospect from application to closing, and where your areas for improvement are.

If you are working for someone who is tracking your statistics, do not think that you don't also need to track and analyze your performance. It is up to you, not your manager, to know your measures and come up with ideas and actions you can take to improve your numbers. It makes sense to know what your manager is watching, so you can watch it also. But be responsible. You can never be a high-income mortgage originator unless you are.

CHAPTER SEVEN

Step 4: Interpreting Credit Reports and Ratios, Building Trust

Congratulations again! You've collected all the data you need to perform a preliminary assessment of the prospect's qualifications for a mortgage. Now it is time to transform that data into valuable information for you to structure the next conversation you have with the prospect—the credit call—in a way to grab his attention, keep his interest, communicate your conviction, build his desire to do business with you, and set up the proposal call.

On the credit call, you use the information collected on the application and credit report to have a conversation with the prospect to:

1. Review the borrower's credit history, credit scores, and key ratios.

2. Inquire about discrepancies or omissions of important information.

3. Zero in on the borrower's motivation priorities for cash flow, cash out, and risk.

4. Identify any likely changes that might impact the borrower's ability to qualify for a loan or that will inform you more fully about her motivational priorities.

5. Identify the problem he has for which you are the solution.

6. Listen for her concerns, clarity, comfort with risk, and expectations.

7. Assess and rate his commitment as a Level 1 (ready to move forward), Level 2 (open and listening, evaluating), or Level 3 (not listening, positional).

8. Establish and verify her readiness to proceed.

That's a tall order for a short conversation, but it is essential that you cover all the points so that you are able to develop a loan proposal that makes sense for, and to, the borrower, and to prepare him to take the next steps with you.

This chapter explains the calculations for Loan to Value, Housing Expense and Debt to Income Ratios and the general guidelines for conforming loans as they regard the key ratios. Next, it describes what you can do for the prospect who is unlikely to qualify for an affordable loan. Then, depending on the borrower's qualifications, you will select from samples of conversations tailored to specific circumstances to set expectations for the future proposal. Finally, we will discuss the masterful sales techniques to ready the prospect to accept your proposal, as we did with the application.

What Does It All Mean? Transforming Data into Information

With the data you gathered on the 1003 application and the credit report, you now have all you need to see how the borrower looks in the eyes of a lender. Three key ratios and several other factors play a major role in underwriting, and determine whether your prospect will be able to get the money on the terms she wants.

Lenders will assess three main categories of risk: credit history, ability to pay, and security interest in the property. Credit history is encapsulated in the credit score, and ability to pay is assessed using two ratios: Housing to Income and Debt to Income. Lenders also consider other factors when assessing ability to pay, such as cash and reserves, and employment stability. Lenders will seek mitigation of ability-to-pay risk in the form of more security (higher down-payment, which results in a lower Loan to Value ratio) or higher interest rates. The security interest is measured by Loan to Value.

You will examine the application data you collected so far, and understand more fully the borrower's financial situation and needs so that you can develop a loan proposal that makes sense to the borrower and to the lender.

Credit History–Credit Scores

The credit score is a picture of how your prospect pays his bills, and how he handles credit. A lender can take one look at a credit score and know if the prospect is a good risk or not. Credit scores range from 350 to 850, and the higher the score, the better it is for the borrower. High scores mean that the borrower will qualify for the best, least-expensive loans available. Low scores mean that the borrowers may not be able to get what they want at a price they can afford.

Scores over 700 are high. Scores between 620 and 700 are not bad, and will still qualify the borrower for a Fannie Mae or Freddie Mac conforming loan. Credit scores lower than 620 mean that your borrower has fewer options, will face higher costs, and has some work to do to improve his financial situation. And scores lower than 550 are going to need a lot of work before they qualify for a loan.

When you have a "tri-merged" report from a credit agency that shows information reported from all three credit bureaus, lenders will generally look at the middle score, ignoring both the high and low scores reported.

No Credit History. Some people do not have a credit history. Young people who are new to their financial responsibilities may never have used a credit card or formally borrowed money, the repayment of which is recorded in transactions reported to credit bureaus. These borrowers, with *nontraditional credit* can still qualify for a loan. They will have to provide other evidence of their creditworthiness, in the form of records show-ing two years of on-time bill payments for a minimum of four creditors. Utilities, phone, and cable TV bills are examples of appropriate documen-tation. If your borrower falls into this category, make a note to discuss it on the credit call.

Credit Inquiries. Every time a creditor or prospective lender pulls a credit report on a prospect, it is recorded in the credit report. If there are more than three inquiries in a 14-day period, the borrower's credit scores will begin to decline by as much as 35 points. For some prospects that drop can mean the difference between qualifying for a conforming loan or not. If that is the case, you can save your prospect some money on the cost of the loan by postponing the loan for 30 days to allow the excess inquiries to drop off.

Overextended Credit. Credit scores drop if the borrower has numer-ous credit cards that are carrying balances at or near the maximum credit limit. It signals to the lender that the borrower is having difficulty paying bills. Credit card balances should be no more than 50% of the credit limit for the borrower's credit score to be unaffected.

Age and Depth of Credit. In general, the longer a borrower has credit, the better, assuming he has made timely payments. Having credit that has been in place for a while is better than newer credit lines. Even if the borrower is seeking a refinance with cash out to pay off credit card debt, it is wise for him to keep the oldest accounts open (again, assuming a recent history of on-time payments) to retain the credit history, even if he locks the cards up and doesn't use them anymore.

Late Payments. Late payments negatively impact credit scores more than any other factor. An occasional 30-day late nonmortgage or nonrent payment is not necessarily devastating to a credit score, but even one payment that is 60-days late or more can damage the borrower's ability to qualify for affordable loans. Late payments give lenders the impression that the borrower is either unable to pay on time, or is not responsible. Neither is likely to encourage them to approve a mortgage. Payment history remains on the credit report for two years, but most weight is given to the most recent 12 months.

Corrective Actions. The best way for a borrower to improve credit scores is to start paying bills on time, and keep doing it. Different lenders report to the credit bureaus at different intervals. Each credit item reported shows the date when the creditor last reported to the bureau. Most recent reporting carries the most weight in credit scoring, so a borrower should pay attention first to the items that are being reported now. He should pay off the most recent smallest bills first, and obtain receipt of payment, as it may take some time for the payment to be reflected on his credit report. Advise your borrower to negotiate with creditors the settlement of long overdue bills for which a lot of interest and penalties may have been added. Often a creditor is willing to settle for a smaller amount in order to close the file. Document any disputes or discrepancies in writing and submit them to the credit bureau, which will note it on the credit report.

Ability to Pay

Lenders use the front end, or housing to income ratio, and back end, or debt to income ratio to assess how easily a borrower will be able to handle a mortgage in addition to other living expenses and financial commitments. Most of the required information is in Section V of the application, shown in Figure 7.1.

Housing (Front End) Ratio. The housing ratio tells lenders what portion of a borrower's income is needed to cover the mortgage and related expenses. It is computed using monthly figures, as

Front End Ratio = Total Housing Expense/Total Monthly Income

You are in a bit of Catch-22 here, because you can't know what loan to propose until you know the housing ratio, and you can't compute the housing ratio until you know what loan you are going to propose.

V. MONTHLY INCOME AND COMBINED HOUSING EXPENSE INFORMATION						
Gross Monthly Income	Borrower	Co-Borrower	Total	Combined Monthly Housing Expense	Present	Proposed
Base Empl. Income*	$	$	$ 0.00	Rent	$	
Overtime			0.00	First Mortgage (P&I)		$
Bonuses			0.00	Other Financing (P&I)		
Commissions			0.00	Hazard Insurance		
Dividends/Interest			0.00	Real Estate Taxes		
Net Rental Income			0.00	Mortgage Insurance		
Other (before completing, see the notice in "describe other income,"below)			0.00	Homeowner Assn. Dues		
				Other:		
Total	$ 0.00	$ 0.00	$ 0.00	Total	$ 0.00	$ 0.00

* Self Employed Borrower(s) may be required to provide additional documentation such as tax returns and financial statements.

Describe Other Income

Notice: Alimony, child support, or separate maintenance income need not be revealed if the Borrower (B) or Co-Borrower (C) does not choose to have it considered for repaying this loan.

B/C	Monthly Amount
	$

FIGURE 7.1 1003 Section V Monthly Income and Combined Housing Expense Information

You can compute maximum housing expense yourself based on knowing that lenders will be most amenable to housing to income ratios of 33% or less. If you know the income, to determine the maximum housing expense that will still result in a front end ratio of 33% or less, make the following calculation:

$$\text{Maximum Housing Expense} = (\text{Monthly Income}/3) - (\text{Taxes} + \text{Insurance})$$

For example: If the borrower earns $72,000 per year, his monthly income is $72,000/12 or $6,000 per month. Maximum housing expense to obtain a housing ratio of 33% is $6,000/3 or $2,000 per month. This $2,000 includes taxes and insurances, which for the purposes of this example, total $400 per month. Then the maximum principal and interest payment the borrower can assume while still meeting the 33% housing ratio is $2,000 − $400 or $1,600 per month.

To test your calculations, use your computed values in the housing ratio formula and verify that your resulting ratio is 33% or less.

$$\text{Front End Ratio} = \text{Total Housing Expense/Total Monthly Income}$$
$$= (\$1,600 + \$400)/\$6,000$$
$$= \$2,000/\$6,000$$
$$= 33\%$$

Debt to Income (DTI or Back End) Ratio. The debt to income ratio gives lenders a picture of the financial demands the borrower faces each month. Not every monthly bill is included in this calculation. Rather, only debt that might interfere with the lender's ability to secure its claim in the event of default is included. You obtain this information from the credit report.

$$\text{DTI} = (\text{Total Housing Expense} + \text{Monthly Debt Payments})/$$
$$\text{Total Monthly Income}$$

The account history section of the credit report (see Table 7.1) includes closed accounts and paid accounts, as well as obligations with minimum monthly payments due. If payments are required for a set, limited time (for example, on a 36-month car loan), the credit report shows the number of payments remaining, along with amount of the monthly payment.

Only include monthly payments if the number of months remaining is more than 10. Credit cards and store charges usually report REV (for revolving credit) in the months remaining column, along with minimum monthly payments. All of these open items must be included in the debt calculation. Be sure to exclude mortgage accounts, as those figures are already in the total housing expense. Lenders typically look for DTI of 38% or less. Again, if you are evaluating the maximum monthly mortgage payment for which your borrower meets the 38% DTI guideline,

TABLE 7.1 Credit Report Credit History

```
     CREDIT GRANTOR       DATE     LAST DT      HIGH     BALANCE CURR
HISTORY
     ACCOUNT NUMBER      OPENED   REPORTD     CREDIT     OWING RATE
30 60 90


  1  FLAGSTAR BANK      12/2004 08/2006      270000      264592 M1
0   0   0
     987654321098
TERMS=360M1554
     MR=11   ECOA=I   B / XPN=01,EFX=01,TU=01
     PP START DT= 08/2006 PP=111111111111
     TYPE OF LOAN: CONVENTIONAL REAL ESTATE
MORTGAGE
     TRANSFER; CURRENT ACCOUNT; FANNIE MAE ACCOUNT; REAL ESTATE
MORTGAGE


  2  CHASE              06/2006 08/2006      15000        9007 R1
0   0   0
     1234567890123456
                TERMS=REV180
     MR=2    ECOA=I   B / XPN=01,EFX=01,TU=01
     PP START DT= 08/2006 PP=11
     TYPE OF LOAN: CREDIT CARD / CHARGE
ACCOUNT
     CURRENT ACCOUNT; CREDIT CARD; AMT IN HIGH CREDIT IS CREDIT
LIMIT


  3  SOVEREIGN BANK     11/2002 01/2005      55000           0 I1
2   0   0
     2468013579246801
TERMS=60M1059
     MR=26   ECOA=I   B / XPN=01,EFX=01,TU=01
       DEL DATES=04/2004
     PP START DT= 01/2005 PP=X11111111121111111111111
     TYPE OF LOAN:
AUTO
     ACCOUNT AUTO
```

you would calculate the number similar to the method used for housing ratio.

$$\text{Max. Mortgage Payment (P\&I)} = (\text{Income}/2.63) - (\text{Taxes} + \text{Insurance} + \text{Debt Payments})$$

Using the previous example, if the borrower's income is $6,000, and debt payments are $200 per month, then the maximum mortgage payment that still meets the 38% rule is:

$$= (\$6,000/2.63) - (\$400 + \$200)$$
$$= (\$2,281) - (\$600)$$
$$= \$1,681$$

Plugging that figure into the DTI formula results in the following:

DTI = (Total Housing Expense + Monthly Debt Payments)/
  Total Monthly Income
$$= (\$1,681 + \$400 + \$200)/\$6,000$$
$$= \$2,281/\$6,000$$
$$= 38\%$$

Employment History. Employment stability and earnings trends are important considerations for a lender. Lenders consider steady employment at the same job or in the same field less risky than frequent or recent changes in jobs or careers. Look at the information you collected in Section IV Employment Information. Make a note to ask the borrower about any job or career changes so that you get a sense for yourself of how stable her earning power is.

Lenders consider self-employed borrowers who have been in business less than two years high risk, which can be mitigated by large amounts of reserves or low LTV.

Reserves. Lenders consider a borrower's reserves if other ratios are less than ideal, to mitigate the associated risk. In general they prefer to see two months worth of mortgage payments available in reserve accounts such as checking, savings, retirement accounts, or other investments. Lenders consider higher reserves less of a risk.

It is important for you to know, on a purchase transaction, where the funds for the down-payment are coming from. A borrower may show

$10,000 in reserves at the time of the application, but if that money is earmarked for the down-payment, you cannot use it to calculate reserves. Remember, the lender is assessing ability to pay after the transaction is complete. If you are not certain what the source of funds for the down-payment is, make a note to discuss it on the credit call.

Security Interest–Loan to Value Ratio

Lenders compute the *Loan to Value ratio* to assess the likelihood that the property will retain its security value over the term of the loan. Loan to Value (LTV) is a calculated number that serves as a guide for determining qualification for different mortgage products.

$$\text{Loan Amount/Value of Property} = \text{LTV}$$

Loan Amount. You recorded the loan amount in Section VII Details of Transaction (see Figure 7.2). If the loan is for a purchase, the loan amount is the purchase price less the down-payment, which you recorded in "a. Purchase Price" and "e. Estimated prepaid items." On a refinance, you recorded loan amount in "d. Refinance."

Property Value. If the mortgage is for a purchase, then use the purchase price of the home from Section VII (see Figure 7.3) as the property value, for now. If the mortgage is a refinance, you recorded the owner's estimated value in Section VI Present Market Value in the Schedule of Real Estate Owned.

LTV is not a final number until an appraisal is done to determine property value. If an appraisal was done within the last 120 days, you can consider that value reliable. In the interest of being conservative from the lender's point of view, on a purchase transaction, if there is a difference between an appraised value and a purchase price use the lower number, which results in a higher (and less favorable) LTV.

VII. DETAILS OF TRANSACTION	
a. Purchase price	$
b. Alterations, improvements, repairs	
c. Land (if acquired separately)	
d. Refinance (incl. debts to be paid off)	
e. Estimated prepaid items	
f. Estimated closing costs	
g. PMI, MIP, Funding Fee	
h. Discount (if Borrower will pay)	
i. Total costs (add items a through h)	

VII. DETAILS OF TRANSACTION	
j. Subordinate financing	
k. Borrower's closing costs paid by Seller	
l. Other Credits (explain)	
m. Loan amount (exclude PMI, MIP, Funding Fee financed)	
n. PMI, MIP, Funding Fee financed	
o. Loan amount (add m & n)	
p. Cash from to Borrower (subtract j, k, l & o from i)	

FIGURE 7.2   1003 Section VII Details of Transaction

Schedule of Real Estate Owned (If additional properties are owned, use continuation sheet.)

Property Address (enter S if sold, PS if pending sale or R if rental being held for income) ▼	Type of Property	Present Market Value	Amount of Mortgages & Liens	Gross Rental Income	Mortgage Payments	Insurance, Maintenance, Taxes & Misc.	Net Rental Income
		$	$	$	$	$	$

FIGURE 7.3   1003 Section VII Schedule of Real Estate Owned

Second Mortgages. In the case of a refinance, if there is a second mortgage on the property (as you recorded in Section V), following review of the credit report, the outstanding principal balance on that loan is added to the loan amount to calculate a *Combined Loan to Value (CLTV)* ratio.

For example, if the borrower owns a $300,000 home and is looking for 200,000 to pay off a balance of 185,000 on an existing first mortgage, plus $15,000 cash out, and there is a $25,000 second mortgage or home equity loan, then a straight LTV calculation would be

$$
\begin{aligned}
\text{LTV} &= \text{Loan Amount} \,/\, \text{Property Value} \\
&= \$200,000/\$300,000 \\
&= 67\%
\end{aligned}
$$

The CLTV more accurately represents the lender's security risk. In the example above the combined loan amount is $200,000 plus $25,000 for a total of $225,000.

$$
\begin{aligned}
\text{CLTV} &= (\text{Loan Amount} + \text{Outstanding Liens}) \,/\, \text{Property Value} \\
&= (\$200,000 + \$25,000)/\$300,000 \\
&= (\$225,000)/\$300,000 \\
&= 75\%
\end{aligned}
$$

An LTV of 70% or less will get the best rates for the borrower, but there are loans available for 100% LTV.

Credit Reports

Credit reports are not perfect. Sometimes borrowers are surprised that accounts they thought were closed long ago still show open balances. Or that a joint credit card from a long-dissolved marriage is still in use by the ex-spouse and showing up on the borrower's report. It is important that you go over each item in the report with the borrower on the credit call. Familiarize yourself with all open items, know what they are for, be clear on the terms, and so on. If you have any questions, get them answered on the credit call. If the borrower cannot explain the item, ask him to investigate and get back to you with the information within a time period that you specify. His reaction to your request will give you an indication of his level of commitment.

Sometimes, particularly in the case of a merged report or a report that includes a co-borrower, the same account can be listed more than once. Check each item, identify potential duplicates, and make a note to verify them with the borrower on the credit call.

If the borrower still shows a high DTI ratio after accounting for likely errors or duplications, or if credit scores are low, start thinking about how you can impact both numbers by structuring a loan to remove some of the debt, or proposing actions the borrower can take to clean up the negative items on his report.

Bankruptcies, Collections and Charge Offs. If the borrower has a history of late payments, it is possible that the credit report will show, in public records, that a creditor "charged off" the debt (wrote it off as uncollectible), or turned the debt over to a collection agency, or that the borrower filed bankruptcy. These events remain on the borrower's credit report for seven to ten years, but may not be devastating, particularly if the borrower's recent payment history is good.

Reality Check: Qualifying the Prospect

At this point, between the application, the credit report, and your initial contact with the prospect, you have enough information to know what challenges you face in securing a loan for this person. Regardless of what the borrower has said to you, you also should have a feeling for what his pressing problem is. The credit call is another opportunity to hone in on what is of interest and importance to the prospect, and to ask questions that will uncover his concerns so you can address them before they become objections to closing the loan.

The questioning or inquiry that you engage in with a prospect is an opportunity (again) to build your relationship as the foundation of trust. Before you can prescribe treatment, or even divulge the diagnosis, your relationship with prospects must be such that they will hear what you are proposing and be open to your recommendations. The credit call, immediately following the application but before the proposal, is the set-up for the proposal you will make to the prospect. If you do what you need to do in the credit call, you should not have any trouble closing the sale and moving the application to submission. If, on the other hand, you do not set the ground work correctly or thoroughly, at some point the borrower will question whether to trust you before he moves forward.

Qualification Rating

Just as the rating for level of commitment allows you to tailor the appropriate actions and conversations for a prospect, a rating system for borrowing qualification provides you with direction as to the tone and content of the credit call. We use a color coding system for qualification (likelihood of approval) based on income and debt ratios, credit score, and loan to value ratios, where green is well qualified and there are no questions or concerns about income, credit, or equity, red is not qualified for any financing options, and yellow is moderately qualified, meaning the borrower may qualify for some options, but there is some concern about income, credit or equity.

Table 7.2 puts the commitment and qualification ratings together to describe nine general classifications for a prospect.

TABLE 7.2 Qualification/Commitment Grid

	Qualify		
Commitment	Green	Yellow	Red
1	Dream client	Service, partnership	Repair
2	Service, trust	Service, trust	Repair
3	Trust, attention	Get tough	Get tougher

Different Strokes. A highly qualified, highly committed prospect is every mortgage originator's dream. You may have a few, and they are likely to be responsible, do what they say, and sail through to closing without much work. Your ability to provide prompt, accurate service is key.

At the other end of the table are the prospects who are in financial trouble and who are unlikely to believe you can do anything for them that won't take advantage of them. You will address the fact that their financial situation is their responsibility, they have a big problem, and if they want your help, they will have to be open to what you say. If you can't get them to the point of a Level 2, you are wasting your time—nothing will ever come of it.

On the other hand, there are people who do not qualify for loans they can afford (Reds), and if they are open to your suggestions and committed to making a financial difference for themselves, these prospects become your loyal customers six months to a year down the line. Invest some time in getting them on the path to credit repair, savings, and cash flow management, and you will have closings in the future. Referrals, too. But it is important that you not waste your time with people who do not follow your instructions to better their position.

Finally, you cannot be the same way with a prospect throughout the credit call. At the start of the call be open, gracious, and give them hope. Be in an inquiry with them about what they want to do and accomplish, without giving them or asking them for any decisions. Then, knowing the problem and what is important and interesting to them, begin to shift the conversation and sell them on your being the one who is on their side to find the best solution. No promises, but the tantalizing hope for a magic bullet. Leave them assured that no one will work harder or better for them than you, and finally, with authority, close them on the next steps, setting up the proposal call.

If at the end of the credit call you still assess your prospect to be a Level 3 commitment, don't let the proposal call be the next step. Have her take action on her own behalf and get back to you before you offer her a solution. Remember, she has nothing at stake, nothing at risk so far.

Before you grant her the benefit of your efforts and expertise, let her show you something that indicates some level of her commitment to alter her financial situation.

The Credit Call

Every borrower is different, and the credit call is designed to move the prospect to "ready" to hear your proposal on what is likely to be the next call. The basic structure of attention, interest, conviction, desire, and close applies to the credit call. Regardless of where the scores tell you that the prospect is in terms of qualifying for a loan, you will use the "bad news, good news" approach to define the problem and set yourself up as the solution.

> *Hi, Joe. This is Randy calling you back from XYZ Mortgage. How are you? Great! There are a couple of things I'd like to go over with you before I prepare some final numbers for you, which I should have the next time we talk. I'll have a couple of ideas that will work for you then.*
>
> *What I'd like to do is educate you as much as possible through this process to help you better understand what lenders focus on and where you match up to their requirements. When a lender does a mortgage for anyone, they focus on three things. The first is your credit, the second is your income, and the third is your equity in your home (or your down-payment for a purchase). There are some other things, but these are the three main things.*

You are establishing the relationship, setting expectations for this call, holding out the carrot for the next call during which you will provide solutions to his problem. You are also establishing the three main topics of this call—credit, income, and equity.

Credit Scores

> *So, with regard to your credit . . . The lender wants to make sure that the odds of repayments are good to excellent. A few years ago they went to a*

credit scoring system. The scores range from around 450 to 850. Fannie Mae and Freddie Mac buy about 90% of the mortgages in the country, and they provide nice low interest rates. They like to see scores above 620.

You will have a slightly different conversation, depending on what the borrower's credit score is. Regardless though, the conversation will set expectations and position you in the light of the problem solver.

Low Credit Scores. Scores below 550 are bad and will severely limit the options, if any, borrowers have. If they qualify, the mortgage is going to cost them a lot more than it would if their credit scores were higher.

> *We call it a credit score, but it is really about integrity. It is about whether you are willing to do what you said you would do. The credit score measures whether you are paying your bills on time. Why is that important? People make money on lending you money, and when you don't pay on time it costs them more money.*
>
> *We have people who have very, very low scores and they want low interest rates, which is ridiculous. Unless your credit scores measure up, on every loan that you do you will spend more money.*

You are setting them up to need you, and not to even think about very low rates.

> *This is where most people with low credit scores are taken advantage of. We see this all the time. People come to us later to refinance, and because they had low credit scores they got themselves nailed by another loan that was not in their best interest, a loan that took them over the coals, and now they can't get out from under with prepayment penalties —I don't want that to happen to you.*
>
> *Your score is <<credit score>>. That is very low compared to what is needed, however we might have some other options for you.*

You have defined a problem (low credit scores) and have held out hope for a solution without giving away too much.

Medium Low Credit Scores. Scores between 550 and 619 are still too low for a conforming loan. These borrowers are likely to qualify for a loan, but are likely to pay a lot more in interest and points, and may need a larger down-payment or lower LTV than other borrowers. Your objective is to raise a problem, set their expectations, and hold out hope for a solution.

> *Credit scores are important. People make money on lending you money, and when you don't pay on time it costs them more money. Unless your credit scores measure up, no matter where you go you will pay more for the loan.*
>
> *This is where most people with low credit scores are taken advantage of. We see this all the time. People come to us later to refinance, and because they had low credit scores they got themselves nailed by another loan that was not in their best interest, a loan that took them over the coals, and now they can't get out from under with prepayment penalties—I don't want that to happen to you.*
>
> *Your score is <<credit score>>, which is not as high as we would like. Let's go over a couple of things that are bringing your score down, so I can make sure I can fit you into a loan, and then we might have some options available for you. Can you tell me about <<any red flags in the last two years>>?*

You have raised the concern, and addressed any attempt to shop around for a better rate than one you can provide. You are establishing yourself as a partner with them in finding a solution, and as an expert in reviewing the details of their credit report. This is the time to raise questions about discrepancies, late payments, maxed out cards, excessive inquiries, bankruptcies, collections, judgments, and so forth.

Medium High Scores. Scores between 620 and 700 are good enough to qualify for a conforming loan, assuming income and equity measures are within guidelines. You want these folks to know they are not too bad off but are not the best, and that you will be getting them the best rates available to them.

> *Your score is <<credit score>> which is not bad, but not the best. Let's go over a couple of things that are bringing your score down, so I can make sure I can fit you into a loan, and then we might have some options available for you. Can you tell me about <<any red flags in the last two years>>?*

Again, as with the medium-low scores, you have raised the problem, and established yourself as the expert partner to provide a solution. You leave them with hope.

High Scores. Scores over 700 are good. These borrowers are likely to qualify for the lowest-cost loans.

> *Your score is <<credit score>> which is good. It means you will have the most options available to you.*

Income

When you review a borrower's income ratios with him, it is an opportunity to ask questions and establish relationship. If you have someone whose commitment is questionable, the credit call gives you an opportunity to ask him to take action before you present a proposal to him. Income documentation will be required for submission with the 1003, so you can ask him to get together W-2s, pay stubs, and so forth to test his commitment.

If the borrower's Housing to Income ratio is higher than 30%, or Debt to Income ratio is above 40%, explore other possible income sources with him. If the borrower is self-employed, this is the time to verify the income the borrower stated to you when you took the application. Ask for copies of tax returns and ask questions about the structure of the business and its revenue and profit.

> *With regard to your income, the bank wants to make sure that you make enough money—verifiable income—to cover your housing expense*

and debts. They want to know you can afford to make the mortgage payments.

If front and back end ratios are within conforming loan guidelines, income is not likely to be an issue for qualification.

> *It looks like you are generating enough verifiable income to qualify for a few different options. This allows us more choices. So it looks like you are fine with regard to income.*

High Ratios. If ratios are higher than 50%, you are not likely to qualify borrowers for a loan they can afford. However, you can improve their future position by offering other services. You want to leave them with hope, regardless of their circumstances.

> *In reviewing your data, I notice that your total income is <<income>>. Is there any other income you earn? (Alimony, child support, investment income, and so forth).*

If ratios are higher than 50%,

> *You do not make enough income, however there might be a few other options available to you. Let's continue.*

For ratios between 40 and 50%,

> *I am not sure we can do an income verified loan. We might have to price an option with a No Income Verification, or stated income, product. The pricing is a little higher, but we might have something you could fit into. Depending on your situation, it could be anywhere from $^1/_4$ to $^3/_4$% higher.*

For high debt to income ratios,

> *I notice you have some debt. Is it recent, or has it been around for a while? Are you paying the minimums or are you paying more each month?*

Do you have a game plan for paying them off? Does your spouse feel the same way? Have you tried in the past and failed? If we could help you with consolidation would you be interested?

You have now either established cash flow as a motivation, or eliminated it as one.

Self-Employed. Get them to do some work and get their income tax returns for the last two years. Often the income they state is not what can be verified with tax returns.

How are you set up as a company? Are you an LLC or a Corporation? Do you file a Schedule C? The income you stated, was it gross or net?

As you get answers to these questions, if you get a sense the borrower is not clear or unwilling to divulge the information, offer the following:

The reason I am asking is that there are different underwriting guidelines for self-employed people. I get the same payment from the lender if your loan is income verified or not. There are some things we can do to get you a better rate. Fax your tax return to me. When do you think you could do that?

If the prospect trusts you, he will agree to your request. If you get a reason it cannot be done quickly, you may not have his trust yet.

Equity. LTV of 80 or lower will give you the best options, whether for a refinance or purchase.

And with regard to your equity (or down-payment if a purchase), basically the bank wants to make sure you have enough equity (or down-payment) for the property. The bank really does not want to lend you 100% of the value of the property. Equity has to do with the amount you borrow compared to the value of the property. We can't determine your equity for certain until an appraisal is done on the property.

For high LTV,

It doesn't look like you have that much equity (money for a down-payment and closing costs) in your property. However, we might still be able to come up with a few options for you that would make a difference. Let us continue.

For low LTV,

With regard to your situation, it looks like you might have enough equity (money for a down-payment and closing costs), however we want to make sure.

Other Topics to Cover. In the credit call, question any red flags that you uncovered in the application or credit report. Always leave them with hope, no matter what the situation looks like. Raising the issue with borrowers now sets expectations and sets you up as the problem solver. In discussing the issues with borrowers, you will also get better insight into their commitment by the way in which they answer the questions. If they are evasive or reluctant to answer, you know that you have an opportunity to build more trust as you go through the issues with them.

As you get some experience, you will learn that there are some lenders who finance only B/C paper. Typically these loans are adjustable-rate mortgages at interest rates that are not in 1/8 increments (.125, .250. .375, .50. .625, .75, .875). Often they carry prepayment penalties, so it is important to see the mortgage note before you propose anything to the borrower.

I notice you have a loan with XXX Mortgage Company. We like to map out the "do-nothing" option, so I need a copy of the note. Fax it to me as soon as possible for me to finalize the numbers for you. When can you do that?

In addition to red flags, take advantage of the chance to nail down the borrower's primary concern and motivation by exploring other information you collected. For example, if the borrower has young dependents, education funding and child care are major expenses that are not considered in the income ratios, but which do impact the borrower's financial situation, particularly cash flow. Ask questions.

> *Does your spouse work? Who takes care of the children during the day? How much are you spending for child care each month? If we could free up some cash for your monthly bills, would you be interested in that? Have you thought about their college education? If we could get you some money out toward that, would you be interested in that?*

If the borrower has outstanding loans (student, auto, etc.) explore his interest in consolidating debt and/or improving cash flow.

> *Would you be interested, if we can swing it, in consolidating your outstanding loans into your mortgage? If we were able to reduce your monthly bills, would that be of interest to you?*

If the borrower is over 50 years old, retirement should be of concern. Look at the borrower's savings and assets.

> *Tell me a little about your spending habits. Would your significant other agree?*

If there is a lot of savings (more than five months of housing expense), inquire as to how that was accomplished. Think in terms of whether it will make sense to use that money to pay down debt or lower LTV when you prepare proposal options.

> *Did you save that amount over time? Or did you get it as a lump sum? How long ago? What plans do you have for that money? If we could increase the equity in your home, or pay off the mortgage before you retire, would that be of interest to you?*

It is also to your advantage to know how long the borrower is planning on remaining in his home so you can balance points against interest rates.

> *What is the longest, very longest time you see yourself in your home?*
> *What is the shortest, very shortest time you would ever consider putting your home on the market?*
> *Does your spouse agree?*

The shorter they plan to be in their home, the less sense points and long-term loans make. By asking these questions now, you are getting the ammunition to eliminate closing costs as an objection later in the process. You will be able, if appropriate, to include points on the basis of what they told you, and offer the pros and cons, leaving the choice up to them.

Get a sense for borrowers' comfort with risk in order to know whether they are open to ARMs and flexible payment options. It can be this simple to find out:

> *On a scale from 0 to 10, in the area of comfort with risk, where would you rate yourself (0 meaning you are very uncomfortable and 10 meaning you are very comfortable). Do you think your significant other feels the same way?*

Setting up the Close

If you have qualified this borrower as RED, meaning you have a concern about credit, income, or equity, set up the close by saying the following:

> *Well, <<credit/income/equity>> is the only concern we have at this point, but we <<don't think or are not sure>> that it will be a big problem. What we are going to do is before we present anything to you is see whether we can fit you into a program based on your circumstances.*

If you have low or no concerns about the borrower's ability to qualify,

It looks like you are in pretty good shape. So hopefully we will have a few different options tomorrow that are going to make a difference for you.

You are ready to close the credit call with the following conversation for everyone:

Hopefully we will be able to come up with one or two options based on the hundreds of different national lenders we work with. Hopefully, we will have something that will make a difference. If we propose something to you tomorrow, it is going to be based on what we can fit you into considering your particular circumstances and situation and usually is only good for that day. The main reason for that is because the rates change every day. Anyone you go to will be pretty close in pricing, because most banks and mortgage companies get their money from Fannie Mae or Freddie Mac, as I've said earlier. So no one should be off the mark with what we will be able to propose for you.

For a refinance, the following conversation and call to action completes the credit call:

The first thing I will do with you tomorrow is show you what it is going to look like if you do nothing at all. The main reason for doing this is because it is very important for us and you to know exactly where you are now, especially if you do nothing at all and stay exactly as you are. Also, it makes it easier to see exactly what difference will be made if you decide to go forward. Hopefully, we will have one or two options that will make a difference for you. One of two things will happen tomorrow. Either it is going to make a difference for you or not. If it is, and you like it, and you are comfortable with it, then I will give you an opportunity at that time to register the loan. We can do this because we already have all your information to register the loan. If not, and we don't have anything for you that makes a big difference for you, then we simply close out your file. It is that simple. Does that make sense to you? Great!

So if we do move forward, at that point what's great is that the only out of pocket fee would be the appraisal, and right now that is <<$>>, and you can pay the appraiser directly at the door. And we have a refundable application fee of <<$>>, that gets credited back to you 100% at the closing. Those are the only fees out of pocket. But we will only get to this point if what we propose to you is something that makes a difference and you feel comfortable and you like it. Does that make sense? Great!

Are there any other questions for me at this time while you have me on the phone? Okay, then I look forward to talking with you tomorrow at <<time>>. Okay, have a great day!

The closing conversation for a purchase is slightly different:

Tomorrow, hopefully, we will have one or two options that will make a difference for you. We do not want you looking at any houses during the time that we are working on your file. We do not want you to do anything that might reduce the number of options we might have available for you. So make sure you continue to make all your payments on time and save your money. Do you understand? Okay, great!

One of two things will happen, either we can do something for you, or we can't. If we can, we will tell you exactly what we can do and tell you exactly what is next. By the way, if we could do something for you, what timeframe are you looking to get into a new home?

Based on what they say, classify their commitment as follows:

1 to 2 months, Level 1

3 to 6 months, Level 2

7 to 12 months, Level 3

If we can get you qualified for a loan, then we will need some additional items to complete the first stage. We normally need a couple of papers signed and then we collect a refundable application fee which is <<$>>. This starts the process and allows us to issue a preapproval letter to your real estate agent, if you are working with someone and allows us to get the paperwork started.

If we can't get you qualified for a loan, then hopefully we might have a few more options available to you. We will also educate and work with you over the next two, three, or six months to get you into a position to do something. Does that make sense? Great!

So if we do move forward tomorrow, we will set a time to get together to sign the initial paperwork and collect the <<refundable>> application fee of <<$>>, okay? Great. Are there any other questions for me at this time while you have me on the phone? Okay, well then I look forward to talking with you tomorrow at <<time>>. Okay, have a great day!

Integrity

Everything is in place to move forward. If you followed the recommendations for building relationship while you took the application, and again during this credit call, the borrower is beginning to get a sense that you are there to serve his interests. *Beware!* You can, with one small slip, undo all the good work you have done so far. Again, it is critical that you follow up with the borrower at precisely the day and time you said you would. Not two minutes later. Not one minute later. On time. Precisely.

You may think this is a bit extreme. It isn't. No one is likely to say anything to you about being a couple of minutes late, and if they did, you would surely give an explanation that would, most likely, go unchallenged. Regardless, when you don't do what you say you are going to do, when you say you are going to do it, this sends a message (no matter how soft a whisper you think it is), that you may not be entirely reliable. It says that other things (what is your explanation?) are more important than the prospect. While you may not think that is the message you are sending, you are, and it erodes the confidence and trust you have worked to build in each interaction.

Be on time. Always. And if the prospect isn't there at the agreed-upon time, again, leave a voice message that has *no* trace of disappointment, annoyance, or any emotion other than confidence and enthusiasm, regardless of how you feel at the moment. If you interact that way with prospects, you earn their respect—and their business. That is what it takes to be a high-income mortgage originator.

CHAPTER EIGHT

Step 5: Determining the Right Product for Your Prospect

The mortgage market is constantly changing. Forty years ago the options for a residential mortgage were limited. Now there are all sorts of ingenious ways to lend money and structure paybacks. Your challenge is to match up your prospect's needs and qualifications with a loan product that makes sense to both the borrower and the lender.

This chapter begins with a nuts and bolts look at loan products and pricing. Then it addresses situations in which each product type is appropriate and well suited. We look at rate sheets and pricing strategies. And we close with a look at what you can propose for unqualified, committed prospects that will, down the road, transform them into loyal, thankful customers.

All loan products are described in terms of common attributes, such as the term of the loan, payment amount, principal, interest, and so forth. They vary primarily in the method and timing of the payback. First we will define the basic attributes, then look at how the different options work together to provide solutions for different prospect situations.

Fixed-Rate Loan Products

Fixed-rate loans have three basic characteristics that distinguish them from other types of loans. First, the rate of interest remains fixed over the life of the loan. Second, the monthly payment remains the same over the life of the loan. Third, the loan is fully paid off at the end of the term (full amortization). Fixed-rate mortgages make sense for people who plan to remain in their homes for a long time and for those who are averse to risk.

Fixed-rate products are defined by the value of the following attributes which are described here:

Term: the length of time (expressed in years or months) over which the loan is repaid.

Interest rate: a percentage of the principal added to the amount to be repaid.

The most popular fixed-rate mortgages are 30-year and 15-year, but 20-year and 40-year fixed-rate products are currently available as well.

The monthly payment for a fixed-rate mortgage is determined by a series of calculations that result in an *amortization schedule*. Easy-to-use online monthly calculators are available at www.tomortgageservices.com. The monthly payment is comprised of two unequal parts: the principal payment and the interest payment. Over the term of the loan the combined amount of interest and principal payment remains constant, but the allocation of the payment to principal and interest shifts drastically.

Assuming a 30-year fixed loan of $150,000 at 5.875%, the monthly payment is $887.31 per month. Principal payment starts small and ends big. Interest payment starts big and ends small. They counterbalance each other to result in a combined payment of $887.31 per month. In the first year of payments, only about 17% of the payment goes to reducing the principal balance, while the remaining 83% goes to interest. Midway

TABLE 8.1   Comparable Rates Fixed Mortgages 30-, 15-, and 40-Year

Based on actual rates 1/29/07	30-year fixed	15-year fixed	40-year fixed
Principal amount	$150,000	$150,000	$150,000
Interest rate	5.75%	5.375%	6.25%
Monthly payment	$875.36	$1,215.70	$851.61
Total payment	$314,255	$217,610	$407,923
Total interest paid	$164,255	$67,610	$257,923
Interest as % of principal	109.5%	45.1%	171.9%

through the last year of a 30-year fixed mortgage, principal payment will account for over 96.6% of the payment, with interest representing the remaining 3.4%.

Comparing Fixed-Rate Terms. In general, the longer the term, the higher the rate of interest, as illustrated in Table 8.1, as lenders assume the risk of changing rates over longer periods. The longer the term, the more interest is paid over the life of the loan, but the lower the monthly payment. In addition to the monthly payments and cost of money over the life of the loan, shorter-term fixed-rate mortgages are attractive to people who want to be debt-free sooner, for example, those who want their home paid for when they retire. The shortened term accelerates equity build up as well.

Table 8.1 shows comparable rates for 30-, 15-, and 40-year fixed-rate mortgages, all on the same day. The 15-year fixed has the lowest rate of interest, but the highest monthly payment. However, it is the least expensive loan overall, as the total interest paid is about 40% of that of a 30-year mortgage.

Adjustable-Rate Mortgages (ARMs)

Adjustable-rate loans have several basic characteristics that distinguish them from other types of loans. First, the rate of interest fluctuates over the life of the loan, resulting in changes to the monthly payment. The adjustments are made periodically over the term of the loan, and are calculated based on an index defined by the loan agreement.

Defining Characteristics

ARMs have several attributes that fixed-rate mortgages do not, all associated with the timing and amount of interest adjustments. ARMs are appropriate for borrowers who expect to move or sell their homes in less than 10 years or for those who need a lower monthly payment at the start of the loan (for example, those who expect their income to increase).

Initial Interest Rate. The rate of interest quoted for most ARMs is usually significantly lower than the rates on fixed-interest loans of equal term (usually 30 years).

Initial Fixed Period. This is the length of time the initial interest rate is in effect before an adjustment can be made. This period can vary from as little as one month to many years.

Adjustment Period. This represents how often (usually once per year) the interest rate can be adjusted following the initial fixed period.

Index. This is an economic indicator that will be the basis for determining adjustments to the interest rate. Common indices are COFI (Cost of Funds Index), TCM (Treasury Constant Maturity), LIBOR (London Interbank Offered Rate), and MTA (Monthly Treasury Average).

Margin. This is the amount by which the index value will be incremented to derive the adjusted interest rate.

Periodic Rate Cap. This is the maximum increase in interest rate for any one adjustment period. A 2% limit is standard.

Initial Rate Cap. This is the maximum increase in interest rate on the first adjustment after the initial fixed period. This can be significantly higher than subsequent adjustment rate caps.

Life-Time Rate Cap. This is the most the interest rate can increase above the initial interest rate over the term of the loan.

Payment Cap. This condition is sometimes found in ARM mortgages, and should not be confused with the rate cap. The payment cap is the highest amount the monthly payment can reach. It is possible that a payment cap will result in a monthly payment that is not enough to cover the principal and interest accrued, resulting in an increase rather than a reduction in the amount owed.

Two-Step Mortgages. A two-step mortgage is a cross between an ARM and a fixed-rate mortgage. A fixed rate is set for some initial period, followed by an adjustment. The remainder of the loan is fixed at the adjusted rate. For example, a 7/23 has a fixed rate for seven years, is adjusted, and then remains fixed again for the remaining 23 years of the loan.

Comparing Apples to Apples

It is difficult to assess in advance the cost of an ARM in comparison to a fixed-rate mortgage. If you wanted to be very conservative, you would assume that the ARM would increase to its lifetime cap in as short a period as allowed. In many cases, the initial cap is the same as the lifetime cap, meaning that at the end of the initial fixed period the interest rate would reach its maximum, and again, being conservative, assume it would remain there for the rest of the loan term.

Table 8.2 compares the principal and interest payments of a 5/1 ARM (fixed-rate for five years, adjustable annually after that) to two fixed-rate mortgages. In the first five years of the ARM, the interest rate is slightly lower than a 15-year fixed. With a lifetime cap of 5% and an initial rate

TABLE 8.2 Comparable Rates 30-, 15-Year Fixed, 5/1 ARM

Based on actual rates 1/29/07	30-year fixed	15-year fixed	5/1 ARM
Principal amount	$150,000	$150,000	$150,000
Interest rate	5.75%	5.375%	5.25%/10.25%
Monthly payment	$875.36	$1,215.70	$828.00/$1,344.15

cap of 5%, at the start of the sixth year when the first adjustment takes place, the interest rate on the 5/1 ARM could jump to the maximum of 10.25% for the remainder of 25 years. At that rate of interest the borrower's monthly payment is higher than a 15-year fixed. Under this scenario it becomes clear that the ARM make sense only if interest rates are definitely stable or declining, or if the borrower does not plan to keep the home longer than the initial period.

Payment Options

A number of options are now available to borrowers that allow flexibility for making mortgage payments on fixed- or adjustable-rate mortgages. These options are great if income fluctuates, or if the borrower wants to reduce the principal balance and build equity more rapidly.

Interest Only

Both fixed and adjustable mortgages are now available with interest-only options. Some loans are set with interest-only payments for some or all of the loan term. For example, a 30-year fixed with interest-only option allows interest-only payments for the first 10 years, and then reamortizes the remaining principal balance over the remaining 20 years of the loan. Other loans are set up to allow the borrower the option to make an interest-only payment at any time over the loan term. These types of payment options are very good for people who have fluctuations in income or periodic major expenses, or for those whose short-term cash flow requirements demand the lowest possible monthly payments for some period. Table 8.3 compares current rates and payments for 10-year fixed, 10-year ARM, and 10-year ARM interest-only options.

You can see that while the interest rate on the ARMs is higher than that on the 10-year fixed, the monthly payments are lower. That is because the principal is amortized over 30 years. The 10-year fixed builds equity

TABLE 8.3   Comparable Rates 10-Year Fixed, ARM, Interest-only

Based on actual rates 1/29/07	10-year fixed	10-year ARM	10-year ARM, Interest-only
Principal amount	$150,000	$150,000	$150,000
Interest rate	5.25%	5.625%	5.625%
Monthly payment	$1,609	$863	$703

the fastest. The interest-only payment option has the lowest monthly payment of the three loans, but no reduction in equity will take place until year 11.

Flexible Payment Option

So-called *secure loans* allow the borrower four options: a 30-year fixed-rate payment, a 15-year fixed-rate payment, an interest-only payment, or a minimum payment, which is less than the interest-only payment. This kind of flexibility is very good for people with erratic income. It is also very dangerous if minimum payments become the norm.

Minimum Payments. ARMs with minimum payment options sound very attractive, with initial rates quoted as low as 1.25%. Because the minimum payment does not even cover the interest due each month, the balance due on the loan increases with each minimum payment made as the unpaid interest is added to the principal balance. In effect, the borrower pays interest on the unpaid interest, as well as on the principal. In a declining real estate market borrowers who rely on minimum payments could easily find that they cannot sell their homes for a price high enough to cover the mortgage balance.

Recasting. Lenders place a limit on the amount of *negative amortization* they allow with a loan that permits minimum payments. When the loan balance reaches a certain value, or at predetermined periods, the lender *recasts* or reamortizes the balance due over the remaining loan term. This new amortization schedule then becomes the basis for calculating payment options.

Biweekly Payments

The basic idea of biweekly payments is to accelerate the repayment of the loan. Normally 12 payments are made annually. With biweekly payments, half the monthly payment is paid every two weeks, resulting in 26 half payments, or the equivalent of 13 monthly payments over a 12-month period. The result is a substantial shortening of the term of repayment—it can be as much as cutting seven years off a 30-year mortgage. With the shortened repayment term comes a resulting significant decrease in the total amount of interest paid. Biweekly payments, particularly for those who are paid biweekly and can arrange for direct payment of the loan from a checking or savings account, are convenient, painless, and economical.

Prepayment

Fixed-rate mortgages generally permit borrowers to prepay the principal balance without incurring penalties. Borrowers can significantly reduce the amount of interest they pay over the term of the loan by making periodic principal-only payments. Combining a biweekly payment plan with the application of the "extra" annual payment to principal-only can result in even greater savings and quicker payoff of a loan than a biweekly payment schedule can on its own.

Balloon Payments

Balloon mortgages offer the low initial interest rates of an ARM, but then require a large final payment of the loan at the end of the period. They are designed to be short-term loans, and often carry a conditional refinancing option to allow the borrower, if qualified, to refinance at the time the balloon payment is made. Conditions include a history of on-time mortgage payments, owner occupancy, no other liens or loans against the property, and restrictions and requirements set by the lender.

Reverse Mortgages

A reverse mortgage, also known as a Home Equity Conversion Mortgage (HECM), provides an extreme twist when it comes to payment options. Available only to people 62 years of age and older with substantial equity in their homes, these mortgages pay money *to* the homeowner on a monthly or as-needed basis. The monthly payments to the homeowner reduce the equity in the home, and interest accrues on the loan. No repayment of principal or interest is required until the home is sold or is no longer the homeowner's primary residence.

Homeowners have several payment choices with a reverse mortgage. They can elect to receive equal monthly payments for life or until they no longer occupy the home (Tenure). Or, they can predetermine the term for which they will receive equal monthly payments (Term). By selecting a Line of Credit payment option, reverse mortgage holders can receive payments at times of their choosing, rather than on a schedule. Tenure and Term options can also be modified to include the Line of Credit option.

Reverse mortgages issued by HUD are federally guaranteed. If the amount owed by the homeowner exceeds the proceeds from the sale of the home, HUD pays the lender the amount of the shortfall. This means that the homeowner will never owe more than the value of the home at the time of sale.

Matching Prospect Goals and Qualifications to Products

As a mortgage originator, you may or may not get involved in creating loan proposals for the prospects you bring through the application and credit call. In my company, until a mortgage originator reaches a level of consistent performance and demonstrates the ability to understand a customer's needs and evaluate loan products in light of those needs and the prospect's qualifications, the file is reviewed by a manager before a proposal is generated.

Qualifications

The most restricting condition you will deal with when matching up borrowers with loan products is the overall qualification of the borrower. Right off the bat, if a borrower's credit score is below 620, your options are going to be limited to subprime loans, which almost always carry penalties for prepayment and sometimes balloon payments. Two-step loans are designated 2/28 ARMs or 3/27 ARMs, where the first number indicates the initial payment period and the second number indicates the remaining years on the mortgage. The prepayment penalty usually applies during the initial payment period. The good news is that many of these programs include a conditional refinancing option. This allows the borrower to use the initial payment period to rebuild credit so that at the time of the adjustment he can qualify for a better loan.

Likewise, borrowers who are self-employed and in business less than two years will likely fall into a more expensive loan. This means higher interest rates, points, and lower LTV ratio requirements.

Credit Grades. Lenders are always concerned about risk. The higher the risk of nonpayment or late payments, the more they will charge for the loan and, in some cases, the more stringent they will be with regard to key ratios and reserves.

Lenders grade borrowers based on payment history, LTV, Debt Ratios, and credit scores, and provide rates based on these grades. The grades are letters (like school grades), where A is the best and D is barely passing. Precise rules don't exist, but Table 8.4 provides general guidelines. Specific guidelines for each lender are available on rate sheets and underwriting guidelines sheets.

Some lenders also specify income documentation levels within the grades and lower maximum LTV and maximum loan amounts as less documentation is provided.

TABLE 8.4   Credit Grades

Grade	Credit Score	Debt Ratio	LTV Max	Delinquencies	Bankruptcy/Foreclosure
A+, A, AA	670 and above	36–38	95–100	No housing, one installment, up to two revolving	None within 2–10 years
A−	650	45	95	One 30-day housing (1×30), couple of 30s on installments and revolving OK, 1–2 60s on installment/revolving	Discharged minimum 2 to 4 years
B	620	50	75–85	1–2×30, 1×60 on housing, 4×30, 2×60 on installment, 5×30, 2×60 revolving	2 to 4 years discharged, reestablished credit
C	580	55	75	3–4×30, 2×60 housing, 6×30, 4×60 installment, 7×30, 5×60 revolving	1 to 2 years since discharge.
D	550	60	65–70	3×30 housing, more on installment and revolving, limit ×90 and 1×120	
E	520 and below	65	50–65	Pattern of ×30, ×60, ×90 lates	Stable employment, may be in bankruptcy

Risk-Averse

If your prospect is averse to risk, then you will probably stay away from the ARMs and stick with fixed-rate products. Fixed-rate products trade off lower monthly payments against shorter term, less interest paid, and faster equity build up. If cash flow is the borrower's primary motivation, then the longer term and lower payments make sense. Interest-only fixed-rate options can get you the extra step in reducing monthly payments, if needed.

If on the other hand, the borrower is looking toward retirement, then a shorter-term fixed-rate will pay the mortgage off sooner, leaving him well positioned for cash flow once his current income level drops. Balance monthly payments against term. If the monthly payment on a 10- or 15-year fixed is too high, you can put the borrower into a 20- or 30-year fixed and use biweekly payments to, in effect, shorten the loan term. You can knock seven years or more off a 30-year mortgage this way.

Length of Time in Home

Assuming you are dealing with someone who has some tolerance for risk, the next factor in deciding whether an ARM is appropriate is the borrower's expectation as to how long he will remain in the home. If you have a prospect who says he is never going to move, then longer-term ARMs or fixed-rate mortgages make sense. In addition, you have the option of adjusting points to buy down rate if cash flow is an issue, as the cost of the points will be amortized over the long term of the loan.

If, on the other hand, the borrower knows it is likely that he will be moving or selling the home in seven years or less, and if he has tolerance for some risk, an ARM can afford him great cash flow advantages with very little risk. A 10/1 ARM can, in effect, be a fixed-rate mortgage for the person who knows he will move within then next few years. Since initial interest rates drop with the shortening of the initial fixed period, you are best off looking at an ARM that has an initial fixed period as close to the borrower's anticipated stay as possible. Always overestimate the borrower's length of stay to be on the safe side, if it falls between ARM initial periods. In other words, if initial periods are ten years or five years, and the borrower plans to stay for seven, go with the 10-year initial period.

If the borrower is going to be in the home for a short period, you will want to price loans with as few points as possible. While the interest rate is slightly higher, due to the short term the borrower will pay less overall for the time he has the mortgage.

Opportunities and Restrictions

Some conditions and circumstances of the loan, the property, or the borrower will either restrict your options, or open up opportunities for alternative loans.

Veterans. Veteran's Administration loans (VA Loans) are available to veterans of the United States armed services who meet certain length-of-duty requirements (see your local VA office for specifics). Loan amounts are limited to $203,000. Qualifications are not as stringent as for conventional loans, and in some cases no down-payment is required for a purchase. The borrower must have a certificate of eligibility obtained from the VA with VA Form 26-1880, Request for Determination of Eligibility and Available Loan Guaranty Entitlement.

First-Time Homebuyers. Questions L and M in the declarations portion of the 1003 ask questions that qualify a borrower as a *first-time homebuyer*. If any of the applicants purchasing the property for their primary residence has had no other interest in a residential property for three years, the applicants may qualify as first-time homebuyers. Under certain circumstances such as divorce, even someone who held a joint interest in a residential property (with a spouse) within the last three years can qualify as a first-time homebuyer if she qualifies as a *displaced homemaker* or *single parent*. To meet the displaced-homemaker qualifications, applicants must not have been in the workforce for several years, have worked in the home caring for it during that time, and be unemployed or underemployed. Single parenthood includes separation, joint custody, and even pregnancy.

The Federal Housing Authority (FHA), a part of the Department of Housing and Urban Development (HUD), assists first-time homebuyers by insuring the mortgage for HUD-approved lenders. Down-payment requirements for FHA loans are lower than conventional loans, and can result in LTVs as high as 97%. The FHA also insures loans for home improvements in some cases.

Self-Employed, Commissioned, Cash Income Earners. Borrowers who are self-employed, earn most of their income from commission or from cash (for example, tips), and those with multiple sources of income from complex investments may find it difficult to document all of their income. Normal full documentation requires pay stubs and W-2s for job holders, and federal tax returns for self-employed borrowers. If the borrower will have difficulty proving sufficient income levels, there are loans that require only limited documentation or no documentation at all. These loans are available for people with good credit and limited LTV. Some lenders require higher asset levels on these loans to mitigate their risk.

Documentation requirement options are numerous and include Stated Income, Stated Assets, No Income Verification (NIV), No Ratio, and No Income/No Assets. Stated Income lenders will generally look to determine if the stated income is in line with assets. With No Ratio and No Income/No Assets loans, neither assets nor income is verified. The added risk to the lender is reflected in appropriately higher rates and more stringent requirements for credit scores and LTV.

Homeowners Aged 62 and Older. For older homeowners with substantial equity in their primary residence homes, a reverse mortgage is an option. Reverse mortgages are an effective cash flow solution for seniors. They can supplement their monthly income from Social Security, or have access to money for medical expenses or home repairs, without the concern of paying it back from monthly income.

There are no asset or income requirements to qualify for a reverse mortgage, although there are restrictions on property value and property type for HUD-issued HEMCs. Full qualifying requirements can be found online at www.hud.gov. Fannie Mae offers a reverse mortgage product that addresses some of the limitations of the HUD HEMC.

Jumbo Loans. If a borrower is looking for more than the Fannie Mae maximum (see Table 8.5), you will have fewer lenders to choose from, regardless of other qualifying criteria. Rates will be higher than conforming loans.

TABLE 8.5   Maximum Conforming Loan Amounts

	Single-Family	Two-Family	Three-Family	Four-Family
48 contiguous states	$417,000	$533,850	$645,300	$801,950
Alaska, Hawaii, Guam, Virgin Is.	$625,500	$800,775	$967,950	$1,202,925

Pricing Loans—Unraveling the Rate Sheet

Assuming you know the borrower's financial situation and have considered his goals, you are ready to start pricing options and calculating the numbers that the prospect will want to hear: rate, fixed or adjustable, monthly payment.

Rate sheets vary from lender to lender. Many of them look as if they were designed to jam as much information into as little space as possible. They can appear confusing, but once you know what the rules of the game are, it is much easier to interpret them. Most rate sheets contain sections by product and have sections for adjustments. Lenders who deal with subprime loans may also include pricing breakdowns by credit grade within product. They may also include documentation requirements and other underwriting guidelines either on the rate sheet or as an addition to it.

Tables 8.6 and 8.7 show rate sheet structures for two different lenders both offering a "Full Doc 2/28" adjustable hybrid product.

As you can see, as LTV rises, rates rise significantly, especially for borrowers with lower credit scores.

Another lender represented rates for the same product as shown in Table 8.7.

Rate sheets for fixed-rate loans are different, reflecting par, above par and below par pricing for different lengths of rate locks. Table 8.8 shows

TABLE 8.6   Rate Sheet A Full Doc 2/28 ARM

Grade	Score	LTV> 65%	LTV> 70%	LTV> 75%	LTV> 80%	LTV> 85%	LTV> 90%	LTV> 95%	LTV 100%
AA 0×30 full/easy/stated to $800K; full doc >$800K–1.5M	700+	5.400	5.450	5.550	5.700	5.850	6.100	6.950	7.500
	680	5.450	5.500	5.650	5.750	5.900	6.350	7.050	7.600
	660	5.550	5.650	5.750	5.850	6.000	6.400	7.150	7.700
	640	5.650	5.750	5.850	5.950	6.100	6.750	7.250	7.800
	620	5.800	5.900	6.050	6.200	6.350	7.000	7.750	8.500
Debt ratio		55	55	55	55	55	55	50	50

TABLE 8.7   Rate Sheet B Full Doc 2/28 ARM

LTV	Mtg hist	70%	75%	80%	85%	90%	95%	100%
DTI		55% w 4500 gmi	55% w 4500 gmi	55% w 4500 gmi	55% w 4500 gmi	55% w 4500 gmi	55% w 4500 gmi	55% w 4500 gmi
Score/grade								
700+	None	5.85	5.90	6.00	6.30	6.55	7.15	7.85
660–699	None	5.90	6.05	6.10	6.45	6.70	7.25	8.00
620–659	None	6.00	6.20	6.30	6.70	7.05	7.80	8.25
600–619	3×30	6.10	6.30	6.45	6.85	7.25	8.00	8.40
580–599	2×30	6.30	6.60	6.75	7.25	7.60	8.25	8.80
500–579 A1	0×30	6.70	6.85	7.05	7.50	7.80		
500–579 A2	1×30	6.90	7.10	7.35	7.90	8.35		
500–579 A3	2×30	7.05	7.35	7.70	8.35	8.95		
500–579 B	1×60	7.30	7.75	8.30	9.15*0x60			

TABLE 8.8   Rate Sheet Conforming 30-Year Fixed with Rate Locks

30-Year	15-Day	30-Day	50-Day
5.625	98.194	98.179	98.158
5.750	99.024	99.003	98.976
5.875	99.688	99.662	99.628
6.000	100.052	**100.021**	99.980
6.125	100.404	100.368	100.320
6.250	101.191	101.150	101.095
6.375	101.732	101.686	101.624
6.500	101.973	101.921	101.853
6.625	102.201	102.144	102.069
6.750	102.659	102.597	102.515
6.875	103.073	103.006	102.917
7.000	103.244	103.172	103.077

the structure of a rate sheet for a national bank offering conforming 30-year fixed mortgages. The actual rate sheet included additional columns for 60-day, 70-day, and 90-day rate locks as well.

In this example, the bolded cell (100.021) is closest to par pricing.

Adjustments. The rate sheet from which Table 8.8 was created has fully half of its legal-size paper jammed with adjustments. They include adjustment by category of states and loan size, low doc loans, cash out and LTV requirements, property type, and mortgage insurance.

Adjustments for the 2/28 hybrids included such items as documentation, second liens, interest-only option, size of loan, purchase or refinance, and specific state requirements.

Pulling It All Together. Once you know what type of loan product is best, you can start comparing rates based on rate sheets and your prospect's particular scores. Be sure to look carefully at the adjustments when computing an interest rate, and don't forget to add in a profit margin for your firm. Once you have an interest rate, you can take advantage of mortgage calculator programs to determine what the monthly principal and interest payment will be with each lender.

What to Do When There Is Nothing You Can Do

Unfortunately, many people find themselves in dire financial straights, and by the time they come to you there may be little you can do for them in terms of finding a mortgage for which they qualify. Most people in this situation have very low credit scores, and one of the things you can do is help them get established on a path to repairing their credit, so that in 6 to 12 months they can qualify for a loan. Time is an asset for all would-be borrowers, if they take the actions needed to position themselves for the future.

Credit Repair Takes Time, Not Money

According to the Federal Trade Commission's web site, borrowers can take most credit repair actions personally at little or no cost. If a borrower with poor credit takes these actions, he can rebuild his credit to the point of qualification for a loan in a relatively short period. Here is what you can recommend:

1. **Get a copy of the credit report.** Borrowers are entitled to one free report per year from each of the three credit bureaus, or if denied credit or employment. Request it online, at www.annualcreditreport.com. If you (the mortgage originator) pulled the report as part of the application process, you can make it available to the prospect.

2. **Correct mistakes, file disputes.** Review the report in detail. Mistakes should be disputed in writing, and the dispute process is free. The credit bureau and the company that reported the item in dispute are responsible, under law, for correcting inaccurate or incomplete credit report information.

3. **Begin good credit habits immediately.** If there are accurate negative items (derogatories) on the report, they can remain there for as long as 10 years. Fortunately, lenders give greater weight to more recent history, so it is important to begin good credit habits immediately.

4. **Bring credit card balances down** to no more than 50% of the credit limit by paying more than the minimum due each month.

5. **Close newer credit cards before older ones.** Leave older ones open, even if the balances are zero. This establishes your depth of credit.

6. **Pay on time.** Never be 30 days or more late, especially with a mortgage, rent, or installment loan payment. Lenders are slightly more lenient with revolving credit delinquencies.

7. **Pay off the smallest recently reported bills first.** This will reduce the number of open accounts, and the zero balances will be reflected more quickly than on accounts that have been inactive (and not reported recently). Get receipts for all payments—it

can take some time for them to show up on the report, and many lenders will accept the receipts as proof of payment.

8. **Offer to settle accounts** which have accrued large amounts of interest and penalties.

Automated Underwriting Tools

Automation provides faster turn around at lower cost. It results in fair, accurate, and consistent evaluation based on the financial facts, blind to factors that are perceived to be prejudicial. Both Fannie Mae and Freddie Mac offer automated underwriting programs for mortgage originators. Competition is growing in the market for automated underwriting systems specifically for subprime lending.

It is worth your while to take advantage of these systems. They provide a heads-up as to whether the ideas you have for a loan product are going to fly with the lender. They can help you avoid ending up with a denial after putting forth a lot of effort with an unqualified prospect.

Keeping Track

At this stage in the process, you are already keeping track of the number of calls you are converting to applications. Immediately following the credit call, rate your prospect in terms of Commitment (Level 1, 2, or 3) and Qualification (Green, Yellow, Red). If your prospect was still at Level 3 after the credit call, make the next call another fact-gathering, relationship-building call, before you propose any options. Unless you can shift the Level 3 prospect to a Level 2, where he is at least open to the conversation you are going to have about mortgage options, you are, wasting your time.

If you find that a good number of applicants are not available for the credit call, or that they decline to move ahead, go back to the application

TABLE 8.9 New Application Log

NEW APPLICATION LOG

X = NEW PURCHASE

Rep:

Last Name, First	Date Taken	Source	Credit Call	Proposal Call	F/Up 1	F/Up 2	F/Up 3	Loan Pack	Submit Dt	Final Status Dt	Outcome
1											
2											
3											
4											
5											
6											
7											
8											
9											
10											
11											
12											
13											
14											
15											
16											
17											
18											
19											
20											
21											
22											

scripts and look at where you are failing to set up the call powerfully. If people come to the calls as planned, but do not move forward, tape your calls and listen to yourself. Are you going through the motions? Or are you using the credit call as a sales tool to build trust, zero in on the problem, and represent yourself as the solution?

Table 8.9 shows the New Application Log, which is where you recorded the application and credit call. If you decide that additional follow-up calls are required to move your prospect to a Level 2 or Level 1, record them in the columns for "F/Up" activity.

If you are working with other mortgage professionals, take advantage of their experience and knowledge. You aren't going to master everything at once. The important thing to remember is that the results you get inform you of the actions you need to take to be a high-income mortgage origina-tor. The more you understand, the better. But knowledge alone will not get you to your goal. You must be willing to practice your craft—salesmanship, genuine interest in the prospect's well-being, creative thinking, and prob-lem solving using loan products—and when you practice, sometimes you make mistakes. Every experience, even if it does not result in a closing, is an experience that moves you closer to your goal. Don't get discouraged, but more importantly, don't quit.

CHAPTER NINE

Step 6: Selling a Proposal That Makes Sense

You have now completed your analysis of the raw data and are ready to put together a proposal based on what you know about the borrower's goals, income, credit, and equity numbers. Two other very important factors come into play that will direct your next actions. The first is the Commitment Level classification (Level 1, 2, or 3), and the second is the Qualification Code (Green, Yellow, Red).

This classification coding was developed to establish a common understanding of where prospects are in relation to moving forward, and to identify the appropriate conversations to have with them to increase the conversion ratios for each mortgage originator.

There is no right place for a prospect to be. Prospects are okay wherever they are in the coding system. The important thing is not where they are. The important thing is that you know where they are, and are therefore able to tailor your conversations with them to provide the assurances they need to be able to move forward with a loan that will help them to meet their goals.

As a salesperson, it is your job to position the prospect before making a proposal. The prospect should be Green or Yellow, Level 1 or Level 2, before you make any recommendations or proposals. Level 3s can't hear what you have to say, no matter how well qualified they are—you might as well talk to stones. And Reds, no matter how well intentioned or committed, are not going to be able to move forward with a loan. Don't shut the door on these folks. You can cultivate your relationship and support prospects qualified as Red to take actions that will move them to a Yellow or Green status. Credit repair and cash flow management programs are available from full-service firms, but we will table our discussion of these services for another time. Now is the time to focus on selling proposals that will lead to loan closings.

It is important to note that the classification system is intended for use in every interaction you have with a prospect or client. Listen to key remarks, questions, and signs that indicate where the prospect's thinking is leading him. The relationship you establish with a prospect is the single most important thing you have going for you. Remember, every other mortgage originator is going to be pretty close to you in terms of product and price. Borrowers will do business with people they respect and have confidence in, unless they are desperate. The classification system allows you to have the conversations that will get prospects on track for a closing and for meeting their goals. Each conversation is very important in establishing trust and professionalism while building relationship.

Again, the foundation for a trusting, confident relationship is integrity: Do what you say you will do, when you say you will do it, the way it should be done. Your word is the most important tool you have, and your primary competitive advantage. If you do not do what you say—you miss or are late for a scheduled call or appointment—you give up your edge. Building a successful mortgage origination practice is not hard when you honor your word in all transactions.

In this chapter you will prepare a comparison of options for your prospect, including a "do-nothing" option in the case of refinances. This comparison is the basis for another conversation with the prospect—the proposal call. The chapter includes script snippets to assist you in structuring the conversation using the enrollment principles of attention, interest, conviction, desire, and close.

Basic Calculations for Comparisons

In spite of all the details you examined in order to come up with options for prospects, there are only a few points that are of interest and importance to them. Monthly mortgage payment is one. The change, if any, in monthly payments and balances of other obligations (cash flow) is another. Secondarily, borrowers are likely to ask about interest rates, principal balances, and points. In the proposal call you focus on the primary motivation or goal the borrower has in seeking a mortgage, and sell him on the benefits of having a new loan, not the features of the loan. That is a very important distinction to remember.

Proposal Analysis Worksheet

Table 9.1 is a worksheet that highlights the prospect's current financial situation, and creates the basis for the conversation to do something, and to do it with you. Enter basic information about the current mortgage at the top, including prepayment penalties and other mortgages or liens, if applicable.

In the middle section list the debts you consider eligible for a payoff or pay down when the loan goes through. This information is on the credit report and the 1003. Total the borrower's monthly payment and balances due on all accounts. Note the terms of the options you will present to the prospect, and calculate the monthly housing expense, as shown.

The Do-Nothing Option

Presenting the do-nothing option does two things. First, it creates a context of free choice without pressure. You give prospects the option to say no to moving ahead, and you give them the information they need to make an intelligent decision. Second, you create a reason to move

TABLE 9.1   Proposal Analysis Worksheet

Proposal Analysis Worksheet

Original Mortgage:

Estimated Value: _____

Date Taken: _____   Credit Score(s) _____

Current P & I _____

Homeowners _____

Taxes _____

PMI _____

Total _____   Balance: _____

2nd Mortgage:

Date Taken _____   Balance: _____

P & I Payment _____

Other Debts:

_____ Payment _____ Balance _____

_____ Payment _____ Balance _____

_____ Payment _____ Balance _____

_____ Payment _____ Balance _____

_____ Payment _____ Balance _____

Combined Total Payments _____

Proposal 1	Proposal 2	Proposal 3
Loan	Loan	Loan
Term	Term	Term
Rate	Rate	Rate
P & I	P & I	P & I
Escrow	Escrow	Escrow
Total:	Total:	Total:

Notes:

forward. They have come this far only because there is something they want to accomplish financially. They can't do that unless they take action. The do-nothing proposal drives home the reality of their present situation and reminds them of their reasons to move forward.

Future Options for Better Choices

Depending on the qualification details, there may not be immediate loan options available. We have already discussed actions the borrower can take to repair damaged credit and mentioned other programs a full-service mortgage organization can offer. Never shut the door entirely, especially with Levels 1 and 2.

> ***Red Level 1 or 2.*** *Listen, Mr. Smith, based on the information we have available at this time, it will be very hard for you to do anything. However, I know you are committed to seeing if you can do something to get into a new home, right? Then there might be a possibility if you are able to come up with additional money for a down payment or get a co-signer for the mortgage. Do you know anyone who would be willing to help you out?*

The presentation of the proposition in an effective sales conversation follows a very simple pattern: Bad news/good news, then take it away—in that order. You have a problem, I have a solution, you may not be able to get it. This very basic recipe leaves people wanting you on their side, working with them. The opening line states the problem in a way that should eliminate shopping around for a better offer. Don't be afraid to nail it down. The conversation holds out some hope to the borrower, but it will require action on his part. Some people will take action, some will not. The ones that do will never forget you.

> ***Red Level 3.*** *Mr. Jones, at this time there are a few issues that really need to be handled with regard to your qualifications. I believe with a little time and working together we will achieve this. How soon were you looking at getting into a new home? Does your spouse feel the same way? If you could possibly achieve that sooner, would you be interested?*

As you engage prospects in interactions with you, you begin to open up a relationship with them, and they begin to trust that you have their best interest in sight. Especially with a Level 3, keep inviting them into the inquiry with you about what they want and what they are willing to do to get it. If they continue to resist, change your tone and stance with them. Let them know that since they are not open to exploring options, you can't help them. At that moment the sale is at risk, and as a salesperson, especially a new one, it is not easy to let go of it. What you learn is that unless you shake them up, the sale is lost anyway and sometimes it is your willingness to walk away that breaks through their resistance and allows them to see you are not trying to take advantage of them.

Moving a Level 3 Up. It is important that you not work with Red Level 3s until you know that they are committed to the process by which you will be able to help them achieve their goals. This borrower has to have something at stake to be motivated to take the actions that will, within a short period, put her in a position to qualify for a mortgage. We use the application fee as an up-front requirement before any additional work is done with this type of prospect. A prospect's willingness to commit a reasonable amount of money to the process is a good signal that she is moving toward listening to us as professionals. And, as incentive to move all the way through the process, we credit the fee back at closing. If we are unable to qualify the prospect within an agreed-upon time frame, we will refund the application fee and close the file.

Spouses. During your interactions with the prospect, evaluate and rate the prospect's spouse or partner. When working with couples, it is very important that they agree with each other, or the loan will never close. You will be surprised at how differently spouses can think about home ownership and finances. Always make your proposal call to both partners. If one partner is unavailable at the time of the call, reschedule. And before you give them the proposition, ask questions to let you know they are on the same page with each other and with you.

Presenting the Choices

Your success reflects your willingness to support prospects to achieve their short- and long-term goals through the mortgage process. If you get a prospect excited about the choices available to him, and the difference that restructuring his finances would make to him and his family, can you imagine how easy it would be for the prospect to move forward? And move forward with you.

In earlier conversations you already explained to the prospect that most lenders get their money from the same place, so everyone should be offering roughly the same pricing. You also explained that on this call you would be presenting options that were valid for today, since programs and rates change daily.

Being able to reference these conversations is important in establishing trust and confidence. The borrower knows what to expect. You tell him what is going to happen, and then it happens. All along, you set expectations and deliver. These conversations minimize the number of surprises the prospect (and you) experience, making the process comfortable and professional so the prospect can move ahead with ease.

When people are comfortable with the process and with you, and you offer them a proposition that fits their short- and long-term goals, they have no reason not to move forward with you. You did the ground work in the application call and the credit call to identify the prospect's goals, which focus on his reasons for the mortgage and the difference it will make for him. You have set the stage for presenting your proposal.

Your job is to keep prospects' vision alive for them. You can't do that if you are attached to the outcome and what they do. Your best results will come only if you remain committed to what they are committed to having in their lives. When people remain in touch with the difference they saw they could make for themselves and their families, it is easy to sell them.

Getting Started. Tempting as it might be, never start a conversation talking about rate, points, or closing costs. We know the prospect is likely to ask. People have been trained to ask, "What's your rate?" and "what are your closing costs?" The answers to those questions won't provide borrowers the information they need to make an informed and intelligent decision, even though they believe the information is important. The information is not important. What is important is that the borrower's problem—the situation that motivates him—is solved.

When you start a conversation talking about rate, you create a basis for comparison—between what you are saying and either what prospects have heard elsewhere, or what they want or expect to hear. They can only assess one as better than another. There is no power for the prospect or for you if you dwell in the conversation about rate rather than the benefit or difference the mortgage will make. When you work through the rate and closing cost questions professionally, without attachment to the outcome, you experience the power you have to make a difference for people. When a prospect asks these questions, will you be prepared, or are you going to react to the questions? Professionals take control and guide the conversation to questions and answers that truly inform the prospect about what is of interest and importance to him.

To be effective, the conversation must focus on the benefits the mortgage provides: being debt free before retirement, or freeing up cash they need monthly. Your job is to have prospects focus on the bigger picture. That is what enables them to move forward.

When prospects are in touch with the fulfillment of their goals, you stand a good chance of being the person with whom they do business. They consider you to be the professional you are, different from others. Clients give referrals because they respect and appreciate the difference you make for them in fulfilling their goals, not because you shaved an eighth of a point off a rate.

The Conversation. At the end of the credit call you had already set a date and time for this, the proposal call. Be on time. Start the conversation by verifying that the conditions are good for the prospect and partner to pay full attention. Then reaffirm your prior conversations with them about their goals and the process.

> *Good afternoon, Mr. Smith. This is Ron from AAA Mortgage. Is Mrs. Smith on the phone with us, too? Okay, good. Is this still a good time to talk? Great.*

If you have not had direct contact with the prospect's spouse until now, the first order of business is to recap for him or her the goals the couple have for the mortgage, and the facts about their financial standing and ability to qualify for a loan. If the partner agrees that the goal you have been working with is one he or she shares with the partner, you are good to go. If they do not agree, ask them if they are willing to entertain the idea of what their partner was looking to accomplish. If he or she is not open, *do not* make the proposal—no decision will be made. Rather, go back over the conversations you had in the credit call, and reschedule another proposal call for the next day.

> *Okay, so we all are clear that you are looking to <<what they want to accomplish>>. I've worked up a couple of options that will do that for you, and I'm going to go over them with you today.*
>
> *As I said yesterday, these numbers are good for today only because rates change daily. So if you see that what I am giving you meets your goals and you like it and it makes sense to you, then I will need a <<$>> fee from you today to register the loan and lock in the rates and get started. If you don't see how what I have for you meets your goals and you don't like it or it doesn't make sense to you, then you won't move forward today, and I will just close your file. That makes sense, doesn't it?*

You have set the expectations for the call and prepared them to be ready for action. You have also closed the door on thinking about it by reiterating that the offer is only good for today.

> *I want to start by going through what we call the "do-nothing" proposal, so that you are clear that you don't have to do anything, and if you don't, where you will be. Then we can go through the other options you have, so that you can clearly see the difference each of them makes for you. At that point, if we make a difference, we'll move forward; otherwise we will close the file.*

Walk them through their present situation, and paint the picture of where they will wind up 5, 10, 30 years from now.

> *Right now you are 6 years into a 30-year fixed mortgage. Your monthly payments are <<x>>, and you have << equity>> equity in your home. If you don't do anything, then you will continue to make this monthly payment for the next 24 years, and in 2031 your mortgage will be paid off, and you will own your home free and clear. You will have paid << in interest>> on your loan of <<loan amount>>. Do you have any questions so far?*
>
> *Okay, as far as your other debt goes, if you continue to pay the minimum due on your credit card, and don't charge any more, you will have them paid off about the same time as your mortgage. So we're clear what the problem is that we want to make a difference with, wouldn't you agree? And if we can make a difference here, then it makes sense to move forward, true? Okay, good.*

At this point you can go ahead and present the two options you have for them beside the "do-nothing" option. When you are done presenting both, ask,

> *Which one makes sense to you?*

This question is a trial close, eliciting an opinion, rather than a decision. The door remains open for discussion, regardless of what they say. If they are enthusiastic about one or the other, you know what direction to take.

> *Great! The first thing we need to do is get together to gather some general paperwork (W-2s, pay stubs, etc). I will come to you to collect these things and also review and have you sign the paperwork I need to send to the lender for qualifications. It will only take about 15 minutes. My job is to collect the documents from you and get your signatures on some additional documentation. I will also leave you a package of everything you sign. It is*

very important that you have your documents ready for me, because I will be doing a few appointments that day. If any questions come up, we will go over them the next day. If everything is fine then I will move forward to order your appraisal and register and lock your loan with the lender to secure the rate and terms. It is imperative that any documents requested be delivered ASAP. Once we receive the appraisal back and have all the paperwork, we will then submit your file to the lender. As long as everything goes smoothly, we should have you closed in about 20 to 25 days. Do you have any questions for me at this time? No, great.

Which works better for you both, Tuesday at 7:00 or Monday at 8:00? Okay, great, see you then.

If the prospects are not enthusiastic about either of your proposals, you have some objections to overcome.

Objections

As you gain experience with proposal calls, you will become familiar with issues that borrowers raise about the options you propose. The most effective way to handle objections in any sales presentation is to close the door on them before they come up in the conversation. While you can benefit from my experience, the most effective closing door conversations are the ones you recognize as needed and create for yourself. Here are some from my experience.

B/C Lenders. *A lender looks at three things when considering whether to lend you money. These three things are employment, credit, and income. These three things are different for every borrower, and how the lenders rate your three criteria determines what rate they will give you.*

There is what is called a nonconforming lender. This lender will lend to you when a conforming lender will not. What's the difference? Well, the good news is that this lender will lend to you, but you will have to pay higher interest and produce more documentation in order for this nonconforming lender to approve your loan. Based on your situation right now, the only way you can get financing is by using a nonconforming lender. We use the nonconforming lender as a stepping stone to improve your credit and establish a good credit history. Nonconforming lenders do not lock the rate, but usually the rates stay the same.

Attorney Fees. Do you have an attorney you would like to use for your closing? We have no problem with you choosing your own attorney, but we have no idea what his fees are going to be, so I will only be able to estimate the cost on the Good Faith Estimate. Also, when it comes to closing and any issues arise, we have found a lot of times we do not have as much flexibility or control over the closing as we would if you were to use one of our approved attorneys. Our only intention in this whole process is to have it go as smoothly as possible with no surprises. I also know our attorneys are very fair in pricing, and if we need something to get handled, we have a lot more control and power to get it done. What would you like to do?

Extra Paperwork. The paperwork we collect when we begin your process is what most lenders ask for. On various occasions however, lenders may request additional paperwork. It is very important that you get these items to me as soon as possible, as any delay may jeopardize closing in time. This is very important, okay?

Credit. It is very important that you do not incur any new charges on any accounts before the closing. It is also important that you do not apply for any new credit before the closing. If you were to do that, it would add to your overall debt and increase your monthly payments, and it might jeopardize the closing. Also, we want to make sure that you continue to pay all your bills on time through the closing. Just because you are refinancing to pay off the bills, we do not want any late payment to get onto your credit report. That includes the mortgage payments that are coming up. Do you understand? Great!

In refinancing transactions, a new lender wants its loan to have a higher legal standing with regard to a security interest in the property than any existing home equity loans or lines of credit. The home equity loan or line of credit has to be *subordinated* to the new loan, and that is often more difficult to accomplish than closing all loans and lines of credit and then reestablishing them after the new mortgage closes.

Subordination (when a second mortgage or HELOC already exists in a refinance transaction). To keep your line of credit (HELOC) can be an involved process. From our experience, it is more complicated to subordinate the line of credit than it is to close the credit line out and then reinstate it after the refinance is complete. More importantly, there is no guarantee that the bank holding the line of credit will subordinate it to the new refinanced mortgage.

If we try to subordinate the line, then I will need the note on the credit line. Next, the attorney's fee for subordination is <<$$>>, and a <<$$>> processing fee, made out to my company, to cover the lender's administrative cost. Any fees left over will be credited back to you at closing. Now the lead time for the subordination process is a week to 10 days. Finally it is vital to have the note and the fees collected at your home along with the other documents when I come out there.

When we have everything, we submit it to your attorney, who then starts the subordination process. The subordination needs to be complete before the loan will close. This is the process for subordination. Unless some extraordinary circumstances exist, we generally suggest to the client to close out the line of credit and open it again after the new mortgage closes. Do you understand what I've just explained? Great. How do you want me to proceed?

Prepayment Penalty. I know that a <<$$>> prepayment penalty seems like a lot. But you want to look at your average savings over 30 years. Your monthly payments can go down, and you can pay off other debt. If you can see that you are saving on a monthly basis, would that make a difference for you?

Higher Rate. The rate is higher, but you want to see what we are accomplishing overall. You said you wanted lower monthly payments.

This loan saves you <<$$>> a month. Does that make a difference for you?

I could get you a lower rate, but you would have to pay too much for it. Really, the primary objective is to save you money on a monthly basis. Can you see that is what we are doing?

Closing Costs. *I know your money is valuable, and I'm not interested in wasting it. These closing costs allow me to offer the rate you are getting, and you make it back through the savings on your monthly payments. What do you want me to do?*

I could reduce the closing costs, but then I would have to give you a higher rate. When you are planning to stay in the home for a long time, it is better to pay a little more in closing costs because you make it up in the monthly payments.

Keeping Track

Congratulations! You have converted your first application. Immediately, update your New Application Log and schedule a follow-up call for the day before you bring the loan package to the clients for review and signature.

If you did not get the sale, write down everything you remember about the conversation. In particular, think about the objections the prospects raised, and whether you were comfortable and confident in your answers. Where do you think you missed it?

Be very clear that if you did not make the sale, there may be several reasons. For your own development, it is important for you to distinguish where in the process you failed so that you can make corrections. Here are some questions to ask yourself:

Did I correctly identify the prospect's most pressing problem/need?

Did my proposal proposition solve the problem?

Had I set up the expectation for a decision in the previous call and at the start of this call?

If your answer to these three questions is yes, then look further at your interactions during the call.

Was I nervous, uncomfortable or uncertain at any point? Why?

Did I do a trial close?

What was the reason the prospect gave for not moving forward?

Did I close at least three times? At what point did I give up?

What did I want to say that I didn't? How could I have said it?

Regardless of the outcome, your experiences are the best teachers you have. Use each one to empower you and inform you about the opportunities for improvement, and it is only a matter of time before you are a high-income mortgage originator.

CHAPTER TEN

Step 7: Creating a Customer Relations System

The secret to your long-term success as a high-income mortgage originator is your ability to build, cultivate, and nurture the relationships you develop with clients as they go through the loan process. Satisfied customers are your best source of business. Most have friends, relatives, neighbors, and colleagues who own homes or who are looking to buy a home. And they all need mortgages.

You may think that since you took the application and sold the loan, that you have finished your job. I have some bad news and some good news. The bad news is that you accomplished the task, but the job is not done. The good news is that if you did what you should have done, when you should have done it, and the way you should have done it, the rest is easy. There is no reason for the loan not to go smoothly, and the client should be highly satisfied. Then, all that is left to do is to remind your clients that you are still around, express genuine interest in keeping them in the best financial situation available to them, and to ask for their business and referrals.

A *word of caution*. Shortcuts you took earlier will bite you over the next few weeks. That piece of documentation you failed to ask for will require phone calls to the borrower and others. That discrepancy you didn't catch between the asset statements and the 1003 will raise a flag with the underwriter, and you will have to go back to the client with more questions and requests for information and/or documentation. The Good Faith Estimate closing costs you assumed the client understood will surprise him at the closing and may cause ill will, or worse, a refusal to close.

Doom and gloom? No. But good customer relations—the heart and soul of a successful mortgage origination practice—don't happen in one interaction. Every interaction is important. Fair or not, a single unpleasant occurrence or incident that brings your professionalism into question can damage or destroy weeks of relationship-building, sometimes to the point where you cannot recover.

The time between the application and closing is critical. Many people question their decisions after they make them, especially where lots of money is involved. If a client has any misgivings, he can turn the slightest misstep into an excuse to back out. Between the application and closing, your job is to keep the borrower informed and to make sure the loan progresses smoothly.

This chapter recommends specific types of ongoing communication with clients to cultivate the relationship you have built with them and to grow that relationship through referrals. It describes communications linked to specific loan cycle events, general marketing, and personalized communications. The next several chapters address keeping the loan progressing smoothly through closing.

Much of the information you need to target your messages to your clients is information that you collected on the loan application. If you took the time to get to know your client, you may have personal information you can reference for additional relationship-building communications, for example, birthday cards for the borrower, and perhaps spouse and children, information about an event of interest to him such as golf or theater. Even if you don't have or don't feel comfortable using this type of information, periodic and regular communication to past customers is essential and makes a difference. The key is to be able to access the information at the right time to generate an effective communication.

One of the easiest ways is to systematize the process of communication by creating letters or other mailings that are tied to events or periods of time. The loan cycle communications fall into this category.

You should be tracking ARM adjustment dates, balloon payment dates, and setting reminders a few months in advance to check in with these customers. These events are opportunities for you and your customers to take stock of where they are and whether there are more favorable options available to them at this time. Target-marketing based on criteria about the client and or the loan product can also result in communication opportunities and can create a need with the customer that might not otherwise be there. As market conditions change in terms of real estate values, interest rates, or new loan products, you can search your criteria to target marketing messages to your past customers.

A Little Technology Goes a Long Way

There are mortgage-industry-specific Customer Relationship Management (CRM) systems, but if you don't have access to one, do not worry. A simple spreadsheet, word processor, and calendar tickler system (all features of Microsoft Office) are all you need to set up an effective and efficient system of communication with your customers.

While it is convenient to have specialized mortgage software designed for customer relationship management, you can accomplish the same goals when you combine disciplined procedures with basic word processing, spreadsheet, and calendar/e-mail software. Learn to modify the letters you can download at www.tomortgageservices.com, and use the sample spreadsheets to record customer information if you do not have access to more sophisticated software. You don't have to be a computer whiz. You just need to know a few basics of each program to create your own CRM processes using these generic tools. It is as easy as A-B-C:

a. Learn to use your word processor's mail/merge features. Most word processors provide step-by-step instructions to help you learn how.

b. Learn basic "sort" and "filter" capabilities in your spreadsheet program. A few keystrokes can help you quickly identify clients who meet selected criteria.

c. Learn to set reminders in your e-mail or calendaring software. Set them, and when they come up as reminders, pay attention to them.

See Appendix E for step-by-step instructions using Microsoft Word, Excel, and Outlook. Truly, that is all you need.

Loan Cycle Communications

We make a point of being in communication at least three times during the application to closing process: The first is when the loan application and go-back (the meeting at which the loan application documents are signed) are completed and the loan file is officially opened. This "open" letter varies slightly depending on whether the loan is a purchase or refinance.

The second series of communications go out weekly while the loan is in process. When the loan closes, another communication and survey are sent out soliciting feedback on individuals and the process, and requesting a referral. Then follow-up letters are sent 3, 6, and 12 months following the closing. Following the one-year anniversary of the closing, we stay in communication quarterly with our customers through a mailed newsletter and/or e-mail short articles we believe are of interest.

Enrollment

All of these communications follow the same basic enrollment strategy outlined for all the marketing and presale conversations. The letters or other communications have to get the customer's attention and address something of interest to him. It is an opportunity to establish again the value you provide. At each opportunity we appreciate the business from the customer, commit ourselves to helping him fulfill his financial goals, ask for feedback, and always ask for a referral.

Loan Cycle Letters

When you take a loan application and complete the go-back, send a letter that thanks the client for his business and states your commitment to have the approval process and closing go quickly and smoothly. Also remind the client that to do that, it is important that he respond quickly to your calls and requests for additional information. Finally, make yourself available to answer questions.

Samples for clients purchasing and refinancing are available online at www.tomortgageservices.com for you to tailor and customize. Figure 10.1 provides a sample Open Letter.

<<Date>>

<<Client Name>>
<<Client Address>>
<<City>>, <<State>> <<Zip>>

Dear <<Salutation>>,

Thank you for submitting your loan application through me. I appreciate your business. You made a smart choice to refinance now, and I will do everything necessary to ensure a quick and smooth approval.

You can help. If there are requests for additional information, I would appreciate your prompt response so we can get your loan through underwriting as quickly as possible. Your prompt return of any information requested will contribute to a smooth closing.

I look forward to working with you. If you have any questions, please don't hesitate to call me at <<your phone number>>. Thanks again for your business.
Sincerely,
<<Your name>>

FIGURE 10.1   Sample Open Letter

If a client refers someone else to you, you should send a letter of appreciation to the referrer, personally thanking him for the acknowledgement of his satisfaction, expressed by the referral. State your commitment to take good care of the person he referred to you. Figure 10.2 is an example of a referral thank you letter that you should tailor to suit your own style.

Optionally, if a purchase transaction involved real estate agents or builders, you may send them letters letting them know you will be handling the mortgage, that you look forward to working with them for a smooth closing, and that you will continue to keep them informed. Again, include your contact information in case they have questions.

Once you send the Open Letters mark your calendar (or otherwise set a reminder) to send out Status Letters every week until the closing. Prior to submitting the application to the lender for approval, the status letter can be a simple checklist of items that remain pending or unresolved. If specific documents are missing, it is important to let the client know what

---

<<Date>>

<<Client Name>>
<<Client Address>>
<<City>>, <<State>> <<Zip>>

Dear <<Salutation>>,

Thank you for referring <<new referral name>> to me. I always appreciate new opportunities for business, and I am particularly gratified to know you thought well enough of me to recommend my professional services. Thank you for your confidence, and know that I will personally ensure that <<new referral name>> receives great service.

Thank you!

Best regards,
<<Your name>>

FIGURE 10.2　Referral Thank You

they are and how to get them to you. List verifications that remain to be conducted as well. When the file processors are ready to submit the file to the lender, let the borrower know that, too. Figure 10.3 shows a status letter requesting additional information.

If the file has been submitted, let the client know that in the status letter. When the loan is approved, send the final Status Letter. Close each letter with your contact information and your availability to answer questions. As soon as you have a closing date, be sure to set a reminder to send the Closing Letter a few days after the closing.

<<Date>>

<<Client Name>>
<<Client Address>>
<<City>>, <<State>> <<Zip>>

Dear <<Salutation>>,

Your loan is in process, and this letter provides you with a status. Things are going well, but we are waiting to receive the following items before submitting the loan for approval by the lender:

_____ Appraisal

_____ Employment Verification

_X_ Tax returns and W-2s for last two years

_____ Most recent quarterly retirement account statements (401(k), IRA, pension, etc.)

_____ Preliminary title report

_____ Other: _____

Please mail this information to me at the address above as soon as possible.

Thank you again for your business. Please contact me at <<Your phone number>> if you have any questions.

Sincerely,

<<Your name>>

FIGURE 10.3   Sample Status Letter

Letters are great as formal documentation and for providing a paper trail of requests for information and a record that progress is being made, but they do not substitute for personal contact. Be in communication by phone or in person frequently with clients to find out by when they will have the documents you need, and what you can do to support them in achieving that goal. When the loan is approved, a congratulatory phone call is in order, at which time you can discuss closing procedures and timing with the client.

Send a Closing Letter after the loan is closed and funded. Congratulate the client on either the purchase of his new home or the wisdom of his refinancing decision, and thank him for the opportunity to serve him. Express your pleasure at how smoothly the process went. Most important, request that clients think of you if they, their friends, or family have financing needs. And of course, close with your contact information and availability to answer questions about the loan or anything else. Figure 10.4 shows a sample Closing Letter.

If the transaction was a purchase and the real estate agent(s) did a good job, you can also acknowledge that in your closing letter to the client, and you can send a closing letter directly to the agent(s) congratulating them and letting them know you enjoyed working with them and look forward to doing so again. The same holds true for attorneys or other closing agents.

All of this thanking and acknowledgement may seem a bit excessive. However, it matters. People remember being appreciated, and they remember the people who appreciate them. Appreciation and acknowledgement are effective tools for building a referral base.

In the first year following the loan closing, we send out mailings at the three-month, six-month, and one-year marks. The Three-Month Letter reminds the client that you worked with him, and thanks him again for the business. It states your intent to stay in touch, and provides contact information and availability to discuss not only his loan, but any questions he might have regarding financing and loans in general. Finally, it closes with a request for a referral should anyone the client knows be in need of a mortgage.

<<Date>>

<<Client Name>>
<<Client Address>>
<<City>>, <<State>> <<Zip>>

Dear <<Salutation>>,

　Congratulations on your new home! I hope you are enjoying it as you unpack and get settled.

　Thank you again for the opportunity to assist you with your mortgage needs. I am happy that everything went smoothly, and am certain that you are, as well.

　If you, your family or friends have financing needs in the future, please keep me in mind. If you have any questions about your monthly payments, interest rate, or anything else, please don't hesitate to call me at <<your phone number>>.
Warm regards,
<<Your name>>

FIGURE 10.4　**Sample Closing Letter**

　　You can also send Three-Month Letters to the supporting players, like real estate agents and attorneys. Remind them of the client and the closing you did, that it went smoothly, and acknowledge their contributions and professionalism in the matter. If appropriate, let them know you are willing to refer business to them, and state your hope that they will do the same. End the letter by looking forward to future business together and include your contact information and availability to answer questions. Figure 10.5 is a sample letter appropriate to send to a client three months following closing.

　　Six months after closing, contact your client again. This time state your commitment to stay in touch, and encourage the client to call you or have anyone he knows call you with questions about mortgage financing, regardless of complexity—offer your time and expertise at no charge, no obligation. End the letter with your contact information and availability,

<<Date>>

<<Client Name>>
<<Client Address>>
<<City>>, <<State>> <<Zip>>

Dear <<Salutation>>,

   Three months ago we closed a mortgage on your home, and I want to say again that I appreciated the opportunity to assist you with the financing.

   I will keep in touch occasionally, and would be happy to help you with any matters related to your financing needs. Please feel free to call me at << your phone number>> to answer any questions you have about your mortgage, loans in general or any other questions you might have. If you have friends or family who are going to buy, sell, or refinance a home, I hope you will tell them about me and ask them to give me a call. It will be my pleasure to assist them.

Sincerely,

<<Your name>>

FIGURE 10.5   Sample Three-Month Post-Closing Letter

and express appreciation for the support he can provide for you to build your business. Figure 10.6 is an example of a letter appropriate at the six-month mark.

    You can also send six-month follow-up letters to the supporting players, reminding them of the transaction, how smoothly it went, and your interest in working with them again through mutual referrals.

    One year following the closing of the loan, send a congratulatory Happy Anniversary Letter to the customer, expressing hope that his goals were fulfilled. Make yourself available to him, his friends, and family to answer questions and provide service. Figure 10.7 provides a sample.

<<Date>>

<<Client Name>>
<<Client Address>>
<<City>>, <<State>> <<Zip>>

Dear <<Salutation>>,

Six months have passed since we closed the mortgage on your home. I want to keep in touch and invite you to call me anytime you—or someone you know—have a question about mortgage financing. It doesn't matter what the question is, I would be happy to provide any information needed.

You are a valued customer, and I offer my services to you, your family, and friends should they ever need real estate financing.

Please feel free to call me at <<your phone number>> to answer any questions you have about your mortgage, loans in general, or any other related topics. If you have friends or family who are going to buy, sell, or refinance a home, I hope you will tell them about me and ask them to give me a call. It will be my pleasure to assist them.

Thank you again for your business and your continued support in helping me build my business. Both are greatly appreciated.

Sincerely,

<<Your name>>

FIGURE 10.6   Sample Six-Month Post-Closing Letter

General Communications to Past Customers

At least four times a year, send out a communication to past customers. The communications can each follow the same basic structure: Express appreciation for the past business and your commitment to stay in touch and be available. Provide information of general interest to homeowners—the actual topic doesn't really matter. Ask for referrals and repeat business. Figure 10.8 provides a template for letters of interest to homeowner clients.

Whether it is through individual letters, a newsletter (there are many companies that provide content), or an e-mail blast, keeping your

<<Date>>

<<Client Name>>
<<Client Address>>
<<City>>, <<State>> <<Zip>>

Dear <<Salutation>>,
    Happy Anniversary! It has been a whole year since we concluded the financing of
your home. I hope that everything you hoped for has been realized and exceeded!
    You are a valued client. Please know that I am always available to answer your
questions—no matter how simple or complicated. I invite you to call me anytime,
and would welcome the opportunity to answer questions and provide service for
your friends, family, neighbors, and colleagues who are considering buying, selling,
or refinancing a home. Do you know anyone?
    Please don't hesitate to call me at <<your phone number>>. I appreciate the
opportunity to serve you.
Sincerely,
<<Your name>>

FIGURE 10.7   Sample One-Year Post-Closing Letter

name in front of the customer is the best marketing strategy you can
implement to become a high-income mortgage originator. We've sent out
information about fire safety, security and safety tips, energy efficiency,
swing set safety, remodeling, landscaping, preparing your home for sale,
major household appliances, job opportunities, local economic and real
estate market conditions, leftover food safety tips (during the holidays),
credit scores, recipes, technology, motivation and history. I've gotten
ribbed by friends for whom I've done mortgages who ask me why I send
them those crazy letters. Here's the reason: It doesn't matter what the
message is—without fail, past customer call-in rates pick up in the days
immediately following a mailing.

    Make calls to past customers a part of your daily outbound calling
routine. As you build up information about your customer base, whether
through a spreadsheet, a paper filing system or by using automated software

<<Date>>

<<Client Name>>
<<Client Address>>
<<City>>, <<State>> <<Zip>>

Dear <<Salutation>>,

   In appreciation of your past business, from time to time I will send you tips and information that I think will be of interest to you as homeowner. I hope you find them useful, and share them with your friends and family. Please keep me in mind when you or someone you know is thinking of buying, selling or refinancing a home.

   <<4 to 10 bullet points on a topic of interest>>

   I look forward in the future to providing you and those you know with the best home financing products and services available.

Sincerely,

<<Your name>>

FIGURE 10.8   Sample Past Client Communication Template

specific to the mortgage industry, you can select customers who meet specific criteria and target them for calls about applicable loan products or about a general mortgage check up to see if there is a way that you can help them save money.

Track Your Communications

Keep records of all correspondence. There are many ways to do this, depending on the technology you have at your disposal and your facility with it. If nothing else, create a paper or electronic folder for each client that contains or references the standard letters you send. Be sure to indicate when the letter was sent, too.

   Track the Responses. If you get a call from one of your past customers, note the date and the subject of the conversation. Ask what prompted the call, and note if he says that one of your mailings had something to do with it.

Cross-Reference Referrals. If you get referrals, make notes in the files of both the referrer and the person they referred. Acknowledge and thank them both.

Use the nice things people say to you or about you to promote yourself. Testimonials, positive quotes, and postings to your web site all speak volumes to someone shopping for a loan. If a customer expresses satisfaction, we encourage our mortgage originators to ask the client to jot a note to the managing loan specialist to let him know. Most clients will say yes. We scan the testimonial documents and put them on our web site next to a picture of the mortgage originator. When the mortgage originator has someone new on the phone, he uses the web site to show himself as a real flesh-and-blood, decent human being, and the person looking sees the glowing remarks others have made. It works to begin establishing trust with a potential customer.

Get a system in place, and work the system. Don't let it slide. Track your actions and the results they produce. Regular communication is the key to building your client base, and a growing base of satisfied customers is the most effective tool you can have toward rapidly becoming a high-income mortgage originator.

PART THREE

Wrap Up

CHAPTER ELEVEN

The Loan Package: Preparing the Loan for Processing

N ow is the time for attention to detail. A properly prepared loan package facilitates the loan's smooth processing, underwriting, and closing, and reinforces your professionalism and goodwill with your client. Done poorly, it creates doubt, mistrust, ill will, and delays in closing that cost you not only this loan, but also the future referrals this customer could have provided to you. High-income mortgage originators take the time to complete this important step thoroughly and accurately, and they reap the benefits of smooth and efficient closings and satisfied customers.

We call the step at which pertinent client documentation is collected, disclosures are explained, signatures are taken, and fees collected the *go-back*. The signed application, disclosures, and other forms that comprise the go-back package contain the information needed by the processing department to submit your loan to a lender, contain the information the lender needs to approve the loan, and contain the information needed to generate most of the closing documents. The go-back is, in many cases, the first face-to-face meeting with a client. It is a very important interaction, both in terms of the loan process and in terms of building relationship.

This chapter presents in detail the many and various forms that comprise the loan package. It provides you with a process for preparing the package, obtaining the needed documents and signatures, and preparing the file for the processor. It also gives you tips on how to track your files and facilitate their movement through to closing.

Uniform Residential Loan Application (1003)

You are already familiar with the 1003 form, having completed sections of it with the client to obtain the information you needed to craft a proposal. Now it is time to fill in any missing or incomplete information that may not have been necessary to this point, but which lenders require to underwrite and approve a loan. The completed 1003 is the first document in the loan go-back package.

I've asked file processors and closing specialists what is the biggest mistake loan originators make, and without fail they say incomplete or inaccurate information on the 1003. There are no shortcuts. What you do not handle correctly at this point *will* come back to bite you, and in some cases, the bite can be fatal to the closing.

Take the time when the client is signing the forms to go over each piece of information on the 1003. The few extra minutes you spend verifying accuracy and completeness before submission will save you hours, days, and even weeks down the road. Delays are costly in terms of time, but even more so in terms of goodwill—with clients, processors, lenders, closing specialists, and attorneys. Never forget that goodwill is your most valuable asset as a high-income mortgage originator.

I. Type of Mortgage and Terms of Loan

Update this information, shown in Figure 11.1, based on the agreed-upon proposal. Make sure the amount (principal), interest rate, term (in months), and amortization type are correct.

Borrower				Co-Borrower			

I. TYPE OF MORTGAGE AND TERMS OF LOAN							
Mortgage Applied for:	☐ VA ☐ FHA	☐ Conventional ☐ USDA/Rural Housing Service	☐ Other (explain):			Agency Case Number	Lender Case Number
Amount $	Interest Rate %		No. of Months	Amortization Type:	☐ Fixed Rate ☐ GPM	☐ Other (explain): ☐ ARM (type):	

FIGURE 11.1   1003 Section I Type of Mortgage and Terms of Loan

II. Property Information and Purpose of the Loan

You may need additional information to complete this section of the application. Ask for the year the house was built. If the mortgage is a refinance, ask the year the owner purchased it, the price he paid, and the amount owed on second mortgages or equity lines of credit. If it is a purchase, the source of funds for the down-payment and closing fees must also be included. (See Figure 11.2.)

III. Borrower Information

You should have all information in this section, with the possible exception of "Yrs. School" for the borrower and co-borrower. I don't have a

II. PROPERTY INFORMATION AND PURPOSE OF LOAN						
Subject Property Address (street, city, state & ZIP)						No. of Units
Legal Description of Subject Property (attach description if necessary)						Year Built
Purpose of Loan ☐ Purchase ☐ Construction ☐ Other (explain): ☐ Refinance ☐ Construction-Permanent			Property will be: ☐ Primary Residence	☐ Secondary Residence	☐ Investment	
Complete this line if construction or construction-permanent loan.						
Year Lot Acquired	Original Cost $	Amount Existing Liens $	(a) Present Value of Lot $	(b) Cost of Improvements $	Total (a + b) $ 0.00	
Complete this line if this is a refinance loan.						
Year Acquired	Original Cost $	Amount Existing Liens $	Purpose of Refinance	Describe Improvements ☐ made ☐ to be made Cost: $		
Title will be held in what Name(s)			Manner in which Title will be held		Estate will be held in: ☐ Fee Simple ☐ Leasehold (show expiration date)	
Source of Down Payment, Settlement Charges, and/or Subordinate Financing (explain)						

FIGURE 11.2   1003 Section II Property Information and Purpose of Loan

Borrower					III. BORROWER INFORMATION				Co-Borrower
Borrower's Name (include Jr. or Sr. if applicable)					Co-Borrower's Name (include Jr. or Sr. if applicable)				
Social Security Number	Home Phone (incl. area code)	DOB (mm/dd/yyyy)		Yrs. School	Social Security Number	Home Phone (incl. area code)	DOB (mm/dd/yyyy)		Yrs. School
☐ Married ☐ Unmarried (include ☐ Separated single, divorced, widowed)		Dependents (not listed by Co-Borrower) no. ages			☐ Married ☐ Unmarried (include ☐ Separated single, divorced, widowed)		Dependents (not listed by Borrower) no. ages		
Present Address (street, city, state, ZIP) ☐ Own ☐ Rent___No. Yrs					Present Address (street, city, state, ZIP) ☐ Own ☐ Rent___No. Yrs				
Mailing Address, if different from Present Address					Mailing Address, if different from Present Address				
If residing at present address for less than two years, complete the following:									
Former Address (street, city, state, ZIP) ☐ Own ☐ Rent___No. Yrs					Former Address (street, city, state, ZIP) ☐ Own ☐ Rent___No. Yrs				

FIGURE 11.3   1003 Section III Borrower Information

good explanation for why this information is part of the 1003, but for the application to be complete it must be filled in. (See Figure 11.3.)

IV. Employment Information

If you have not already done so, get the complete mailing address for the borrower's (and co-borrower's) employer. Include a work phone number, as the closing department will need this information when verifying employment. Get job titles and positions correct, again for use in employment verification. (See Figure 11.4.)

V. Monthly Income and Combined Housing Expense Information

This section should already be complete, because the information contained in it was needed to compute DTI ratios when coming up with the

Borrower			IV. EMPLOYMENT INFORMATION		Co-Borrower	
Name & Address of Employer	☐ Self Employed	Yrs. on this job	Name & Address of Employer	☐ Self Employed	Yrs. on this job	
		Yrs. employed in this line of work/profession			Yrs. employed in this line of work/profession	
Position/Title/Type of Business	Business Phone (incl. area code)		Position/Title/Type of Business		Business Phone (incl. area code)	

If employed in current position for less than two years or if currently employed in more than one position, complete the following:

FIGURE 11.4   1003 Section IV Employment Information

V. MONTHLY INCOME AND COMBINED HOUSING EXPENSE INFORMATION						
Gross Monthly Income	Borrower	Co-Borrower	Total	Combined Monthly Housing Expense	Present	Proposed
Base Empl. Income*	$	$	$ 0.00	Rent	$	
Overtime			0.00	First Mortgage (P&I)		$
Bonuses			0.00	Other Financing (P&I)		
Commissions			0.00	Hazard Insurance		
Dividends/Interest			0.00	Real Estate Taxes		
Net Rental Income			0.00	Mortgage Insurance		
Other (before completing, see the notice in "describe other income," below)			0.00	Homeowner Assn. Dues / Other:		
Total	$ 0.00	$ 0.00	$ 0.00	**Total**	$ 0.00	$ 0.00

* Self Employed Borrower(s) may be required to provide additional documentation such as tax returns and financial statements.

Describe Other Income	*Notice:* Alimony, child support, or separate maintenance income need not be revealed if the Borrower (B) or Co-Borrower (C) does not choose to have it considered for repaying this loan.	
B/C		Monthly Amount
		$

FIGURE 11.5   1003 Section V Income and Combined Housing Expense Information

proposal. If income is marginal for loan approval, ask about child support and alimony income, and whether the client is willing to include that income in his application. (See Figure 11.5.)

VI. Assets and Liabilities

Double-check the information recorded in this section against the credit report. Make sure the numbers match up after adjustments or corrections to the credit report. Debt to income ratios factor heavily into approval, so make sure the liabilities are accurate.

Access to the full value of pension and 401(k) retirement accounts is granted over time, with a percentage of the value awarded or *vested* each year, usually over a 3-, 5-, or 10-year period. A very common mistake is to assume 100% vesting in a retirement program, when the actual vested amount may be significantly less. This can throw reserve ratios totally out of whack and can result in denial of a loan. Don't let this happen to you. If a pension plan or 401(k) plan is included in assets for reserve calculations, ask how vested the borrower and co-borrower are in the plans and adjust the asset values accordingly.

VI. ASSETS AND LIABILITIES				

This Statement and any applicable supporting schedules may be completed jointly by both married and unmarried Co-Borrowers if their assets and liabilities are sufficiently joined so that the Statement can be meaningfully and fairly presented on a combined basis; otherwise, separate Statements and Schedules are required. If the Co-Borrower section was completed about a non-applicant spouse or other person, this Statement and supporting schedules must be completed about that spouse or other person also.

Completed ☐ Jointly ☐ Not Jointly

ASSETS Description	Cash or Market Value	Liabilities and Pledged Assets. List the creditor's name, address, and account number for all outstanding debts, including automobile loans, revolving charge accounts, real estate loans, alimony, child support, stock pledges, etc. Use continuation sheet, if necessary, Indicate by (*) those liabilities, which will be satisfied upon sale of real estate owned or upon refinancing of the subject property.		
Cash deposit toward purchase held by:	$			
List Checking and savings accounts below		LIABILITIES	Monthly Payment & Months Left to Pay	Unpaid Balance
Name and address of Bank, S&L, or Credit Union		Name and address of Company	$ Payment/Months	$
Acct. no.	$	Acct. no.		
Name and address of Bank, S&L, or Credit Union		Name and address of Company	$ Payment/Months	$
Acct. no.	$	Acct. no.		
Name and address of Bank, S&L, or Credit Union		Name and address of Company	$ Payment/Months	$
Acct. no.	$	Acct. no.		

FIGURE 11.6   1003 Section VI Assets and Liabilities

If the borrower includes rental income among his assets, verify the calculation of Net Rental Income by checking the amount of PITI on the rental property from bank statements, tax receipts, and insurance payments. Again, a mistake in income can have a huge impact on whether a loan is approved, particularly if the ratios are marginally acceptable. (See Figure 11.6.)

You will need the addresses and account numbers for the asset accounts, which the borrower can obtain from the account statements.

Good Faith Estimate

The Good Faith Estimate (GFE) is mandated by RESPA to inform the borrower, in advance, of fees and costs associated with obtaining the mortgage loan. By law, you must provide the borrower with the GFE within three days of the application. It contains much of the same information, and in the same basic format, as the HUD-1 Settlement Statement that attorneys will produce as part of the loan closing. The GFE has nine sections, each dealing with a set of related fees. Standard fees are numbered within each section for consistency, and match HUD-1 section and line numbers. Specify any additional charges that may not be standard on the blank lines in each section. (See Figure 11.7.)

The information provided below reflects estimates of the charges which you are likely to incur at the settlement of your loan. The fees listed are estimates-actual charges may be more or less. Your transaction may not involve a fee for every item listed. The numbers listed beside the estimates generally correspond to the numbered lines contained in the HUD-1 or HUD-1A settlement statement which you will be receiving at settlement, The HUD-1 or HUD-1A settlement statement will show you the actual cost for items paid at settlement.

800	ITEMS PAYABLE IN CONNECTION WITH LOAN:			1100	TITLE CHARGES:	
801	Origination Fee @ % + $	$		1101	Closing or Escrow Fee	$
802	Discount Fee @ % + $	$		1102	Abstract or Title Search	$
803	Appraisal Fee	$		1103	Title Examination	$
804	Credit Report	$		1105	Document Preparation Fee	$
805	Lender's Inspection Fee	$		1106	Notary Fee	$
806	Mortgage Insurance Application Fee	$		1107	Attorney's Fee	$
807	Assumption Fee	$		1108	Title Insurance	$
808	Mortgage Broker Fee	$				$
810	Tax Related Service Fee	$				$
811	Application Fee	$				$
812	Commitment Fee	$				$
813	Lender's Rate Lock-In Fee	$				$
814	Processing Fee	$				$
815	Underwriting Fee	$		1200	GOVERNMENT RECORDING AND TRANSFER CHARGES:	
816	Wire Transfer Fee	$		1201	Recording Fee	$
				1202	City/County Tax/Stamps	$
900	ITEMS REQUIRED BY LENDER TO BE PAID IN ADVANCE:			1203	State Tax/Stamps	$
901	Interest for days @ $ /day	$		1204	Intangible Tax	$
902	Mortgage Insurance Premium	$				$
903	Hazard Insurance Premium	$				$
904	County Property Taxes	$				$
905	Flood Insurance	$		1300	ADDITIONAL SETTLEMENT CHARGES:	
		$		1301	Survey	$
1000	RESERVES DEPOSITED WITH LENDER:			1302	Pest Inspection	$
1001	Hazard Ins. Mo. @$ Per Mo.	$				$
1002	Mortgage Ins. Mo. @$ Per Mo.	$				$
1004	Tax & Assmt. Mo. @$ Per Mo.	$				$
1006	Flood Insurance	$				$
		$			TOTAL ESTIMATED SETTLEMENT CHARGES:	$
"S"/"B" designates those costs to be paid by Seller/Broker.				"A"designates those costs affecting APR.		
TOTAL ESTIMATED MONTHLY PAYMENT:				TOTAL ESTIMATED FUNDS NEEDED TO CLOSE:		
	Principal & Interest	$				
	Real Estate Taxes	$		Payoff Payment		$
	Hazard Insurance	$		Estimated Closing Costs		$
	Flood Insurance	$		Estimated Prepaid Items/Reserves		$
	Mortgage Insurance	$		Total Paid Items (Subtract)		$
	Other	$		Other		$
	TOTAL MONTHLY PAYMENT	$		CASH FROM BORROWER		$

FIGURE 11.7 Good Faith Estimate

Items Payable in Connection with Loan (800)

The costs included in this section relate to the loan and the processes and fees needed to bring it from application to close. Instructions for the HUD-1, available at www.hud.gov, provide guidance for completion of the GFE.

801—Loan Origination Fee. This is the fee or points charged by the lender to process or originate the loan. If the fee is based on points, show the points (as a percentage of the loan) as well. If the lender pays a CLO (Computer Loan Originator) fee, record it here as an item to be repaid to the lender by the borrower.

802—Loan Discount. This is points paid to the lender to reduce the interest rate on the loan. Show points as a percentage of the loan amount, in addition to the actual dollar amount.

803—Appraisal Fee. Appraisal fees vary depending on the value of the home and the appraiser. Typical costs are $250 to $350 dollars. Include the amount of the appraisal fee only if it is to be paid at the closing. If the borrower pays the appraiser directly at the time of the appraisal, the cost is indicated as POC (Paid Outside of Closing).

804—Credit Report. The fee for a credit report is usually $20–$25 dollars, and may be payable to the broker or lender.

805—Lender's Inspection Fee. It is used (rarely) for special inspection requirements. Include fees for normal pest inspections (termites) in Additional Settlement Charges.

806—Mortgage Insurance Application Fee. If mortgage insurance (PMI) is required and a fee for the application is charged, record it here.

807—Assumption Fee. Use this only with a purchase where the borrower is "assuming" payment of an existing mortgage.

808—Mortgage Broker Fee. This is not the broker's profit (disclosed in the section labeled Compensation to Broker), but rather any specific fees for brokering a deal that will be paid back to the lender.

809—Tax-Related Service Fee. If the lender pays a fee to a servicer to set up escrow and payment of taxes, list that fee here for the borrower to pay back to the lender.

Other Fees in This Section. Other itemized fees charged to the borrower and paid to the lender in connection with the loan include, but are not limited to processing fees, underwriting fees, wire transfer fees, rate lock fees, and flood certificate fees.

Title Charges (1100)

This section of the GFE contains fees for the closing documents related to title and charges by attorneys. Title transfer fees (for a purchase), title search fees, and title insurance fees all fall into this section. Itemize attorney fees, notary fees, and other closing agent fees related to title in this section.

Government Recording and Transfer Charges (1200)

Record government charges for recording deeds, liens, and transfers in this section.

Additional Settlement Charges (1300)

Use this as a catch-all category for items that do not fit into other categories. Pest inspection fees are typically recorded here.

Items Required by Lender to Be Paid In Advance (900)

In almost every situation the first mortgage payment will be due 30 or more days after the closing. The lender will collect some of the interest at the closing to cover the period between the closing and the first payment.

Some of the following monies may not be paid to the lender, but the lender requires the borrower to pay them at the closing, in advance of when they are due to third parties. Homeowner's insurance premiums (Hazard Insurance), PMI payments, real estate taxes, and other taxes are commonly included in this section.

901—**Interest**. Record the per diem rate of interest and the number of days between the closing and first payment. Compute the amount of interest to be paid at the closing and record it here.

902—**Mortgage Insurance Premium**. Enter the amount required by the lender to be prepaid for PMI.

903—**Hazard Insurance Premium**. To protect its security interest the lender will require that a certain number of months of homeowner's premiums be prepaid by the borrower. Enter the number of months, monthly amount, and total prepayment at closing on this line.

Reserves Deposited with Lender (1000)

Use this section to record fees that will be held in escrow by the lender. The total amount the lender can collect at the closing to hold in reserve is limited under RESPA 3500.17(b). If the itemized totals (below) exceed that amount, make an adjustment to bring the total amount collected for reserves into conformance with the RESPA requirements. The adjustment amount will always be either 0 or negative (to reduce the total amount collected for reserves).

1001—**Hazard Insurance Premium**. If the lender will be paying the homeowner's insurance premiums on behalf of the borrower, enter the number of months, monthly payment, and total amount required at closing as an initial reserve here.

1002—**Mortgage Insurance Premium Reserves**. If PMI is required enter the number of months, monthly payment, and total amount required by the lender as a reserve and due at closing.

1004—**Taxes and Assessment Reserves**. This is the amount of property tax reserves the lender requires at closing to be held in escrow until the taxes are due.

Other items in this section. Other items include Flood Insurance Reserves, School Taxes, and any other monies the lender expects to collect at closing to be held for future payment of borrower obligations related to the secured property.

Compensation to Broker (Not Paid Out of Loan Proceeds)

This section records the Yield Spread Premium and other compensation paid to the broker. The monies are not paid by the borrower to the broker, but are *paid outside of the closing* (POC) by the lender. Disclosure of broker compensation is required under RESPA. Direct (retail) lenders do not have to disclose the equivalent profits they build into their fees and rates. Typical broker compensation ranges up to 4% of the amount of the loan.

Total Estimated Funds Needed to Close

This section summarizes the others and itemizes the purchase price (if applicable), loan amount (principal), estimated closing costs (Sections 800, 900, 1100, 1200, 1300), estimated prepaid items/reserves (Sections 900, 1000), and any amounts paid by the seller (for a purchase).

Total Estimated Monthly Payment

This section itemizes principal and interest, other financing (principal and interest), hazard insurance, real estate taxes, mortgage insurance, association dues (for condos), and the total monthly payment expected.

Truth in Lending Disclosure Statement

In the late 1960s Congress passed the Consumer Protection Act, which included the Truth In Lending Act. The Truth In Lending Act (TILA) required that all offers of credit include the annual percentage rate, which differs from the "advertised" rate of interest by including additional fees and charges as part of the financing amount. The law intended that the annual percentage rate (APR) provide the consumer with a way to compare apples to apples in the face of differences in closing costs and other fees associated with mortgages and other loans advertised at the

TABLE 11.1   Truth in Lending Disclosure

Annual Percentage Rate	Finance Charge	Amount Financed	Total of Payments
The cost of your credit as a yearly rate.	The dollar amount the credit will cost you.	The amount of credit provided to you or on your behalf.	The amount you will have paid after you have made all payments as scheduled.
%	$	$	$

same rates of interest. The Truth in Lending Disclosure is one of the forms requiring a borrower's signature prior to submitting the loan to a lender. (See Table 11.1.)

Amount Financed. This is the amount of the loan principal, minus the following types of fees and charges associated with the cost of obtaining credit: credit report fees, administrative fees, interim interest (901). Do not deduct payments out of closing such as Yield Spread Premium. Also, any costs or fees that would have to be paid even if the transaction were cash, rather than credit, remain in the amount financed: title fees, recording fees, prepaid items.

Total of Payments. This is the principal plus interest that the borrower will repay over the life of the loan. Use the actual principal amount (as opposed to amount financed), rate, and term to determine this number. Use the payment schedule calculator at www.tomortgageservices.com to calculate the total cost of the loan.

Finance Charge. Compute the finance charge as the difference between the Total of Payments and Amount Financed.

Annual Percentage Rate. The APR is the rate of interest that would result in the monthly payment of the actual loan, if the amount of the loan were the Amount Financed rather than the principal amount. Use an APR calculator, but understand the example in Table 11.2.

The monthly principal and interest payment for this loan, assuming $100,000 at a fixed rate of 6% for 30 years is $599.55. The total payments are $215,838.44. The amount financed adjusts the loan amount by the costs for credit: origination fees, interim interest, and administrative fees.

TABLE 11.2   APR Amount Financed

Item	Amount	Adjust for APR
Loan Amount	$100,000	$100,000
Origination Fee 2%	$2,000	−$2,000
Interim Interest	$1,000	−$1,000
Administrative Fee	$275	−$275
Title Fees	$525	$0
Attorney Fees	$500	$0
Recording Fees	$85	$0
Amount financed (for APR calculation)		$96,725

Fees that would be paid even if this were a cash transaction (title fees, attorney fees, recording fees) are not deducted. The amount financed comes to $96,725. The APR—the rate at which $96,725 results in a monthly payment of $599.55 is 6.30%. To check, use a monthly payment calculator, using $96,725 as the mortgage amount and 6.30% at the rate for 30 years, and you will get a monthly payment of about $599.

Using these examples, Table 11.3 shows the completed Truth in Lending Disclosure.

The Truth in Lending Disclosure also details the insurances required, monthly payments, late charges, prepayment penalty, and the borrower's ability to have someone else assume the mortgage. The disclosure also specifies whether the loan is an adjustable-rate or whether a balloon payment is part of the loan. The Truth in Lending Disclosure specifically states

TABLE 11.3   Truth in Lending Disclosure

Annual Percentage Rate	Finance Charge	Amount Financed	Total of Payments
The cost of your credit as a yearly rate.	The dollar amount the credit will cost you.	The amount of credit provided to you or on your behalf.	The amount you will have paid after you have made all payments as scheduled.
6.303%	$119,113.44	$96,725.00	$215,838.44

that the borrower is giving a security interest in the property. Borrower and co-borrower must both sign the disclosure statement.

Final Touches

If the company you work with has automated systems, there are probably only a few steps you need to take to print the set of documents that comprise the loan package. If your company deals in more than one state, know that each state has its own regulations governing mortgage transactions. Know what they are and be responsible for getting all loan submission documentation signed. In the case of automated systems, the information you enter from the 1003 forms the basis for all the other forms—so again, accuracy and completeness are very important. This section gives you an overview of the content and purpose of those forms.

In addition, for conforming loans, it makes sense to run the package through one of the automated underwriting systems provided by Fannie Mae, Freddie Mac, or third parties. While rules vary slightly, it is an excellent way to red flag any underwriting issues and to resolve them before submitting the package for approval.

1003 Section VII. Details of Transaction. Now that the Good Faith Estimate is complete, there is one more section of the 1003, shown in Figure 11.8, which you must revisit before it is complete and ready for the borrower's signature.

Affidavit of Occupancy. This form affirms whether the borrower intends the subject property to be a primary residence, secondary residence, or investment property.

Anti-Coercion Statement Disclosure. This tells the borrower that a lender cannot dictate who the insurance provider will be.

Fair Credit Reporting Disclosure. This document says that you will order a credit report and the results will be available to the borrower. It

VII. DETAILS OF TRANSACTION	
a. Purchase price	$
b. Alterations, improvements, repairs	
c. Land (if acquired separately)	
d. Refinance (incl. debts to be paid off)	
e. Estimated prepaid items	
f. Estimated closing costs	
g. PMI, MIP, Funding Fee	
h. Discount (if Borrower will pay)	
i. Total costs (add items a through h)	

VII. DETAILS OF TRANSACTION	
j. Subordinate financing	
k. Borrower's closing costs paid by Seller	
i. Other Credits (explain)	
m. Loan amount (exclude PMI, MIP, Funding Fee financed)	
n. PMI, MIP, Funding Fee financed	
o. Loan amount (add m & n)	
p. Cash from/to Borrower (subtract j, k, l & o from i)	

FIGURE 11.8   1003 Section VII Details of Transaction

also specifies the borrower's right to information regarding credit reports that result in credit denial.

FHA Loan Disclosure (if applicable). This form describes the interest policy on prepaid FHA loans.

Government Loan Disclosure (if applicable). This disclosure tells the borrower his rights under federal Right to Financial Privacy Act of 1978 and advises him that HUD has a right to access his information.

Servicing Disclosure Statement. It explains RESPA requirements for notification to the borrower if the broker or lender transfers servicing rights. It also outlines how to resolve complaints and states the lender's estimate of the likelihood that it will transfer servicing rights, based on the lender's capabilities and past performance.

Mortgage Loan Originator Agreement. This is a disclosure and agreement between the borrower and broker/originator regarding the relationship between originator and lenders, and the ways in which broker compensation may be paid by the lender, the borrower or both.

Borrower's Certification. The borrower certifies that he has applied for a loan and knows it is a crime to provide false statements.

Borrower's Authorization to Release Information. It informs third parties that the borrower grants the broker or lender the right to obtain information regarding assets, employment, income, credit, tax returns, and so forth.

Borrower Signature Authorization. With this document the borrower authorizes the lender to verify information regarding employment, income, assets, and credit for the purpose of processing the loan application.

Equal Credit Opportunity Act. This is a disclosure to the borrower that creditors cannot discriminate based on race, color, religion, national origin, sex, marital status, or age. It also informs the borrower that alimony and child support income do not have to be disclosed for loan purposes.

Housing Financial Discrimination Act of 1977 Fair Lending Notice. This notifies the borrower that lenders may not discriminate based on neighborhood characteristics or trends, race, color, religion, sex, marital status, or national origin or ancestry.

Private Mortgage Insurance Disclosure. If the loan requires PMI, this disclosure explains that PMI protects lenders against default. It says that under some circumstances PMI will automatically terminate and that in some cases the borrower has the right to cancel PMI.

Notice to Applicant of Right to Receive Copy of Appraisal Report. This notifies the borrower of his right to receive a copy of the appraisal, and specifies procedures for requesting the copy.

Flood Disaster Protection Act of 1973. This is an acknowledgement by the borrower that flood insurance may be required, and that if so, he will pay it.

Notice to Home Loan Applicant Credit Score Disclosure. This notifies the borrower which credit agencies reported scores used for the application, what the scores were, and what key factors each indicated affected their scoring.

Privacy Policy Disclosure. This explains the originator's information privacy policy, what information may be gathered, and with whom it may be shared. It provides the borrower with the opportunity to opt out of certain information sharing policies and promotions and/or sales of other products and services.

Tax Information Authorization (Federal Form 8821). This is an authorization by the borrower for the IRS to make available tax records to the lender.

Request for Transcript of Tax Return (Form 4506-T). This signed form authorizes the IRS to provide transcripts of the borrower's tax returns.

Application Fee Disclosure Agreement. This is a statement by the borrower agreeing to pay the application fee. It also specifies the terms under which the originator will credit or refund the fee.

Agreement Concerning Nonrefundability of Advance Fees. (CT). This spells out for the borrower what fees will not be refunded if the borrower withdraws the application or is denied credit. The application fee, appraisal fees, and credit report fees are typically named.

Interest Rate Disclosure. This details the terms of the proposed loan and the borrower's decision to request a rate lock or allow the stated rate to float.

Information About Procedures for Opening a New Mortgage Loan Account. This document discloses the information about the borrower that is collected under the USA Patriot Act. The information includes name, address, date of birth, and other identifying information.

Certification of Identity. This is a statement by the originator that he collected the information required under the USA Patriot Act.

Notices to Mortgage Loan Applicants. This is a collection of other statements and disclosures including notification that the application package is not a loan commitment.

Dos and Don'ts While Loan Is in Progress. This form is not legally required, but it spells out actions that can impact the loan's approval. Signature indicates notification to the borrower.

Automated Underwriting

Fannie Mae (and Freddie Mac) provides comprehensive Findings documents following a run through of an application for a conforming loan. The automated underwriting systems provide immediate feedback on loan risk acceptability, eligibility requirements, and guidelines for changes in interest rates.

Most importantly, they specify the verifications required and the conditions the borrower must meet for approval. This gives the borrower a task list of things to do to bring the loan to closing. It tells you when the loan must close for the application to remain valid. It tells you also:

- That mortgage insurance is or is not required.
- What income verification documentation is required.
- Rental income documentation required, if applicable.
- The amount of assets that must be verified.

- The nature of the verification of assets required (bank deposits or statements, explanation of large deposits, source of funds for down-payments on a purchase).

- Whether the borrower(s) qualifies as a first-time homebuyer.

- Any other conditions the borrower must meet before the loan qualifies as conforming.

Request for Documentation

In order to complete the loan package documents, you would have had to ask the borrower to look for particular documents (for example, mortgage statements or bank statements). There are other documents to include with the loan package, and before you meet the client for signatures, it is a good idea to give the borrower a list of items to have prepared for you to take with you.

Some of the standard documents you will collect at the go-back are:

Last month of pay stubs or social security or retirement award statements.

Last two years of W-2s (if employed) and/or tax returns.

Three months of bank statements.

Last quarter 401(k) or other retirement statements.

Copy of driver's license, green card or social security card.

Current mortgage statement.

Copy of mortgage note and addendum.

Application fee.

For buyers or owners of rental property, lease or rental agreements and mortgage statements, and if not on the mortgage statement, insurance and tax payment documentation.

Court orders or divorce decrees if alimony and/or child support is paid or is received and included as income in the application.

Bankruptcy and/or foreclosure documents if discharged or filed in last four years.

Note and mortgage statement for second mortgage, HELOC, or home equity loan.

For a purchase, the sales contract and copy of initial deposit.

Cancelled rent checks for last twelve months if borrowers have been renting.

If self-employed, year-to-date profit and loss statement, business tax returns for last two years, accountant letter or business license proving two full years of self-employment.

Making It Official

You have done everything you need to do at this point. You have meticulously completed the forms for the go-back package, you have requested the documentation for the borrower to provide, and you have confirmed your appointment with the borrower to review and sign the documents and give you the application fee. Minimize the calls to the client immediately prior to the go-back to avoid the opportunity for them to cancel. All that is left at this stage is to conduct the go-back.

If you conduct the go-back in person (and I recommend that you do, if possible), it may be the first time you meet the client face to face. Whether you review the documents in person or over the phone, consider it another opportunity—and a key one—to establish yourself as a competent, committed professional in the eyes of the client.

The most important thing on the go-back is to be on time and to have what you need to complete the transaction. Map out your directions in advance. Getting lost is no excuse for not being on time. Leave extra time for peak periods during the day—the rush-hour traffic does not excuse tardiness. If you are going to more than one go-back on the same day, plan your time to not rush, and map out your route in advance. Have the contact information of all the borrowers you will be seeing handy with you.

Dress professionally—you will be entering someone's home or business, and you should show respect by dressing appropriately, arriving on time, and being professional.

Go Back Presentation Script

Hi, Mr./Mrs. _____, my name is _____ from _____. My job tonight is to gather some documents and signatures and go over a few disclosures and to leave you a package on everything you have signed. My intention is to complete this process in no more than 15 minutes. If for any reason you have a few questions, which sometimes clients do, I or my manager, _____, will be available tomorrow morning. Our intention is to make this process easy and comfortable, and with no surprises. Unless they are good surprises! Okay, great.

The first thing I am going to need is the documents I asked you to gather. Where are they? Great.

Review each document, and attach supporting documentation. Do not make a major deal of it if documents are missing, but ask for them, and if it is possible to get them on this visit, do so.

Great! The next thing we will do is get your signatures on a few documents. I'll briefly go over each form, and you'll be getting a copy of everything you sign. The first form is _____.

Brief the borrower on each form and disclosure and have him sign and initial where indicated. Co-borrowers must do the same. If there are any changes requested by the client, just cross out the error, handwrite the correction, and have the borrowers sign their initials where the change was made. Don't make a big deal out of anything. Corrections are good—it means potential delays and problems have been eliminated.

Always be polite. Don't be afraid to say, "I don't know" even when you do know. Remember, the goal is to complete the process thoroughly in fifteen minutes. If you are there longer, you are probably talking about things that don't make a difference. You can be charming, personable and efficient, and professional. Those are the characteristics of the high-income mortgage originator.

After the process is complete, leave the borrower a copy of the documents he signed. Let him know that he will receive all original documents and the appraisal at the closing. Also let him know that in the next day or so an appraiser will contact him to schedule a time to do the inspection. Let him know that it is very important that he schedule it as soon as possible because you need it to submit the loan to a lender for approval. Explain also that often lenders make conditional approvals, which means that you may request additional documentation. If so, let him know it is important that he respond quickly. Finally, thank the borrower for the opportunity to do business with him and let him know you will be talking again shortly.

Upon returning to the office with a go-back package, update all asset, liability, and income data, make any necessary corrections based on the documentation, order the appraisal, lock the rate if appropriate, and turn the file over to a file processor.

When It Doesn't Go According to Plan

On occasion, you will have a client who gets upset and wants to back out. If the client is inappropriate with you or is upset with the process, attempt to support him to continue the process, but do not force the issue. If the client does not want to move forward, close the file, do not leave any documentation at the home, and tell him that you and your manager will contact him the next day. Let the client know that if he cannot resolve the issue with the manager, you will just withdraw the file and close it out. Remember that regardless of how it turns out you want the client to have a good experience with the process.

Tracking

Keeping statistics on go-backs allows you to look at whether the process for setting up the appointment and preparing the client is working, and if not, where adjustments should be made. We use the Go-Back Assessment Form (Figure 11.9) to record a few key facts.

Each of the questions on the assessment refers back to a specific point that should have been made in the proposal call (and in some cases, earlier calls as well) to prepare the client for the go-back. Promptness, preparedness, and readiness for the application fee are all related to specific points that were supposed to be made. If the client was not prompt,

---

Go-Back Assessment Form

Client Name: File Number:

Originator:

Scheduled date and time for appointment:

Arrival time: Departure time: Total time:

Was the client on time?

Was the client prepared?

Did the client appear concerned?

Did the client appear apprehensive?

Did the client have many questions?

Did the client know about the application fee in advance, and was he prepared to pay it?

Additional comments and notes:

Next actions:

FIGURE 11.9 Go-Back Assessment Form

prepared, and ready to pay the fee, you know that you did not get those points across in your proposal call. It may well be that you said what you were supposed to say, but the point did not get across.

It may not seem like a big deal—after all, what difference does starting a few minutes late make? It makes an impression (and not a favorable one) regarding the level of commitment and professionalism. What difference does it make if the client didn't have all the paperwork ready or available—they are going to get it all within a day or so anyway. Again, it's not about the promptness or the paperwork in and of itself—it is a red flag about the level of commitment the client has to the loan. Is it a serious problem? It will be unless you take corrective action. Use it as an opportunity to present once again for the borrower the reason he is doing the loan—the difference that having the loan is going to make for him financially. In other words, keep enrolling him into his vision for what the loan will provide. Being late or unprepared indicates faltering enrollment—he has lost sight of that vision. Knowing that, you can have the enrollment conversation to get him back into committed action.

Concerns and apprehensions on the part of clients are usually a reflection of a loss of confidence—in you. If you have doubts about your ability to make the difference with clients, they will sense it. If you try to push them or force them, rather than enroll them, they will resist and have a right to be concerned. Use the results of these questions to inform yourself of what actions you need to take to rid yourself of concerns and to practice the enrollment conversations you need to master to be a high-income mortgage originator.

Rate the client's commitment using the three-level scale. Is the client still eager to go ahead (Level 1)? Or is she now more cautious and questioning (Level 2)? Or is she resisting your advice on how to move forward (Level 3)?

If you think the client is a Level 3, you must address the relationship before you move on. Can the deal go forward? Yes. But unless you take care of the commitment level at this stage, you stand a higher than average likelihood that the deal will fall apart further along in the process, after you (and others in the process) have invested even more time, and possibly money.

Use the results to inform yourself about where you can improve your performance, efficiency, and enrollment skills. You aren't going to do things perfectly all the time. If you can objectively evaluate your performance via the results, you can learn, you can develop, and you can improve—you can be a high-income mortgage originator.

CHAPTER TWELVE

Brokers and Lenders: Identifying and Serving Their Needs

Your work, if you did it as you were supposed to, is done. Your loan is ready for processing. At this point you turn it over to the capable and competent hands of many other mortgage professionals who have a part in guiding the loan through to closing. File processors, underwriters, closing specialists, and attorneys each play a major role in reaching the following milestones remaining in the loan process:

Submission. The broker or file processor makes sure all documentation is complete and submits the file to an underwriter.

Approval. The underwriter evaluates the loan and approves it for closing. He may stipulate that the approval is conditional upon certain requirements being met and will specify what they are. Additional documentation may be required. The file processors and closing specialists prepare for and schedule the closing.

Scheduled. The closing is scheduled with the borrower, closing agent (usually an attorney), and in the case of a purchase, the seller's representatives.

Closed. The closing is the official carrying out of the transaction where all final documents are signed, title transfers take place, and monies are settled. Once the closing takes place, there is a three-day waiting

TABLE 12.1   In-Process Tracking Sheet

Client Name	Go Back Date	Appraisal Date	Lock Exp. Date	Submit Date	Approval Date	Closing Schedule Date	Closed Date	CRM Set Up

period (during which the client can withdraw) before the funds for the loan are distributed.

Although you may have completed the bulk of your work, you have a very heavy interest in observing these processes. If you missed anything in the steps leading up to this point, you will be called in to set things right. You won't receive your commission until the loan is closed and funded, so keep watching, keep track, and stay in communication. Table 12.1 provides a simple tracking sheet for you to use.

Processing to Submission

Set up a system to track your loan's progress through submission, approval, and closing. You will receive your commissions following the closing and funding of the loan, so it is important for you to know when all your hard work is going to pay off for you.

Within two business days of the go-back, submit the completed, corrected, and up-to-date file documents to the file processor who will *register* the loan with the lender. This puts the lender on notice that a file is pending submission. If a rate lock is needed and you haven't requested it yet, this is the time to do it.

The file processor checks the file for completeness and accuracy, and assures that the documents are organized according to a preestablished convention. Certain documents are attached to the left side of the folder in a particular order, and certain documents are attached to the right side of the folder, also in a particular order. Extra documents may be included but usually are turned face down, so that anyone handling the file knows they are nonessential. Instructions for file organization may be different for conforming loans than for nonconforming loans.

Table 12.2 shows examples of file preparation instructions for nonconforming and conforming loans. Your file processor has something similar—it is in your best interest to find out what the requirements are and adhere to them faithfully.

Remember, you may not think it is a big deal if one or two items are out of order, but for the file processor who has to deal with you and all your mortgage-originating colleagues, and who has to verify the completeness of the file, order is essential to the smooth flow of files to lenders.

The file processor reviews the file and makes sure all paperwork requested for the initial underwriting is included and properly organized. The file is held pending receipt of the appraisal. When the appraisal arrives, the file processor uses the valuation and real estate tax data it contains to recompute LTV and DTI ratios to ensure that they still meet the guidelines of the loan product proposed. If he has access to an automated underwriting system, the file processor may run the application through it using the new appraisal information.

Low Appraisals

On occasion the appraisal results in new LTV and DTI ratios that leave the borrower unqualified for the loan product as proposed and agreed upon. If this is the case, the file processor notifies you, and you go back and talk with the borrower. This conversation is very important. You will either retain the client's trust, or you will lose the deal. It all depends on how enrolling you are in the conversation. Remember, back in Chapter 9 we said it was important to include in your proposal conversation the fact that nothing was final until the appraisal came in. If you had that

TABLE 12.2 File Document Organization

Nonconforming Loans	
Outside Cover	
1. Loan Submission Sheet	

Inside Cover (Left side) Top to Bottom	Right Side Top to Bottom
1. Commission Report	1. Nonconform Prequal/Pricing Sheet
2. Mortgage Statement	2. Credit Report
3. Application Fee	3. Original 1003 signed
4. Request for Appraisal	4. Good Faith Estimate signed
5. Go-Back Disclosures	5. Truth in Lending signed
	6. Add'l docs per lender pricing sheet

Conforming Loans	
Outside Cover	
1. Loan Submission Sheet	

Inside Left Cover, top to bottom	Right Side, top to bottom
1. Lock Confirmation and Request, rate sheet	1. Final Checklist and Commission Report
2. Application Fee and Appraisal Fee	2. DO, DU or LP findings (File Mgr)
3. Request for Appraisal & Confirmation	3. Tri-merged credit report
4. Mortgage Statements	4. Program Guidelines
5. Disclosure Notices	5. Signed Application, Good Faith Estimate and Truth in Lending
	6. Last month of pay stubs
	7. Last 2 years W-2's, all borrowers
	8. Last 2 years Tax returns, all borrowers
	9. Last 3 month Bank Asset Statements
	10. Quarterly Statements for Retirement Accts, IRA, 401(k), etc.
	11. Misc. (contracts, divorce decrees, leases, bankruptcy papers, business license)
	12. Other Misc.
	13. Appraisal
	14. Signed Disclosures

Note: Any additional paperwork not required on initial submission is to be turned **face down** at the bottom of the left hand side of the file.

conversation with the client, you have something you can reference back to. If you didn't, you have some explaining to do.

In either case, prepare some good news to go along with the bad news you are going to deliver to the client. Before you call, be sure to compare the agreed-upon loan parameters with the difference the appraisal caused. Usually it is a matter of increase in interest rate, or points or down-payment, or some additional documentation. Remember the secret formula to an effective sales call: Bad news, good news, I can solve your problem.

Chances are that even with a less favorable appraisal than expected, the borrower will still be better off than in the do-nothing scenario for a refinance.

In the case of a purchase where the appraisal comes in lower than anticipated, there are a few options. The buyer and seller can negotiate a new price, the buyer can borrow less by making a larger down-payment to keep the LTV at the desired level, or the appraisal can be disputed if there is evidence that the comparable properties are questionably comparable.

Next Steps

The file processor updates the 1003 with the appraisal information, reprints the 1003, Good Faith Estimate and Truth in Lending documents, and adds them to the file with the appraisal and with the signed versions of those documents.

The file then goes to the closing department for initial submission to the lender. Most closing specialists also check the file before submitting it to the lender. Closing specialists have good working relationships with lenders and understand the submission processes and demands unique to each lender. Closing specialists are the liaison between you and the lender at this point. Do what they ask, when they ask, the way they ask you to do it.

When asked what advice they would give to mortgage originators, both a file processor and closing specialist said without hesitation that attention to detail on the 1003 was the single most important element to a successful closing and a satisfied customer. Both cited example after example where discrepancies, omissions, and errors caused delays, ill will, denials, and withdrawals.

Among the most common pitfalls and mistakes are the following:

- The borrower is not fully vested in his 401(k) or other retirement assets, so their value toward reserves is diminished.

- The mortgage originator repeatedly goes back to the borrower for requests for additional documentation and information. Eventually the borrower stops returning calls and pulls out of the deal altogether.

- Verification of employment reveals that continued steady employment is questionable.

- The borrower cannot prove enough income based on earnings records.

- The borrower cannot prove where the assets came from.

Submission to Approval

Many wholesale lenders have automated submission processes that allow the capture of application information, sometimes seamlessly from automated application systems, and go directly and immediately into automated underwriting systems. Approval can be immediate.

Underwriters have the ultimate decision-making power to approve or deny a loan, or to set conditions that must be met for the loan to close. The underwriter verifies that the loan application complies with all of the guidelines required for the selected loan product.

Even with lenders using automated underwriting systems, there is still a human element that comes into play in many cases. While the computer makes a decision based on the information on the loan application, the underwriter makes sure all supporting documentation is included and agrees with the information on the 1003. If anything is missing or if the documentation brings up questions or discrepancies, your loan is delayed until the documents are straightened out, or the loan is denied or resubmitted. Delays are unnecessary. Do what you should do, the way you should do it, when you should do it. The last thing you want to do is go back to a borrower who is anxiously awaiting a decision to let him know the process has ground to a halt waiting for him to provide different or additional documentation. It can damage or destroy the goodwill and trust you worked so hard to build up to this point.

Conditions to Close

Underwriters often impose *conditions to close* as part of the approval. This is also known as an approval *with stipulations*. The conditions or stipulations must be met to the underwriter's satisfaction before the loan is *cleared to close*. At this point you may have to go back to the client with a request for additional information, but at least you have the good news that the loan has been approved, and can close once the documentation is provided.

Closing specialists say the biggest problem they have is chasing down mortgage originators who need to chase down clients for additional documentation. As a mortgage originator and a professional colleague, keep the closing department informed of your actions to obtain the needed documentation. Let them know you called and left a message, even if you were unable to reach the client. Let them know the client told you it would take a couple of days to find the needed documents. Let them know the information will be faxed, or is in the mail. Not only does this communication let the closing department know you are on top of things, it keeps you on top of things knowing that you have to communicate some activity every day until the issue is resolved.

Compensating Factors

With your understanding of the concerns that underwriters address, you can present your borrower's case in the best possible light, even if everything is not perfect.

Will the borrower be able to pay?

Will the property retain sufficient value to secure the loan?

Can the loan be sold on the secondary market and/or for servicing?

Regardless of the guidelines that govern an underwriter's assessment, and regardless of the programming with which automated underwriting systems determine approval or denial, underwriting is not a black or white affair. If there is one weak ratio or unmet criterion, the borrower may compensate for it with very strong criteria in three other areas. In spite of Fannie Mae back end ratio limits of 36%, people with ratios as high as 60% have been approved for Fannie Mae loans, because they had extremely high credit scores, had been employed at their current job for a very long time, and had assets substantially above the required reserves.

The Account Exec–Your New Best Friend

Relationships between originators, brokers, and lenders are obviously very important. A managing loan specialist broker said his business goes to the account executive (AE), not the lender; if the AE moved from one lender to another, the broker's business went with him. The manager explained that a good AE knows the ins and outs of the lender's processes and systems, and often can suggest ways to use the systems to the best advantage. Very often, particularly with borderline cases or where approval criteria are marginal, a savvy AE can tell you what is needed to get the approval. He can, in some cases, also negotiate the conditional approval if the conditions as specified cannot be met. A good account executive greases the skids, saving you and the borrower delay and aggravation.

Use all of your knowledge of the industry and the concerns and responsibilities of each of the players to present your borrower's circumstances in the best possible light. Going that extra step is the difference between just doing a job and being a high-income mortgage originator.

Approval to Close

Upon receipt of an approval or a conditional approval, the closing department returns the file to you. Review the approval, and check that the pricing and terms of the loan are consistent with the original documents.

The closing department returns to you the conditions to satisfy before the loan can be cleared to close. Get on the phone, and start hunting these items down. The longer you delay, the longer it will be until you get paid. Keep the closing department apprised of all your efforts and progress to satisfy the conditions. Be sure to reference the file in a way they will recognize (file numbers, client names). When *all* conditions have been satisfied, return the file to the closing department. *Do not do this piecemeal!* You will drive everyone—the closing specialist, the borrower, the lender, and yourself—nuts.

The closing department forwards all documentation to meet the conditions for closing to the lender. If any other conditions arise, the lender notifies the closing department, and the cycle repeats.

Upon final approval and sign off on the conditions by the lender, the lender *clears the loan for closing*. Your closing specialist orders the title, payoff, and insurance information needed for the closing. Closing specialists appreciate a mortgage originator who provides complete and accurate contact information for payoff of the existing mortgage and for the insurance company. Take the extra few minutes before submitting the loan to know that the names and phone numbers you provide for these items are accurate. The closing department does everything it can do to get your loan closed as quickly as possible, and to get the cash flowing into the borrower's hands, the company's hands, and your hands. Do your job. Get the information they need before they need it.

The closing specialist coordinates the date, time, and place of closing with the attorney and borrower, and informs you as well. At that time, the closing specialist also provides the Settlement Statement to you. Compare the HUD-1 Settlement Statement to the Good Faith Estimate. Promptly communicate any discrepancies, particularly with respect to money needed to bring to the closing, or proceeds from the closing going to the borrower. The worst thing you can do is have your client arrive at a closing unprepared for the closing requirements. It destroys relationships faster than anything and is the single biggest reason borrowers refuse to close. And it's all avoidable.

Verification of Employment (VOE)

Very close to the closing, the lender requests a verification of employment. The form (Fannie Mae Form 1005) asks not only for current employment and earnings information, but for projected earnings and pay raise history. If overtime or bonuses are included in the application as sources of income, the VOE will confirm, by the employer's estimates, whether their continuance is likely. In addition, projected salary increase is asked, as well as last increase, indicating a trend to the lender.

The form also asks if the employee was off from work for any length of time. If the answer is yes, then it could explain year-to-date earnings indicated on pay stubs being lower than declared income. It can also create trouble, as in the case of a construction worker who failed to disclose a back injury that had kept him out of work for months. While still employed under workman's compensation, the likelihood of retaining a steady income source in that line of work was not adequate for the lender to approve the loan. Consider yourself forewarned—and be forearmed to ask the questions of your borrower before you get to this point in the process.

Prepare Your Client for Closing

Once your client's loan has been cleared to close and the closing is scheduled, it is time for you to make sure your client is fully aware of what will take place. Of particular importance is any money the client may need to bring to the closing. If funds are required, and the borrower does not have them available, the closing cannot be completed.

Also, let the borrower know that any funds they are expecting to receive at the closing will not be available until three business days later, as required by the Consumer Protection Act's *right of rescission* period during which the borrower can cancel the transaction. Again, borrowers who are expecting to cash a check the same day will be disappointed if they walk out of the closing empty-handed. All you have to do it make sure they know what to expect.

Keeping Track

With only one or two loans in the pipeline you don't need much in the form of reminders or support structures to keep you on top of what you need to do for each file. However, when you start building the volume of your business, it is very important that you establish a way to track where each file is, what the appropriate next action is, and when to take it. Failure to follow up is a terrible and costly mistake. Every delay is an opportunity for the deal to fall through, and letting things fall through the cracks is like leaving money on the table. Worse, you miss the opportunity to build your base of satisfied customers.

Table 12.3 is a bird's eye view of your files in the pipeline. Refer to it daily and keep track of your activities as you move the file from one stage to another.

If you update this chart daily and refer to it, you will be able to see clearly which files need action on your part. You can move a file from

TABLE 12.3　Closing Activity Tracking

Client	In Process	Submitted	Approved	Conditions	Cleared	Scheduled	Closed	Notes

"In Process" to "Closed" within two weeks without working hard at all. If files are taking longer than that, look at the results to inform you about which processes and preparations you can improve. The longer files hang around, the less time you have to turn your attention to taking care of past customers and building your client base. Moving files quickly and efficiently is the hallmark of a high-income mortgage originator.

CHAPTER THIRTEEN

The Wrap Up: Closing the Loan

You are in the final stretch toward the closing. With the assistance of file processors and closing specialists, your client's attorney should have everything he needs to conduct the closing to everyone's satisfaction. Once again, if you have prepared your client properly, there will be no surprises at the closing. If you have kept him informed and repeatedly assessed and responded to his commitment level, there is no reason for him not to move forward.

Many of the documents signed at the closing are the same or similar disclosures, notifications, and acknowledgements that the borrower signed at the go-back. This chapter quickly reviews the closing documents, and focuses on those that are new or different at this signing so that you can effectively prepare your client for the closing.

Preparing Your Client for the Closing

The client needs to know where and when the closing will take place, how much money he needs to bring to the closing (and what forms of payment are acceptable), and how much, if any, money he will get when the rescission period expires. If there are any outstanding documents that are part of the conditions for closing, it is your job to make sure the client has them at the closing.

This is a time of excitement and possible anxiety for your client. When you speak with him, listen for and assess his level of commitment. Is he excited and open (Level 1); cautiously optimistic (Level 2); or anxious, doubtful, and resistant (Level 3)? This is another opportunity to remind him of the benefits that will come from the mortgage, and to shift the Level 3 to a Level 2. Take the time to address any concerns now, before the closing.

HUD-1 Settlement Statement Preparation

The HUD-1 Settlement Statement is the final financial reckoning for the loan transaction. The closing attorney (who charges a document preparation fee) prepares it and makes it available for review 24 hours before the closing.

All fees, charges, costs, and disbursements are recorded in this one document. As with the Good Faith Estimate, the HUD-1 lists itemized costs and fees within groupings and with standard item numbers. (Refer back to Chapter 10 if you have questions about that portion of the HUD-1.) The charges should not be significantly different between the Good Faith Estimate and the HUD-1 Settlement Statement. If they are, inform the client as quickly as possible and explain the reason for the differences.

The HUD-1 also includes a cover page that summarizes the payoffs of other loans and debt, and adjustments between buyer and seller in a purchase transaction. Figure 13.1 illustrates.

Section 100 Gross Amount Due From Borrower. This section includes the purchase price of the property (purchase only) and the price of any personal property (fixtures, furniture, etc.) that are included with the sale. The total of the settlement charges (itemized on the next page of the HUD, in agreement with the GFE), and a list of debts and loans to be paid off are stated here. Adjustments for items the seller paid in advance (for example, fuel, taxes) are included in this section as well.

A. **Settlement Statement**	**U.S. Department of Housing and Urban Development**	OMB Approval No. 2502-0265 (expires 11/30/2009)

B. Type of Loan

1. ☐ FHA 2. ☐ FmHA 3. ☐ Conv. Unins. 4. ☐ VA 5. ☐ Conv. Ins.	6. File Number:	7. Loan Number:	8. Mortgage Insurance Case Number:

C. Note: This form is furnished to give you a statement of actual settlement costs. Amounts paid to and by the settlement agent are shown. Items marked "(p.o.c.)" were paid outside the closing; they are shown here for informational purposes and are not included in the totals.

D. Name & Address of Borrower:	E. Name & Address of Seller:	F. Name & Address of Lender:

| G. Property Location: | H. Settlement Agent: | |
| | Place of Settlement: | I. Settlement Date: |

J. Summary of Borrower's Transaction		**K. Summary of Seller's Transaction**	
100. Gross Amount Due From Borrower		**400. Gross Amount Due To Seller**	
101. Contract sales price		401. Contract sales price	
102. Personal property		402. Personal property	
103. Settlement charges to borrower (line 1400)		403.	
104.		404.	
105.		405.	
Adjustments for items paid by seller in advance		**Adjustments for items paid by seller in advance**	
106. City/town taxes to		406. City/town taxes to	
107. County taxes to		407. County taxes to	
108. Assessments to		408. Assessments to	
109.		409.	
110.		410.	
111.		411.	
112.		412.	
120. Gross Amount Due From Borrower		**420. Gross Amount Due To Seller**	
200. Amounts Paid By Or In Behalf Of Borrower		**500. Reductions In Amount Due To Seller**	
201. Deposit or earnest money		501. Excess deposit (see instructions)	
202. Principal amount of new loan(s)		502. Settlement charges to seller (line 1400)	
203. Existing loan(s) taken subject to		503. Existing loan(s) taken subject to	
204.		504. Payoff of first mortgage loan	
205.		505. Payoff of second mortgage loan	
206.		506.	
207.		507.	
208.		508.	
209.		509.	
Adjustments for items unpaid by seller		**Adjustments for items unpaid by seller**	
210. City/town taxes to		510. City/town taxes to	
211. County taxes to		511. County taxes to	
212. Assessments to		512. Assessments to	
213.		513.	
214.		514.	
215.		515.	
216.		516.	
217.		517.	
218.		518.	
219.		519.	
220. Total Paid By/For Borrower		**520. Total Reduction Amount Due Seller**	
300. Cash At Settlement From/To Borrower		**600. Cash At Settlement To/From Seller**	
301. Gross Amount due from borrower (line 120)		601. Gross amount due to seller (line 420)	
302. Less amounts paid by/for borrower (line 220)	( )	602. Less reductions in amt. due seller (line 520)	( )
303. Cash ☐ From ☐ To Borrower		**603. Cash** ☐ To ☐ From Seller	

FIGURE 13.1   HUD-1 Settlement Statement

Section 200 Amounts Paid By Or In Behalf Of Borrower. The principal amount of the new loan is recorded here, and credits for items unpaid by the seller (for example, taxes) are listed here as well.

Section 300 Cash At Settlement From/To Borrower. This reconciles the amounts in Sections 100 and 200. If the amounts paid into the transaction (loan amount, etc.) exceed the gross amount due from the borrower, this section will show cash due to the borrower, otherwise it will show the amount of money the borrower has to bring to the closing.

Section 400 Gross Amount Due To Seller. This shows the transaction from the seller's point of view. The purchase price of the property plus personal property included in the transaction are shown. If the seller is paying off debt, it would be listed here too, as would adjustments for items the seller paid in advance. For a refinance, this section is empty.

Section 500 Reductions In Amount Due To Seller. This section contains the offsetting entries to Section 200, Amounts Paid By Or In Behalf of Borrower. If the borrower is given credit for these items (taxes, for example), then the seller will pay this amount or count it as a deduction from sums payable to the seller.

Section 600 Cash At Settlement To/From Seller. Similar to Section 300 Cash At Settlement From/To Borrower, this section shows how much money the seller will bring to the closing or receive in cash proceeds after funding.

Preparing Your Client for the Closing

Why is this information important to you? Because if you are uncertain when you call your client to prepare her for the closing, you will create uncertainty, doubt, concern, and possible mistrust at the moment the client is going to take final action on one of the most important financial decisions she will make in her lifetime. That's the only reason. Your job is to make sure the client is comfortable in her understanding of the costs and the money she is getting or paying at the closing. The only reason a borrower will pull out at this point is if she is unpleasantly surprised. Your job is to avoid the surprises, and to keep reminding the client of the difference the mortgage is going to make for her.

Just because you go through the numbers with the client, doesn't mean she is comfortable or understands. Sarah, a closing specialist, has saved many a deal that fell apart at or immediately following the closing. She says, "For many borrowers, the events leading up the closing are stressful. If there were some bumps along the way, or the originator had to go back for additional documentation a lot of times, the borrowers' nerves get frazzled, and they stop listening. They think they hear or know what is going on, but they may not have it right. In spite of the fact that the originator and attorney both go over the Settlement Statement, some borrowers are unprepared or unhappy with what they think the numbers say. When a deal falls apart at this point, there is a lot of emotion. I'm able to get the borrower on the phone and be an impartial listener and explainer of the facts and the numbers. I spend as much time as I need to with them until they understand and their emotions no longer have the better of them. I always give them the option to pull out, but also remind them of why they got into this in the first place—the difference the mortgage is going to make for them. I've never lost a deal when I am able to get the client talking and listening. They always move forward. It should never get to this point if the originator prepares them properly from the beginning."

It is all enrollment. If you ever find yourself in a situation like this, be a fly on the wall as the closing specialist saves the deal. You will learn a lot about where your relationship with the client broke down.

Other Closing Documents

Any documents that include numbers involving closing costs may be adjusted from the go-back documents based on the information in the HUD-1. The Truth in Lending Disclosure is one such document. Other documents repeated from the go-back package are the 1003, Name Affidavit, Notice of Right to Cancel, Request for Taxpayer Identification Number and Certification, RESPA Servicing Disclosure, Affidavit of Occupancy, Borrower's Certification and Authorization, Privacy Notices, and Compliance Agreement.

The following additional documents are part of the closing package.

Mortgage Note. The formal agreement between the borrower and lender is spelled out in the Note. It includes the borrower's promise to pay, the rate of interest, time, place and amount of payments, charges the lender can levy if payment is overdue or defaulted, obligations of co-borrowers, and governing jurisdiction for the document.

Deed. This document spells out the lender's security interest in the property, including the right to foreclose and sell the property.

Payoff Letter. Typically this is a letter to the former mortgage lender that accompanies the check that will prepay the balance due on the old mortgage. If other loans are being paid from the proceeds, payoff letters are included for each. The letters request a written release of the lien, which the former lender is required to provide within 60 days.

First Payment Letter. This specifies the date and amount of the first payment, and includes payment coupons with payment instructions for the first several payments. This allows time for the servicing company to establish the account and send all necessary forms and documents to the borrower without interfering with the first few payments.

Loan Closing Disclosure Acknowledgement. This document has the borrower acknowledge that the loan process conformed with RESPA requirements, including Good Faith Estimate, Truth in Lending, no discrimination, servicing transfer notification rights, escrow requirements, insurance rights and obligations, and that the agreement is binding.

First Lien Letter. This notifies the lender that the closing has taken place and that the mortgage is a valid lien against the property.

Hazard Insurance Authorization and Requirements. This states the policies of the lender with regard to minimum insurance requirements and the lender's right to secure insurance (for which the borrower will pay) if the borrower fails to obtain or maintain adequate coverage.

Hold Harmless Mortgage Survey. This is a waiver of well/septic inspection and report and release of the lender from obligation or responsibility for the status of insulation.

Tax Information Sheet. This document lists the types and amounts of town, county, school, and other property-related taxes to be paid by the borrower.

Flood Insurance Notification. This document informs the borrower that the lender will monitor flood zone boundaries, and that if the property is or becomes part of a flood zone that flood insurance will be required. It authorizes the lender to obtain the insurance, and obligates the borrower to pay for it.

Hazard Insurance Information for a Refinanced Loan. This is notification to the borrower's insurance company of the new Mortgagee Clause information (for the new lender).

Show Me the Money

Loan closed, job done. It is time for you to get your compensation. How much will you make? It is up to you to know and understand the compensation plan your work falls under. Just as your clients don't like surprises at closing, you will not like an unpleasant surprise in your paycheck.

First, remember that your commission is probably not payable until after the loan is funded, which is three business days after closing. In addition, the company you work for may have a payment cut-off period, so if your loan misses it, your payment may take longer to show up in your paycheck.

Compensation plans are as varied as mortgage companies. They range from simple straight commissions, to minimum performance standards to qualify for commissions. There is no right or wrong compensation plan. It is up to you to know what your plan is and what you can do to maximize your income within its parameters.

Keep track of what your commissions should be on each loan that closes. When you receive your compensation, reconcile your records to the amount you received so you are clear that you understand and are responsible for your compensation. If you cannot reconcile the amounts, set up an appointment with the person who handles commission payments to have him walk you through the calculations until you are satisfied.

When you know your compensation plan and you have the experience of originating mortgages and guiding borrowers through closings, you have a good set of tools to map out your route to becoming a high-income mortgage originator. Start with how much you want to make. Don't worry that you may not see how it will be possible to achieve—if you don't start thinking big you will never become big.

You have been tracking your actions and results at every step. Start working backwards from the compensation on one loan and what it took to generate that, and then see what actions you would have to take to reach your financial goals. At some point you will see that it is physically impossible for you to do it on your own, operating the way you do now. If you continue to track and use the results you produce to inform you, you will see opportunities to operate differently to produce the results you want. You will have to be willing to let go of what you know for the sake of trying new things—in pursuit of your high-income goals. And, most likely, you will not be able to do it on your own. What I know is that it is much easier to reach new heights of success when you have a team, than it is on your own.

On your own you will eventually reach peak capacity. You will have to leverage yourself and depend on others to move beyond your top performance levels. The tools you have to manage yourself are designed for you to manage others with as well. Track and look at what the results tell you to boost performance. The next chapter looks at your options for advancement.

CHAPTER FOURTEEN

Next Steps toward Your Future

You've been through the whole loan cycle, congratulations! You're in business, originating mortgages. You're in control, tracking, measuring, following up with leads, prospects, and customers. Your days are varied and full of human interest and, with some perseverance and good habits, full of money and commissions.

You may already be wondering about the future Or, you may be basking in your accomplishments and may not be thinking yet about what comes next. It doesn't really matter where you are—there are career options available to you, especially if you have had some success, (which, if you have followed the practices in this book faithfully, you should).

Do you experience satisfaction, challenge, and reward as a mortgage originator? Whether the answer is yes or no, now that you have some experience, you can start to look around at the industry and the types of companies and positions that are open to you from a different perspective from what you had when you first began originating mortgages.

As you can see by what we've covered in the book, there is a lot to the mortgage business; it is not something you tackle lightly. You don't just go into mortgage origination to see how it turns out: There is a lot to learn, there is a lot to know. It takes a total commitment to succeed, and it takes years of experience to be able to be in your own business. My advice is to take two to three years working for a good company and getting yourself well-grounded before you open your own business.

This chapter looks at the pros and cons of going it alone, versus working for someone else, and provides questions to ask a prospective employer, should you choose that route.

Starting from Scratch

I'm a big supporter of entrepreneurship. I think being in business is the best way there is to make a very good living—and the most challenging. The United States Census Bureau reports that over half the businesses that employ people fail within five years. The most challenging part of launching a business is generating sales, and you now have a tremendous advantage over most people opening shop for the first time. But don't underestimate the amount of work, time, money, and uncertainty you have to deal with to launch and run a business. It is extremely difficult to do on your own. And as much as dealing with other people can be a headache, without a team you have to shoulder the entire burden, and at times it feels very heavy. If you are going to consider starting a brokerage firm, look for other people who will share the costs and the work to get it off the ground.

Start-Up Laundry List

You need a place to work. It can be a small office or a room in your home. You need a computer with Internet access and a printer, a phone, and a fax machine/copier. You need filing cabinets. You are already looking at a couple of thousand dollars of investment before you add office supplies, such as paper, ink and postage, or utilities such as electricity, heat, and air conditioning. If you want an Internet presence (and I recommend that you have one), you need a web site (add in more one-time and ongoing costs). And unless you want to hand write your applications, you need mortgage origination software and a subscription service to a credit agency to pull credit reports.

In some states, originators must register under a broker or lender. In others, they must be licensed. That means examinations (and fees). And if you set yourself up as a business entity with limited liability (also highly recommended), welcome to the world of tax-ID numbers, quarterly filings, and taxes just to operate a business. And find an accountant—when the time comes to file your tax returns, you will be glad you did.

Unless you plan to do the job of processor and closing specialist as well as mortgage originator, you will have to hire people. You are now an employer. Even if your staff is part time, welcome to the world of payroll and withholding taxes, W-2s or 1099 filings for contractors. Consult an accountant for the IRS guidelines that determine who qualifies as a 1099 contractor. If your staff doesn't meet the requirements, you as an employer are subject to substantial penalties and costs (another good reason to establish yourself as a limited liability entity).

Once the infrastructure is in place, you can start marketing. Buy lists, and get ready to stuff envelopes, affix stamps, and send out your mailings. Or start making those cold calls.

By now it should be clear that striking out on your own is not a trivial undertaking. On the other hand, if you have ever worked for a boss who was not the most wonderful and understanding person on the face of the earth, then you know that in spite of all the challenges, being your own boss provides freedom and flexibility. Responsibility and freedom go hand in hand in business.

Finding the Right Firm

Throughout this book I have alluded to the practices and philosophies that I believe make a successful mortgage business. Practices, policies, and strategies vary tremendously from one company to another. Not everyone agrees with the principles I have put forth in this book. These techniques and practices are not designed for the quick buck, but are designed to create a foundation on which to build for the long term, and to implement structures to support growth and continuous improvement.

Mortgage origination is a career with very few barriers to entry. You don't need a lot of money or advanced educational degrees to get a job or start working in this field. That makes it very attractive to many people who look at a booming refinance market and see an easy way to make a lot of money quickly. When the market is hot, everyone in the business looks good. If you want to get in, make your bundle and get out, then it matters not the type of firm for which you go to work. And, it makes sense, if you can afford it, to go for the biggest bucks you can get—usually a commission split of the loan's profits.

If on the other hand, you are in this business for the long haul, as I am, then focus on stability, longevity, and training when you look for an employer. The immediate payoff may not appear to be as attractive as other offers, but consider the growth potential, financial security, and future earnings you will be able to achieve with a firm that is committed to long-term growth through referrals.

Interview Questions for You to Ask

When you seek a position with a mortgage firm, remember that employment interviews are two-way. They will assess and evaluate your knowledge, experience, and personality. You should be interviewing them to determine whether their way of doing business is aligned with your goals and style. Consider asking the following questions when interviewing an employer for a position as a mortgage originator.

How long has the company been in this business? When the mortgage business is good, it is good for everyone in it. Everyone makes a lot of money. When the supply of money is plentiful, it is easy to sell to people with bad credit. Mortgage companies expand and grow at astonishing rates when almost anyone can qualify for a mortgage. But markets change quickly. In this most recent downturn, companies with 8,000 employees went out of business seemingly overnight. Across the country, thousands of smaller companies folded each month.

Consider that a firm that weathers the bad periods is one that will flourish in good times. A firm that has survived and grown through slow markets is flexible and adapts to changing market conditions. Unless you want to look for a job when the next downturn occurs, give this matter considerable weight when choosing an employer. For the pros—the companies that have a long-term business strategy—downturns are an opportunity to build the business. Only the pros do well in bad markets when good credit is needed to qualify for a loan. People with good credit are harder to sell, but when you sell to people with great credit you have customers for life. That is how you build your business. That means when the market slows again (and it will), you have a good chance of keeping your position and even advancing.

What training is provided? Even if you consider yourself fully trained, this question is important. Especially when you are starting out, it is important to have people to work with from whom you can learn the fine points of mortgage products and salesmanship. A company that invests training resources in its employees is a company that is in the game to build and grow in the long term. Even if you are enjoying some success now, everyone in any business can benefit from the teachings of someone with more experience. You can always improve—and your earning power is limited only by what you imagine you can achieve and what you are willing to do to meet your goals.

Not many companies are willing to train extensively, because they know they are training their competition. Don't get involved with a company that is not willing to train you because they are concerned about your leaving. Go with a company that is willing to train you, willing to take the time, willing to make the effort. I am never concerned about people going out on their own because I give them a reason to stay—fair and steady compensation, a great work environment, and unlimited opportunity for advancement.

What types of marketing programs does the company undertake? Don't assume anything. Find out how leads are generated. Are they provided to you? Do you have to pay for them? Are you going to be expected to generate your own leads? Will you receive additional compensation for the leads you generate? Who pays the cost of marketing? Are there eligibility or performance requirements to participate in the company's marketing programs? Is effectiveness rewarded for closing company-generated leads?

What percentage of the client base is from referrals and repeat business? This tells you the degree to which customer service is valued and practiced within the company. Again, if a company is in the game for the quick bucks, cultivating repeat business and referrals is not a priority. On the other hand, a high percentage of repeat customers and referrals tells you that the company builds on its reputation, and must be customer-focused and ethical to be successful in that way.

How will my performance be measured? It is important to know what is expected of you, what the rewards are for exceeding expectations, and what the penalties are for falling short. While most people resist measurements, without them your future depends on the goodwill of those who make the salary adjustment decisions, rather than on objective performance measures.

Is there an opportunity to have others work for me? A firm that is committed to growth will have a career path that allows you to advance and manage others, and be compensated accordingly. Again, be clear about the criteria to qualify for advancement, the compensation structures, and the earning potential. It may not happen overnight, but you could build a team of high-income mortgage originators and boost your income without increasing your work load. How great is that?

Conclusion

You have at your disposal all the tools you need to be a successful, high-income mortgage originator. There is no magic to make it happen suddenly. Consistent action over time will pay off if you follow the guiding principles and practices of this book.

With that, good luck, have a great journey and a great prosperous future. Send us an e-mail, and let us know how the book has helped you.

Downturns in the Mortgage Cycle

Although I alluded to it at the beginning of the book, this chapter wasn't planned, but because of the collapse in the subprime mortgage business in early 2007, I would be remiss not to include it.

Sometimes due to circumstances beyond your control staying in business may be impossible because your sources of funds have all dried up. If you have been in the game any length of time, you know that in cycles of approximately 10 years the game gets called and is restarted, and thousands of mortgage companies go out of business. A Connecticut company that looked like it would be around forever—with 8,000 employees in a brand new high-rise office space—literally went out of business overnight.

When these things happen, some originators are destroyed. I remember when it happened to me over 20 years ago when I was with a bank mortgage company. When they lost their funding, my fellow originators and I were out of a job. But we still had our personal mortgages to pay, car payments to make, food to buy, tuition to fund, children and families to support.

When you go through this the first time, it is devastating, and you think it is just a unique set of circumstances. But if you stay in the business any length of time, you realize it is all a normal part of the mortgage business. Funding dries up overnight, and you can't place your loans with any wholesalers, who start getting more restrictive on their approvals. You start getting fewer approvals and more conditions. If you have never gone through it, you are sure you chose the wrong career. As time goes on and more and more wholesale lenders close up shop, remember that this is a trillion dollar business, and as many as 20,000 firms close in a month.

Most people are not prepared for the game to end this way. The downturn is the culmination of many lenient practices by lenders that sometimes give 110% financing, allow no money down, and put borrowers into adjustable-rate mortgages for which they qualify at the low introductory interest rates, but for which they cannot make payments as time goes by and their payments increase. These borrowers fall behind and eventually cannot make the payments. You will see more and more homes for sale—all warning signs to get ready for the collapse and the foreclosure start.

People try to refinance into a fixed-rate mortgage, but cannot because of prepayment penalties or low appraisals due to the glut of homes for sale. You will see more and more mortgage companies going out of business and conservatively, tens of thousands of people will lose their jobs.

What to Do

If you are a high-income mortgage originator working for the right company, you will actually be set to reap the rewards that the situation now makes available. But first there needs to be a total change in your mindset. You had better have been trained to sell from a totally different position—one put forth in this book—which most originators are not. You will no longer have easy fast closings—they will take more time and effort and demand more profit. Yet because your competition is weak, you have the opportunity to expand and grow. When every one else is drowning around you, you will be sailing along smoothly. Good luck and good sailing, from one high-income mortgage originator to another.

Key Mortgage Industry Resources on the Web

www.dnc.gov   Do Not Call regulations and guidelines.

www.fanniemae.com   Guidelines on conforming loan requirements and underwriting considerations, and for 1003 Uniform Residential Loan Applications.

www.fdic.gov   The Federal Trade Deposit Insurance Corporation web site is the source of information related to consumer protection (Truth in Lending) regulations.

www.ftc.gov   The Federal Trade Commission oversees Fair Credit Reporting policies and regulations.

www.hud.gov   The Department of Housing and Urban Development is responsible for RESPA regulations. This site provides information for completing the Good Faith Estimate, HUD-1 Settlement Statement, and the forms.

Glossary

Adjustable interest rate. This is a rate of interest that changes (is adjusted) over the term of a loan, at agreed upon intervals.

Adjustable-rate mortgage (ARM). This is a loan product that includes an adjustable interest rate. Most begin with a very low monthly payment at the beginning of the loan term. ARMs are particularly attractive to people who expect their income to rise, and in times of high interest rates when rates are expected to decline.

Application. This is a form that a borrower completes that contains information a lender uses to qualify the borrower for a mortgage. The most commonly used application is the Uniform Residential Loan Application, also known as Form 1003 or simply "the ten-oh-three."

Application fee. This is a fee (usually a flat rate) charged by a mortgage originator to a borrower to cover the costs of completing and processing a mortgage application.

Appraisal. This report, issued by an appraiser, determines the property's value. The report also contains information about the how the value was determined, including information about comparisons to other properties used to determine value.

Appraiser. This is a licensed real estate professional responsible for determining the market value of a property.

Assets.   These are things of positive monetary value such as cash, the value of real estate, jewelry, resale value of an automobile, investments, savings, and so forth. Assets are reported on a loan application and are offset by liabilities to compute net worth. Assets and net worth are indicators of financial stability and health.

Bankruptcy.   This is the legal status of insolvency or inability to pay bills that protects the debtor from pursuit by creditors through collection actions, liens, or other legal remedies for default.

Binder.   In a real estate transaction, when a seller accepts an offer, the binder is a sum of money and a preliminary agreement regarding the terms of the transaction. Real estate binders often specify a time limit in which the borrower must obtain a loan commitment, or the seller is released from the agreement.

Bridge loan.   This is a short-term loan product, usually needed to secure a home purchase prior to the sale of the borrower's present home. Proceeds from the sale are used to repay the bridge loan at the time when the sale of the present home goes to closing.

Cash flow.   This is the amount and timing of income and expenses, usually for one month. If expenses (cash outflow) exceed income (cash inflow) for a particular time period (usually one month), cash flow is negative. If income exceeds expenses, cash flow is positive. Cash flow is an indicator of the borrower's ability to bear the monthly mortgage payments.

Closing.   This is a legal transaction that marks the conclusion of the purchase or refinance mortgage transaction. It consists of title transfers, funds transfers, distribution of fees, and signing of many documents.

Closing documents.   These legal papers are required to conduct and conclude a real estate or mortgage transaction. Examples of closing documents are title, contract, appraisal, mortgage note, disclosures, truth in lending, and so forth.

Collection action. This is a legal proceeding initiated by a lender to force repayment of a loan that is in default. Collection actions are reported on credit reports, and negatively impact credit scores.

Comps or comparables. These properties are used to compare to a property for which a mortgage is being sought. The basis for comparison consists of age, style, location, recent sale, and condition.

Conforming loan. This is a mortgage loan that meets the qualification standards set forth by Fannie Mae and Freddie Mac.

Contract (real estate). This legal document spells out all the final terms and conditions for the purchase or sale of a home. This document is signed at the closing to conclude the transaction.

Credit. Examples include "His credit was excellent"; "I have good credit." This usage refers to the interpretation of the credit scores and credit reports issued by one or more credit bureaus, and is a short-hand way of indicating the strength or weakness of the borrower's ability to qualify for a loan.

Credit bureau. There are three organizations that collect and report an individual's financial transaction history. Information is gathered from merchants and lenders regarding outstanding loan balances, monthly payments, and the timing of payments received from the individual. Each credit bureau weights the information differently to compute a credit score.

Credit inquiry. This is a request for a credit report. Too many inquiries in a short period raise questions about the financial stability of the individual and can negatively impact credit scores.

Credit report. This is provided by one of three credit bureaus about an individual; it documents loan balances, monthly payments, credit card balances, liens and judgments, and record of on-time payments. The credit bureau rates all the information on the report to calculate a credit score, which is an important factor in determining for which loan products a borrower qualifies.

Credit score. This is a computation based on information contained on a credit report and reported by one of three credit bureaus.

Discretionary income. This is the amount of monthly income remaining after all monthly expenses are paid; it can be used at the borrower's discretion. It is computed as income minus expenses.

Documentation of assets. This is requested by lenders to support information provided on the loan application; it refers to bank statements, brokerage account statements, mortgage statements, and statements from other financial accounts such as stocks, investment accounts, retirement accounts, 401(k)s and so forth.

Down-payment. This is the lump sum of money that the borrower is paying toward the price of a home. The difference between the price and the down-payment is the amount to be borrowed.

Economic index or indices (plural). These are generally accepted standards of measure of economic conditions. They are used as a baseline on which mortgage interest rates are based.

Employment history. This is the record of a borrower's employer(s) names and addresses, and the length of time the borrower worked there. If the borrower has been at the current job less than two years, prior employment information is likely to be requested by a lender. It is used as a measure of the borrower's financial stability. (see also Self-employment history).

Equity. This is the value of the home minus the unpaid balance of the mortgage(s).

Escrow agent. This person or institution provides escrow services to both parties as part of a transaction involving the transfer of assets.

Float. This term refers to allowing the interest rate available for a loan to fluctuate.

Float down. This is an agreement between borrower and lender that an agreed-upon rate of interest is guaranteed, unless rates drop, in which case the agreed-upon rate will drop.

Good Faith Estimate. This is a preliminary disclosure of closing costs, fees, and other charges likely to be settled at the closing. Required by RESPA, it protects borrowers from unanticipated fees and charges levied by lenders and others.

Home equity line of credit (HELOC). This is a line of credit based on borrowers' equity in their homes.

Home equity loan. This is a loan secured by borrowers' equity in their homes; it is also known as a second mortgage.

Income. Money received or owed to a borrower, it consists of wages, overtime pay, interest, dividends, alimony, child support, rental receipts, and so forth.

Income verification. This is a process by which a lender is assured that information a borrower provides regarding their income is true. It may entail the collection of W-2s, 1040s, and documentation of assets for review.

Judgment. This is a legal ruling obligating action, usually to pay. A judgment against a borrower is reported on a credit report and is considered unfavorable for purposes of the credit score.

Key ratios. These are comparative standard measures used in the mortgage industry to assess the risk of a loan and the qualifications of the borrower. Examples are Loan to Value (LTV), Debt to Income (DTI) and Front End Ratio.

Liability. This is a financial obligation borne by a borrower, usually representing a promise to pay in the future. Examples are loan balances, unpaid real estate taxes, and so forth. Liabilities offset assets in the computation of net worth.

Lien.   This is a claim of a right or interest in a property owned by another. A mortgage is a type of lien.

Line of credit.   This is an amount of money a lender agrees to make available to a borrower in advance of a loan. Lines of credit allow homeowners to borrow money as needed, similar to a credit card.

Loan commitment.   This agreement by a lender is a promise to fund a mortgage for a specific property, made prior to closing.

Loan product.   This is the set of terms and conditions under which a lender agrees to lend and a borrower agrees to repay a loan. Common loan products include fixed-rate mortgages, adjustable-rate mortgages, home equity loans, and home equity lines of credit.

Loan to Value (LTV).   This key ratio is used in the determination of loan qualification. It compares the principal amount of the mortgage to the appraised value of the property in the following formula:

$$(\text{Principal}/\text{Value}) * 100 = \text{Loan to Value ratio (LTV)}$$

In general, the lower the ratio, the less the risk to the lender since a drop in the value of the home is less likely to reduce the lender's security interest in the property.

Mortgage broker.   This professional, unaffiliated with any one lender, arranges mortgages on behalf of borrowers. A broker has relationships with many lenders, and is therefore able to shop the loan for the most favorable terms.

Mortgage originator.   This professional is responsible for generating loan applications and acting as liaison between borrower and lender. Also known as loan originator and loan specialist, the mortgage originator generally works with or for a mortgage broker or a lender to secure financing for borrowers.

Nonconforming loan.   This is a mortgage loan that does not meet the qualification standards set forth by Fannie Mae and Freddie Mac. These loans are deemed riskier than conforming loans, and are therefore more expensive (offer less favorable terms to the borrower) than conforming loans.

Offer. In a real estate transaction, an offer is a price and closing date (along with other conditions of purchase) proposed by a prospective buyer to a seller for the purchase of real estate.

Payment history. Reported by merchants to credit bureaus regarding the timeliness of payments received, this information is included in credit reports and used in the calculation of credit scores.

Piggy-back. This double mortgage transaction usually consists of a residential mortgage (either purchase or refinance) and a home equity loan or line of credit. Borrowers will piggy-back a second mortgage or HELOC to secure availability of funds at specified rates.

Preapproval. This is a process by which a borrower applies for and receives approval for a mortgage prior to identifying a specific property for which the mortgage will be obtained. Preapproval assures buyers that they will be able to obtain financing for homes within a certain price range.

Prequalification. This is a preliminary assessment of the amount of money a lender is willing to lend.

Primary lender. This is a bank, mortgage banker, or finance company that sells mortgages to the public, either directly (retail) or through mortgage brokers (wholesale).

Prime rate. This is the cost of money that banks charge their premier customers. Prime rate is one of the key indices upon which mortgage rates, and adjustable interest rates are based.

Principal. This is the amount of money loaned to a borrower. The amount of money a borrower repays on a loan will include the principal plus interest.

Private mortgage insurance (PMI). This is insurance for the lender against default of mortgage payments by the borrower. PMI is usually required by a lender when the borrower's down-payment is less than 20% of the home's value.

Processor.   This is a mortgage professional responsible for the completeness, accuracy, and organization of the documents in a loan file between the loan application and underwriting.

Property value.   This is the worth of the property for which a mortgage is being obtained, based on the lower of sale price or appraisal.

Purchase.   This is a mortgage transaction with a transfer of property title from one party to another.

Rate lock.   This is a firm and unchanging agreement by a lender to fund a loan at a specified rate of interest. A rate lock remains in effect through closing, unless it expires sooner.

Rate of interest.   This is a percentage of the principal used to compute the amount a borrower must repay on the loan. It is also known as interest rate or rate.

Rate sheet.   This price list is issued by a lender, detailing terms and conditions of loan products they offer for sale.

Real estate agent.   This is a representative for a real estate buyer or seller working under a real estate broker to bring buyers and sellers together.

Real estate broker.   This licensed professional represents either a buyer or seller in a real estate transfer transaction. A broker brings together buyers and sellers, and is responsible for managing the activities of real estate agents.

Refinance.   This mortgage transaction does not involve the transfer of property between two parties.

Residential mortgage.   This is a loan for the purchase or financing of a dwelling containing four or fewer housing units.

Retail lender.   This is a bank or other lending institution that deals directly with borrowers.

Reverse mortgage. A mortgage available to senior homeowners that pays out equity to the homeowner. Repayment of the loan is not due until the homeowner moves or sells the house.

Secondary market. This term usually refers to Fannie Mae, Freddie Mac, or Ginnie Mae, organizations that buy loans from primary lenders.

Secured loan. This kind of debt is backed by collateral to ensure repayment or restitution of the borrowed amount. A mortgage is a type of secured loan. The property is collateral on the loan, and should the borrower default on payments, the lender has a right to dispose of the property in order to be repaid.

Stated income. This type of loan application bypasses income verification. It is used primarily for self-employed persons who attest to the validity of the information provided, but who are not required to produce the documentation needed for income verification.

Subordination. A legal term to describe the reduced priority of a party's claim in favor of a higher-priority claim by another party. Second mortgages are subordinate to first mortgages, meaning that the first mortgage holder's security interests come first. In a refinance, when the first mortgage is paid, the second mortgage has precedence over the new loan, unless the second mortgage is subordinated (usually a requirement for refinancing).

Tax returns. The term generally refers to IRS form 1040 and supporting documents, filed annually by U.S. tax payers. Copies of tax returns are required by lenders in some cases to verify the borrower's income.

Term (of a mortgage). This is the time period over which the loan is repaid. Terms of 30 years, 20 years, 15 years, or 10 years are common for residential mortgages.

Title search. This is research into the current and past ownership of a property as well as the transactions that transferred a property from one owner to the next. A title search is conducted prior to a mortgage closing to assure the lender that the borrower has full rights to assign an interest in the property (a lien) to the lender in exchange for the mortgage.

Underwriter. This mortgage professional determines whether to approve a borrower for a mortgage; the underwriter uses key ratios and other inputs to assess the risk assumed by the lender in approving the borrower and the loan.

Wholesale lender. This sort of lending institution works exclusively through mortgage brokers.

A Day in the Life of a Mortgage Originator

8:30–10:00 A.M. The morning begins with calls related to loans in process. You call an employer for a verification form for one of your clients. Or you follow up with an appraiser prior to receiving the written report. You lock rates and gather loan documentation to keep the process going. And you call clients to let them know what's going on, to stay in touch and answer any questions or concerns they have.

10:00–11:00 A.M. Once the in-process files are moving, you turn your attention to generating new applications, beginning with calls to past customers. You may have sent out a mailing which you are following up on. Or you are just calling to see how they are doing, offer your services, and ask for referrals. Or you call past customers who are in mortgages that had a short fixed rate that is about to convert to adjustable, to let them know their options and what you can do for them. You call clients who recently closed a loan, to ask how it went and to ask for referrals. Staying in touch is very important—a satisfied customer is the best marketing and advertising you can have.

11:00–12:00 NOON. Next, you move on to generate new business. Cold calls keep you sharp, so that when someone calls you in response to your marketing efforts, you are on your game and can convert the incoming call to an application. You keep statistics of your calls—how many people you spoke to and how many applications you took—and you track your improvement over time. You tape-record your presentation and listen to your interactions to train yourself in the sales techniques you learn in this book. You quickly develop a keen ear for the things that work and the things that don't, and become masterful on the phones. (I know it may seem hard to believe, but I promise you, if you do this, you will overcome your anxiety and develop mastery.)

12:00–1:00 P.M.   Next, your activities center on processing applications, pulling credit reports from today's applicants, reviewing yesterday's credit reports, and discussing the reports with prospects to set them up for the next steps in the process. In these credit call conversations, you develop relationships with prospects based in trust and integrity. You also learn to know if the prospect is ready to move to the next step, and if not, what you need to do to get him ready.

1:00–3:00 P.M.   Next, you turn your attention to preparing proposals for prospects. You review rate sheets, evaluate the prospects' motivation and qualifications, call lenders for quotes on different loan products, and prepare alternatives and recommendations. You call prospects to review the proposals with them, and to ask for the go-ahead, thus closing the sale. You track your conversion ratios and take corrective actions as needed.

3:00–4:00 P.M.   Later, you prepare loan packages for the proposals you sold, schedule appointments to review the package with the client, obtain signatures, collect application fees, and ask for referrals. You may visit clients' homes to obtain signatures and review the loan package documents, and then return to the office to submit the package to a processor.

4:00–5:00 P.M.   You'll prepare for upcoming closings you have scheduled and reconcile the closing settlement statement with the Good Faith Estimate. You call your clients to prepare them for the closing, and ask for referrals. You update your records for future correspondence with your client to set up a schedule of automatic, regular communication with them.

6:00–8:00 P.M.   On occasion, in the evening you attend a networking event, put on a seminar for first-time homebuyers or a credit repair program, or take a course to improve your knowledge and skills.

APPENDIX D

Overview of the
Loan Process

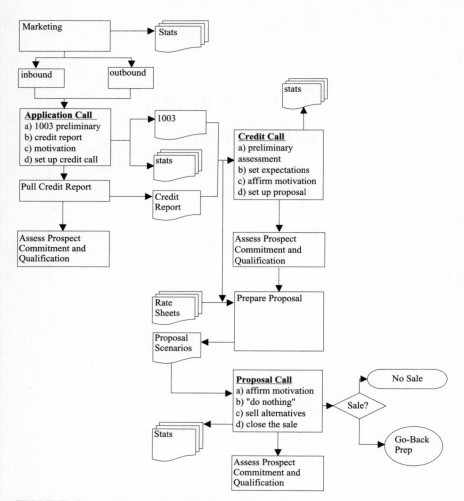

FIGURE D.1   Loan Process Overview Pre-Sale

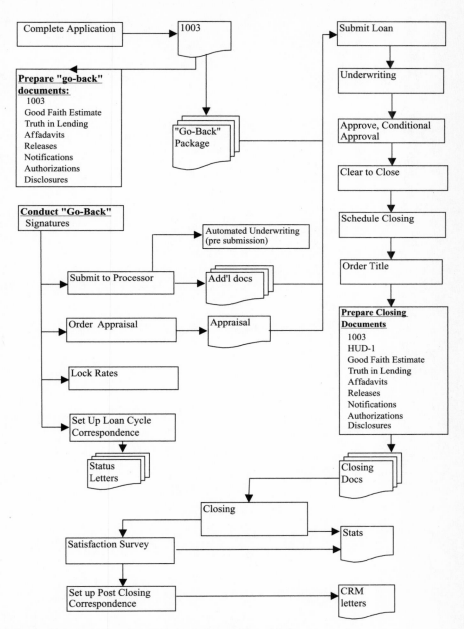

FIGURE D.2   Loan Process Overview Post-Sale

Comparison of Loan Instruments

TABLE E.1   Comparison of Loan Instruments

Characteristic	Fixed-Rate	ARM	Two-Step (A)	Two-Step (B)
Term				
Amortization Period	X	X	X	X
Initial Fixed Period		X	X	
Adjustment Period		X		X
Rate				
Initial	X	X	X	X
Initial Rate Cap		X		X
Periodic Rate Cap		X		X
Life Time Cap		X		X
Index		X		X
Margin		X		X
Payment Amounts				
Fixed Amount P & I	X		X	
Variable P & I		X		X
Payment Options Available				
Principal & Interest	X	X	X	X
Interest Only	X	X	X	X
Minimum Payment	X	X	X	X

(Continued)

TABLE E.1 Comparison of Loan Instruments (*Continued*)

Characteristic	Fixed-Rate	ARM	Two-Step (A)	Two-Step (B)
Payment Frequency				
Monthly	X	X	X	X
Bi-weekly	X	X	X	X
Additional Principal	X	X		X
Prepayment w/out Penalty	X	X		X

Key Ratio Calculations

Loan to Value (LTV)

= Amount of Loan / Value of Property
    Where Amount of Loan = principal amount borrowed
    Value of Property = Appraised value
Or   Value of Property = Lower of appraised value or purchase price of new home.

DTI and Housing Ratios

See Table F.1 for definition of terms.

Housing or Front End Ratio

= Total Monthly Housing Expense / Total Monthly Income

Debt to Income (DTI) or Back End Ratio

= (Total Monthly Housing Expense + Monthly Debt Payments)/ Total Monthly Income

Average monthly earnings (commissions, bonuses, overtime)

= Total amount earned in that category for the last two years of earnings / 24

TABLE F.1 Elements for DTI Calculation

Total Monthly Housing Expense	Monthly Debt Payments	Total Monthly Income (Gross)
First mortgage P & I	Monthly installment loans (with more than 10 months remaining)	Monthly gross wages
Other financing P & I	Revolving credit minimum payments	Average monthly overtime (based on two years of earnings)
Hazard Insurance (homeowners, flood)	Alimony paid	Average monthly bonus (based on two years of earnings)
Real Estate Taxes	Child Support paid	Average monthly commission (based on two years of earnings)
Mortgage Insurance	Direct payroll deductions for health, savings, retirement, dues, charitable, etc.	Alimony received (optional)
Homeowner Assn. Dues		Child Support received (optional)
Other Home Ownership Expenses		Net Rental Income

Net Rental Income

= (Gross rental income $*$ .75) − (Housing Expense on Rental property)

APPENDIX G

Quick Ratio Guidelines for Conforming Loans

TABLE G.1   Maximum Conforming Loan Amounts

	Single-Family	Two-Family	Three-Family	Four-Family
48 contiguous states	$417,000	$533,850	$645,300	$801,950
Alaska, Hawaii, Guam, Virgin Is.	$625,500	$800,775	$967,950	$1,202,925

Key Ratio Guidelines

Housing (Front End) Ratio – 33% or less;
DTI (Back End) Ratio – 38% or less;
LTV – 80% or less to qualify without PMI;
Credit Scores – about 620 or higher.

Using Microsoft Office for Customer Relations Management

You don't have to buy expensive Customer Relationship Management software to have a system that keeps you in touch with your customers. Using basic office tools—word processing, spreadsheet, and e-mail—and disciplined procedures, you can make communicating regularly easy and professional. Familiarize yourself with the key features of Microsoft products that will help you achieve your goal.

Mail Merge for Personalized Letters

Creating a personalized form letter uses the Mail Merge features of your word processor. There are two pieces to the process—your form letter or template and the list of recipients for whom the letter will be personalized. The letter template contains the text of the letter, and special placeholders for the information that is being customized for each recipient. The recipient list typically has name and address information, as well as any other details specific to each recipient, for example, the date of their closing.

Creating the Letter and Recipient List

Compose the letter as you would any normal letter, but leave out the name and address information for now. Save the letter.

Using Excel, create a spreadsheet to contain the recipient list and any other customized information that you want the letter to contain. Each customer's information must be contained on one row, and there should be no blank rows or intermediate header rows in the sheet. Make sure your Excel file has column titles that Word will recognize, like "First" for first name and "Last" for last name, "Company" for company name, "State" for State, "Zip" for zip code. This will make the actual merge process much simpler.

Merging the Letter with the List

The actual generation of the customized letters for printing involves two steps to combine the template with the recipient list. Microsoft provides a "wizard" to guide you through the process.

Open your letter. With the letter open,

Go to *Tools* → *Letters and Mailings* → *Mail Merge*

A panel will open up on the right to guide you through the process. Choose *Letter* when asked what type of document you are creating. Click *Next* at the bottom of the panel, and you have the choice of selecting your current document or one of several templates. Use the current document.

Click *Next* at the bottom of the panel to see choices for selecting recipients.

Then, in the merge panel in Word, select *Use an existing list* and just click under that on "*Browse*" and open your recipient list spreadsheet file.

Your spreadsheet will open, allowing you to select all recipients or you can filter some out by clicking the arrow next to any of the headings to select by city or state, and so forth. You can also click the box to the left of the row to select or deselect any name individually. Click *Next* at the bottom of the panel to get to the next step.

You may edit your letter, if needed. To add the special placeholders for the personalizing information from your recipient list, click the location in the letter where you want the address block to be. Then click on *Address Block* in the Mail Merge Panel to select what elements you want to include. Then click on the *Greeting Line* in the panel to select the format you want to use including rows that have missing or invalid names.

Click *Next* to preview your letter. You can always back up to a previous step if you want to change something.

Once satisfied with the letter, click *Next* to complete the merge.

Then click *Edit individual letters*. This will create a file (a new Word document) containing all the completed, customized letters. Review and make any edits that may be necessary before printing. For example, sometimes zip codes with a leading zero will only have the remaining 4 digits. If that happens, you can use *Find and Replace* under *Edit* to correct the issue.

Searching Through Your Client Base

Spreadsheets such as Microsoft Excel have capabilities beyond basic math functions. Features that allow you to sort rows based on the data in a column, and to filter your view of rows based on data content, make these programs simple-to-use databases that provide quick access to specific data about your clients.

Sort

Sort is a function that groups rows in a database according to data that they share in common. For example, if your customers live in several states, by sorting on the STATE column in your spreadsheet, all residents of one state would appear together in the list, followed by all residents of the next state (alphabetically) and so on.

To sort a list of names or businesses in Excel, highlight the complete list from the top left to the bottom right of all the information, including the titles of columns. Then on the menu, select *Data → Sort*

In the *Sort window*, click the circle next to *Header row*, if not already selected.

Use the drop-down arrow to select the column to sort by, such as "Company." If you want to sort within that group, use the next drop down box to select the next group, such as "Last Name." You can select one more subgroup if you wish.

You may want to sort by different groups for the whole list rather than as subgroups. That is, the whole list by "Last Name." You can do that by repeating this process or you can use the Filters discussed next.

Filter

Filters are very helpful to separate out sections of your list that meet a criterion you have without changing your spreadsheet or needing to sort the list first. And you can copy your filtered list to a new worksheet if desired.

First add headings to your list, if they are not already in the file.

Then select the whole row containing the headings by clicking on the row number on the left side of the worksheet.

From the menu, select *Data → Filter → AutoFilter*

Excel adds drop down arrows next to every heading you have.

Now you can click on any arrow to filter your list by city, business, etc. You can also click an arrow and sort by that column, ascending or descending.

Best of all, you can select *Custom* from the arrow and filter by more than one criteria at a time or select all those with a certain word or phrase. For example, to show only Customers that have "ARM" in their Mortgage Type, click the arrow next to Mortgage Type and click (Custom . . .), then in the *Custom* window, click *contains* on the left drop down arrow and type "ARM" in the box on the right side.

You can get subgroups with filters by selecting the first group you want and then selecting the second group from the heading desired. Or after selecting the first group, use the arrow for the second group to sort by that heading.

Note: If a drop-down arrow doesn't show items that you know are in the list, it is likely that you need to remove a filter from one or more of the headings. Excel changes the color of the arrow from black to blue when a column is filtered. You can look for the blue arrow, or if you want to turn off all filters without having to check each heading, go to the menu and select *Data* → *Filter* → *AutoFilter*. All the data will show and the arrows will be gone.

Setting Reminders

Microsoft Outlook, in addition to providing e-mail services, includes calendar and reminder features that are very useful for triggering activities that can be scheduled in advance. It is very easy to set up a series of reminders to send out your loan cycle letters at specified intervals, and then not worry about it again until the reminder pops up.

Set Up Reminders in Outlook Calendar

To set a reminder, you create an "appointment" in the calendar. Click on *Calendar* and select from the menu *New* → *Appointment*. An appointment window will open. In the Subject line, put the client name or file number and the name of the letter you want to send to them. From the drop-downs provided, select the date and time you want to send the letter. You set up the reminder (a pop-up box) by checking the reminder box in the *Appointment* window. Then click the arrow to set how much time ahead of the appointment you want the reminder to show up.

When the date and time come and you have Outlook open, a pop-up reminder will appear. When you have completed the task, click on the item in the pop-up window and then click *Dismiss* to remove it.

Set Up Reminders in Response to E-Mail Messages

For any message that is sent or received that you want to follow up on, you can have a reminder automatically pop up at a date and time of your choice.

Highlight the message of interest in your Inbox or Sent Mail and right-click your mouse. Then select *Follow up → Add reminder . . .*

Then in the *Flag for Follow Up* window, click the drop-down arrows of interest to set a date and time to follow up.

Once you have completed the task you can click the Completed box on the item. That puts a check mark in the flag column in your inbox showing that you completed the task. *Note:* You can click on the flag column in your inbox to sort by flag to see all notes you want to follow up on and all you have completed.

INDEX